DISTANT SECRETS

SECRETS

*Unravelling the Mysteries
of Our Ancient Past*

DISTANT SECRETS

Unravelling the Mysteries of Our Ancient Past

by Ronald Schiller

A BIRCH LANE PRESS BOOK
Published by Carol Publishing Group

Library of Congress Cataloging-in-Publication Data

Schiller, Ronald.
    Distant secrets : unravelling the mysteries of our ancient past /
by Ronald Schiller.
        p.   cm.
    ISBN 1-55972-004-2 : $17.95
    1. Antiquities. 2. Excavations (Archaeology) 3. Man,
Prehistoric. 4. Civilization, Ancient. I. Title.
    CC165.S33   1989
    930--dc20   89-22087
                                                CIP

To
LILLIAN

Contents

viii*Contents*

(*Homo sapiens sapiens*) in Africa and Israel; how the species spread to Asia and Europe to supersede Neanderthal man; the theory that all people living on earth are descendants of a single woman who lived in Africa 200,000 years ago; how the various races of mankind may have evolved.

mids, no two of which are alike. Did they have a grim purpose?

important artistic legacies. Yet they came very close to being destroyed during China's recent Cultural Revolution.

Putting Together the Pieces
of the Past

This volume is not a history of human origins and civilizations. Each chapter deals with a specific aspect of past human achievement or experience about which so much more has been learned in recent years as to render obsolete the accounts of them written a generation ago.

I have visited all of the sites described, usually in the company of the scientists who discovered them, or who are now in charge of the researches being conducted at them. Some of the opinions expressed, and remarks they made, appear here in print for the first time. The reader is taken along to the ancient sites in Africa, Europe, Asia and the Americas, to experience vicariously the labor and frustrations as well as the satisfactions and joys of archeological exploration.

In effect, the book offers a series of intriguing detective stories in which scientists and prehistorians search for clues to a mystery, then try to fit them together to reach a solution. As in fictional detective stories, there are weapons and bodies, plots and counter-

1

plots, false leads and surprise endings. The difference, of course, is that our sleuths investigate real events that have profoundly influenced human history.

One of the first such detectives was Nabonidus, the last king of Babylon. In the sixth century B.C., he excavated the long defunct city of Ur in Mesopotamia and displayed the objects found in a museum. When a cloudburst washed away the earth to reveal a forgotten temple in the city, a scribe recorded in cuneiform on a clay tablet that the discovery "made the king's heart glad, and caused his countenance to brighten." Even before that, several Greeks, including Solon, who later became ruler of Athens, and Herodotus the historian, had visited Egypt to find out what they could about the pyramids and other monuments. Later, Roman emperors, whose own coins are avidly collected today, collected ancient Greek coins. Savants also theorized about the development of civilization. In 52 A.D., a Chinese historical compilation speculated that before reaching their present level of culture, men had passed through ages of stone, bronze and iron, the same designations that are used today.

Archeology as we understand it, however, did not begin until the Renaissance in 16th century Italy, when nobles, cardinals, popes and other men of wealth, began collecting ancient Greek and Roman statuary, and sponsored excavations to find more. The interest was vastly stimulated a century later by the discovery of the cities of Herculaneum and Pompeii, which had been buried under volcanic ash by the eruption of Vesuvius in 79 A.D. The buried cities became literal "art mines" from which great quantities of classical statuary and other objects were extracted.

The excitement spread to other countries where "antiquarians," as they were then called, began investigating the relics of their own national pasts. The Scandinavians explored the dolmen tombs of their Viking ancestors, in which they found runic inscriptions and a surprising quantity of gold objects. In France, some of the megalithic tombs of Britanny were excavated, and reports were published, illustrated with engravings of the skeletons and grave goods they contained. In England, John Aubrey, among others, dug into ancient burial barrows and studied the circular henges that dot the British isles, including Stonehenge. He attributed them to the Druids of Roman times. We now know they are very much older.

The fever also reached the New World. In 1784, Thomas Jefferson excavated Indian mounds on his estate in Virginia, and decribed his findings in his *Notes on the State of Virginia*. In 1793, William Henry Harrison, later elected ninth President of the United States, dug into mounds near Cincinnati, Ohio. Unable to believe that they could have been built by the Indian "savages" he saw around him, he ascribed them to "an unknown race."

By this time, the term "archeology" (Greek for the "the study of ancient things") had come into general use. When Napoleon invaded Egypt in 1789, he brought with him 167 archeologists and artists to study and record what they saw. Although the French soldiers referred to them as *les ânes* (the asses), their reports become the basis of modern Egyptology. Among the relics they discovered was the Rosetta Stone, a slab of black basalt dating to 196 B.C., on which an inscription was engraved in three ancient scripts. By comparing the understandable Old Greek text with the Egyptian hieroglyphs above it, a young French prodigy, Jean Francois Champollion, was able to decipher the Egyptian characters— after 14 years of study.

The 19th century was an era of memorable archeologists and spectacular discoveries. It has been called "the golden age of archeology," although its glitter has somewhat tarnished in recent years. Among the notable achievements of the century were the rediscovery of the magnificent Mayan pyramids and cities of Honduras and Yucatan by American lawyer John Lloyd Stephens and British artist Frederick Catherwood between 1839 and 1943; the unearthing of the Biblical city of Nineveh in Mesopotamia by Frenchman Paul Emile Botta in 1842, and of the Assyrian capital at nearby Nimrud by English explorer Austen Layard five years later. An event of far reaching importance was the decipherment of the cuneiform script of the Middle Eastern civilizations by British scholar Henry Rawlinson in 1846. Another was the finding of the first great Stone Age paintings in a cave near Altamira, Spain by Marcellino Sanz de Sautuola in 1879.

The most celebrated exploits of the century were the excavations of Troy, Mycenae, and other fabled cities of ancient Greece, between 1870 and 1876, by retired German businessman Heinrich Schliemann, who used Homer's *Iliad* and *Odyssey* as his guide books. (Schliemann had made much of his fortune in California during the gold rush of 1849.) These finds were followed by the excavation in 1877 of the cities of the Sumerians, the most ancient civilization of the Middle East, by French diplomat Ernest de Sarzec; the many discoveries and first accurate surveys of the pyramids of Gizeh made in 1880 by Flinders Petrie, the most famous of all Egyptologists; and the excavation of the legendary palace at Knossos in Crete, where Hercules fought the bull, by Britisher Arthur Evans in 1899, which revealed the existence of the hitherto unknown pre-Greek Minoan civilization.

Despite their achievements, the 19th century excavators are not generally admired by modern archeologists. Some are regarded as little better than grave robbers, who "shoveled their way into the past," destroying more than they recovered in their search for precious objects and imposing monuments. Heinrich Schliemann is described as "a complete stranger to any archeological skill," who may have left the cities he excavated in greater ruin than he found them.

The exploits of Giovanni Belzoni, a former circus strong man, who excavated in Egypt in the early 19th century on behalf of the British government, were particularly horrendous. After breaking into one tomb he wrote: "Every step I took I crushed a mummy in some part or other....I could not avoid being covered with bones, legs, arms and heads, rolling from above."

French Egyptologist Auguste Mariette excavated by blasting the ruins of a fallen temple near the Sphinx with gunpowder. In Mesopotamia, Austen Layard set gangs of native workmen digging into ancient mounds without supervision in his haste to seize their treasures before his rivals could get to them.

And what treasures they found! Under a citadel wall in Troy, Schliemann uncovered a priceless 4,000-year-old hoard of gold jewelry and other objects which he mistakenly announced had been secreted by the last king, Priam, before the city fell. In the ruins of Mycenae he discovered another invaluable cache of gold objects, including a death mask which he believed to be that of Agamemnon, leader of the Greek forces against Troy, although it is far older. A great deal of gold was uncovered in the Mesopotamian excavations as well.

Despite local laws forbidding the export of antiquities from the countries in which they were found, most of the portable treasures, as well as a great many statues and friezes, were smuggled to western Europe. The greatest haul was made by Lord Elgin in 1803. With the connivance of the Turkish officials who then ruled Greece, Elgin removed the magnificent but deteriorating marble friezes and statuary that adorned the Parthenon in Athens. He took them to England, where they have been beautifully displayed in the British Museum ever since. Many justify the removal of the "Elgin marbles" and other ancient statuary on the ground that if they have remained where they were, they would have been destroyed by neglect, vandals and the elements.

By far the greatest contributions to archeology in the 19th century were made not by excavators but by scientists, culminating in the landmark books written by British geologist Charles Lyell and naturalist Charles Darwin. Prior to that time, archeological thinking had been straitjacketed by the universally-accepted strictures of the Bible, whose geneologies indicated that the world and the first man, Adam, had been created a mere 6,000 years earlier.

Thus, the skeletons of extinct animals and primitive humans that were found in Europe, such as those recovered from the Neander valley of Germany and the Cro-Magnon rockshelter in France, were held to be the remains of men and creatures drowned in Noah's flood. The ancient chipped flint tools that farmers dug up with their plows were believed to have been made by elves, or to have been "generated in the sky by a fulgurous exhalation conglobed in a cloud by the circumposed humour." But such notions were no longer tenable after the 1833 publication of Lyell's *The Principles of Geology*, which proved that the earth's strata and the fossils they contained had been formed over a span of many millions of years. And the Biblical geneologies collapsed after Darwin demonstrated in *The Origin of Species* (1859) and *The Descent of Man* (1871) that humans had evolved from more primitive species a very long time before Adam.

With the shackles of myth struck off, archeology emerged in the 20th century as an arduous science instead of a pleasant hobby. There were still a few major finds made by adventurers and wealthy amateurs, such as Hiram Bingham's 1911 discovery of the long-forgotten Inca city of Machu Picchu in Peru, and the 1922 excavation of Tutankhamen's tomb in Egypt, with its vast treasure, by Lord Carnarvon and Howard Carter. But archeologists today are more concerned with reconstructing ancient societies and cultures than in finding monuments and artifacts of great museum value. The work has become a team effort, involving anthropologists, biologists, chemists, botanists, geologists and climatologists, among others.

Archeological activities are no longer confined to the classic civilizations of the Old and New Worlds. They are now conducted in almost every corner of the globe. In fact, in many countries and U.S. states, they have become legal necessities. Before roads, dams and other large public works are undertaken, local authorities must engage archeologists to survey the ground in advance, so that nothing of historical value is destroyed before it can at least be studied.

Modern archeologists are also much more concerned with preserving what they find. Excavations are filled in after the researchers have completed their investigations, instead of being abandoned to the mercy of pillagers and the elements. In some cases digging is avoided altogether. The pre-Roman Etruscan tombs of northern Italy, and a crypt at the base of the Great Pyramid at Giza which houses a 5,000-year-old wooden boat, were explored by lowering a periscope and floodlights through a small hole drilled through the roofs of the vaults, then photographing or televising their contents.

Nor is archeological exploration confined to the land, as it once was. Outlines of prehistoric buildings, cities and roads are graced through infra-red photographs taken from airplanes. Photographs returned by space satellites are studied to detect sites that may lie on the banks of ancient rivers or seacoasts that have disappeared. With the development of the aqualung by Jacques Cousteau in 1943, and the building of small research submarines, underwater archeology has also burgeoned. The many ancient sunken ships that have been found, and the cargoes they carried, tell us a great deal about past cultures that was previously unknown. In the opinion of University of Pennsylvania archeologist Salomon Reinach, "the richest museum of the ancient world lies at the bottom of the Mediterranean."

The number of archeological discoveries made in recent decades is staggering. It would require several pages merely to list them all. Many of the most important are described in this book. But there are others. Whole unsuspected civilizations have been unearthed: the 2500 B.C. Indus civilization of Pakistan and India; the equally ancient cultures of Siberia and Russia; the earliest known civilization of Middle America, the Olmec; and new finds in Belize in Central America that have pushed Mayan origins back several millenia. Some of the earliest cities in the world, dating back to the Stone Age, have been excavated, including Jericho in Palestine, Ugarit in Syria, Catal Huyuk in Turkey; and later ones such as Lagash, the 14th century B.C. capital of the Hittite empire.

Rich hoards of gold are still being found. One discovered in a fifth century Moche tomb in Peru in 1988 is said to rival Tutankhamen's treasure in value. Another recovered earlier from Bronze Age graves in Bulgaria is described as "the earliest assemblage of gold objects to be unearthed anywhere in the world." Cambridge University archeologist Colin Renfrew calls the find "as significant as Schliemann's discovery of the gold treasure of Troy a century earlier."

Other major events were the discovery of the 2,000-year-old Dead Sea scrolls in Qumran, Israel, and the excavation of the fortress of Masada where the Jews held out against the Romans in the first century A.D.; the finding of the tomb of Philip of Macedon, Alexander the Great's father, in northern Greece; new discoveries at Stonehenge and other sites in the British Isles; the decipherment of the Minoan Linear B script by British philologist Michael Ventris, and of the Mayan hieroglyphs through the efforts of several scholars. There were also the finding of a great archive of cuneiform tablets in the ruins of the pre-Biblical city of Ebla in Syria; the unearthing of the Great Pyramid of the Aztecs in Mexico City; and of the huge terra cotta armies arrayed in the tomb of the first emperor of China in Xian. Most significant of all have been the discoveries in Africa of the remains of hominids almost four million years old, and of stone tools manufactured two million years ago (described in Chapter 1 of this volume), which have totally changed our concepts of human evolution.

Each of these discoveries has made international headlines, for there is abroad in the world today an insatiable curiosity about man's past. Stimulated by popular books and television shows on the subject, by the speed of jet planes and prosperity in the advanced nations, travel to archeological sites has assumed boom proportions.

When I first visited the Parthenon in Athens on a fine morning in 1966, there were scarcely a dozen people there. On my last visit in 1983, the streets around the temple were jammed with tourist buses for blocks and the hilltop itself seemed as crowded as a commuter station during rush hour. Similar crowds can be found at other sites from Peru to India. I had little trouble in gaining permission to enter the painted cave at Lascaux in France in 1970. But the humidity caused by the perspiration of thousands of visitors has done so much damage to the prehistoric murals, that visitors are no longer allowed to see them, and must content themselves with looking at replicas. Stonehenge may now be viewed only from a distance, the streets of Pompeii and Herculaneum are periodically closed to control the crowds, and there is even talk of keeping people off the Great Wall of China to protect it from the daily pounding by thousands of feet.

Despite the inconveniences, archeological travel can be an enormously rewarding experience. Reading about historic places, seeing pictures of them or visiting museums are inadequate substitutes for actually "being there." To understand an ancient culture and evoke the sense of participating in it, one must experience it three-dimensionally, to be surrounded by its aura, to see the grooves worn into its cobblestones by human feet, the centuries-old graffiti inscribed on its walls, and feel oneself being carried back in time.

Sooner or later the realization dawns that the buildings, decorations and cooking utensils you are looking at were produced by people very much like us, with the same needs, fears, pleasures and problems. Standing in the cold, dank atmosphere of a cave dwelling in the side of a cliff, one relives the concern parents must have felt in keeping their children warm and safe. In examining the grooves, brushstrokes and occasional mistakes, made in ancient statuary and paintings, you can almost feel the chisel or paintbrush in your own hand. The occasional fingerprints left thousands of years ago on pottery and mud bricks by the people who made them are so poignant they can move you to tears.

One also leaves ancient sites with an appreciation of the boundless creativity of the human mind. Mankind is slandered by the idea advanced by various writers ignorant of archeology that such remarkable structures as the pyramids, Stonehenge, and the like, could only have been built by advanced aliens from space, with the aid of laser beams and anti-gravity devices. The space helmets they purport to see on Mayan reliefs, and the landing strips for flying saucers in Peru, are nothing of the kind. There are still unsolved mysteries surrounding many of the ancient monuments, as shall be related in the pages that follow, but the solutions, when found, will reveal that they were unquestionably built by men—unaided.

Archeology also offers a needed anodyne for the worries that beset people today, particularly the uncertainties created by threats of nuclear annihilation and overpopulation, of global pollution and the greenhouse effect. The ancient monuments provide evidence that the human species has been around for a very long time and that it can survive the problems it faces today as it did in the past.

This, I believe, is the subconscious reason for the increase in archeological travel. It explains why books and television shows about ancient peoples and cultures have grown so popular, and why people spend large sums of money for the privilege of being allowed to labor like slaves under the broiling sun at archeological digs from Arizona to Israel. We are looking for reassurance and continuity.

—Ronald Schiller

CHAPTER 1

The Search for Our Earliest Ancestors

(5 million to 100,000 years ago)

EXACTLY HOW the tragedies in Africa occurred is not known. The little family in the Afar Desert of Ethiopia, three to five adults and two children, appeared to have been camped in a gully, when caught in a flash flood and drowned. The remains of the adult and five-year old child in the Laetoli Valley of Tanzania lay in a thick layer of volcanic ash. But whether they died in the fiery downpour, or the ash covered their bodies afterward, cannot be ascertained.

Also not known is whether the deaths attracted much attention at the time, since they occurred between 3.8 and 3.2 million years ago. But the discovery of what was left of their skeletons, in 1972 and 1975, created worldwide headlines and revolutionized our knowledge of early man.

For though these were by far the earliest hominid (manlike) beings yet found, they were more advanced, physically, than had been believed possible. Although their brains were a good deal smaller than ours—less than 450 cubic centimeters (27½ cubic inches) vs. 1,400 CC for an average modern adult brain—they were larger than those of apes. Their legbones indicate that they walked upright without difficulty, and some are so modern in structure as to be almost indistinguishable from our own. Unmistakably, these incredibly ancient creatures were our ancestors, progenitors of the genus *Homo* (man).

The landmark discoveries, added to others a few years earlier, have almost totally destroyed the theory of man's descent that was accepted as scientific fact a generation earlier. And one of the intriguing things about the finds is that most of them were made by the members of a single remarkable family, known to their envious colleagues as "the lucky Leakeys."

As late as 1959, anthropologists were convinced, on the evidence of human skulls and other bones found in Java and near Peking, China, that man had evolved in eastern Asia some half-million years back in the form of *Homo erectus* (upright man), and had subsequently drifted westward, reaching Europe some 300,000 years later. About 125,000 years ago, the theory continued, he had evolved into the Neanderthal type (named for the German valley where his remains were first discovered). Neanderthal was a brutish looking fellow, heavy-boned, slope-headed and chinless, still bearing the monstrous browridge of his forebears.

Then suddenly, seemingly from out of nowhere, about 40,000 years ago, men of modern type, *Homo sapiens* (wise man), appeared on the scene. Whether he had evolved from Neanderthal, or represented a new wave of invaders from the east, the authorities were not sure. But whatever his origin, *sapiens* superseded, or exterminated, his more primitive cousins and remained to populate Europe and the rest of the world.

Although Charles Darwin had predicted that Africa might prove to be the birthplace of mankind, the continent south of the Sahara played no part in the evolutionary drama devised by his successors. Because the inhabitants of the region were so many millenia behind those of Europe, the Middle East and the Orient, in their cultural attainments, it was regarded as a geographic cul-de-sac into which men had drifted at some comparatively recent date in prehistory.

The first jarring note to this universally accepted scenario was sounded by South African Professor Raymond Dart, a neurologist and self-taught fossil expert at the University of Witwatersrand in South Africa. In 1923, he identified the skull of an infant creature that he claimed to be halfway between man and the apes, which he named *Australopithecus* (southern ape). Although possessing a pro-truding snout, like a chimpanzee, with a brain no larger, it pos-sessed certain hominid characteristics. Its teeth were arranged more in an oval, like man's, rather than in the elongated rectangle of an ape's; it lacked the fang-like canines that all apes possess; and from the position of the *foramen magnum*—the hole through which the nerves of the spinal cord enter the skull—it was evident that its head was balanced on the neck in human fashion, instead of jutting forward.

In the years that followed, hundreds of additional australopithe-cine fragments turned up at other sites in Africa, indicating that there were at least two types of the man-apes living side by side, the slender-boned creature of the kind Dart had found, now called *Australopithecus africanus*, and a heavier-boned variety referred to as *A. robustus*. It was impossible to date their skeletons with any accuracy, however, for instead of lying in strata that might give some clues as to their age, they were all imbedded in breccia, a concrete-like agglomeration of rock and sand. But on the evidence of the fossils of long-extinct animals mixed in with the man-apes, Dart judged them to have lived two million years ago. Since they lacked claws or fangs, Dart postulated that the puny creatures used sticks, stones and bones, to defend themselves against predators, and to kill small game and birds, and that they probably hunted in packs, as wild dogs, hyenas and African bushmen still do. Their favorite weapons, he believed, were the shoulder blades of ante-lopes, since many of the crushed baboon skulls found in caves in which the australopithecines lived bear the singular indentations such an implement would make.

These fantastic assertions by the neurologist from South Africa, of all unlikely places, were ridiculed for nearly 35 years. Because he lacked academic credentials in paleoanthropology, Dart was regarded as a mere dabbler in the field. At an anthropological meeting held in 1955, the first to which he was ever invited, Dart was given exactly 20 minutes to present his evidence. Whereupon the assembled savants dismissed the australopithecines as extinct primates of comparatively recent date, unrelated to man.

But vindication was not long in coming. In 1959, the husband-wife team of Louis and Mary Leakey, aided by their three sons, found in Olduvai Gorge, in the Rift Valley of Tanzania, the skull of an exceedingly ugly, hyper-robust hominid, bearing a bony crest on its head, like a gorilla's. They named the creature *Autstralopithecus boisei* in honor of Charles Boise, one of their financial backers (although among themselves the Leakeys referred to it as "old boy"). This time the evidence could not be ignored, nor its age doubted, since the skull lay in a stratum of volcanic ash which potassium-argon dating proved, positively, to be 1.8 million years old—almost the same age Dart had postulated.

The *boisei* find was more than a matter of luck, since Louis Leakey had been looking for such a skull for 28 years. Although educated in England, with a Ph.D. from Cambridge University, he was born in Kenya in 1903 and grew up speaking the language of the Kikuyu tribe before he learned English. His 1933 marriage to a young British archeology student, Mary Nicol, caused a scandal since the two had been living and working together before Louis' divorce from his first wife. The ebullient anthropologist's professional reputation was equally clouded since he had made previous claims to very early hominid finds, which had been disproved. But the discovery of *boisei* erased all past errors and propelled him to the forefront of his profession.

Two years later, the Leakeys' oldest son Jonathan made an even more startling find, the first of a series of skull fragments and limb bones of more advanced hominids with a much bigger braincase, averaging 642 CC in volume. Although just as old as *boisei*, their facial features were less massive and the tops of their heads were smooth, their teeth were more the size of our own molars, and their feet had already developed along human lines, with the big toe close to the other toes, not widely separated as in apes. The crude stone choppers and remains of a rudimentary stone shelter found in the same stratum, led the Leakeys to christen the new type *Homo habilis* (skillful man).

With these stunning revelations the traditional theory of man's evolution collapsed. It was apparent that he had been on earth at least four times longer than had been believed possible, that Africa was probably his birthplace, and that in place of a single lineage, three or more species of near-men had coexisted in the same place at the same time.

But while the theorists were still arguing about which of the creatures belonged on the family tree, another bombshell exploded. In 1972, shortly before his father's death, second son Richard Leakey and his native assistants unearthed on the shore of Lake Turkana in northern Kenya the fragments of a shattered skull lying in a stratum dated at around 1.8 million years old, which was catalogued as number 1,470. When Richard's wife, Meave, had pieced them together after several months work, an astoundingly modern-looking head emerged. Although classified as a *Homo habilis*, and of the same age—1.8 million years—its features were considerably more advanced. It had no browridge to speak of, its 800 CC braincase was far larger, and the area of the skull where speech is controlled was so well developed that the creature might even have been able to talk.

There were other surprises as well. The smallness of the teeth indicate that, unlike its big-molared australo cousins, 1,470 was a meat eater. The hip and leg bones found in the stratum show it walked fully erect. And though less than five feet tall, the skeleton below the neck was similar to our own, proving that the bodies of modern humans had evolved long before their heads.

At this point, two non-Leakeys entered the evolutionary sweepstakes, American paleoanthropologist Don Johanson and French geologist Maurice Taieb, leaders of a joint French-American expedition. In 1974 in the badlands of the Afar Desert of Ethiopia, at the northern end of the Rift Valley, they made a sensational find—the ribs, arms, leg bones, and parts of the skull of a 3.5-million-year-old female, 3½ feet tall and aged about 19 at the time of her death. They named her Lucy, after their favorite Beatles song, "Lucy in the Sky With Diamonds." This was the oldest, most complete skeleton of an erect-walking human ancestor yet discovered.

The following season in the Afar, Johanson and Taieb came across 150 fossil bones, including hands, feet, arms, legs and skull fragments, of an entire family of hominids. When sorted out they appeared to be the remains of three to five adults and two children, two and four years old. From the way the remains were jumbled together in what appeared to have been the bed of an intermittently flowing stream, the explorers first surmised that the group had been resting or sleeping in a gully when it was caught and drowned in a flash flood 3.2 million years ago. The skeletons, which Johanson called the "First Family," were dated at around three million years. It was evident that they too had walked upright, and their reconstructed hands were so well-articulated that they probably could have wound a wristwatch or shuffled a deck of cards without great difficulty.

But Johanson and Taieb did not retain their lead in the hominid race for long. Two years later, in 1977, the expedition headed by then 62-year-old Dr. Mary Leakey, unearthed from the volcanic ash of the Laetoli Valley, 50 miles south of Olduvai in Tanzania, the teeth and jawbones of the oldest pre-humans yet discovered, dated at 3.8 million years. One had belonged to an adult, another to a child about five years of age, whose canine teeth were pushing up through the milk teeth. Thus in four short years of search, between 1973 and 1977, man's ancestry had been pushed back almost two million years in time, and the science of paleoanthropology had been propelled a quantum leap forward.

Noting the resemblance between the Laetoli bones and those of Lucy and the First Family, Johanson and his co-worker, Tim White, concluded that they represented a single species, which they labelled *Australopithecus afarensis*, after the place Lucy had been found. This strained relations with the Leakeys who doubted that

Johanson's people were members of a single species, or that they were necessarily related to the Laetoli residents a thousand miles away and more than a half million years older. (Besides, it is considered bad manners in the profession for anyone but the discoverer to name the fossils he or she finds.) Nevertheless, most anthropologists agree that the sets of bones are much the same, and the *afarensis* designation is now generally accepted.

The rivalry between Richard Leakey and Don Johanson dominates the hominid drama. Although both are tall men, of the same age, they are quite different people. Johanson, born in the United States in 1943, has had a thorough academic training in science, earning a doctorate from the prestigious University of Chicago. He is open-faced, exuberant and gregarious. Leakey, born and raised in Kenya, is sharp-featured, close-mouthed and reserved. At his camp at Koobi Fora, on the shores of Lake Turkana where I and other guests spent our after-work hours in the rooms assigned to us—"slave quarters" we called them, although they are quite comfortable—we could see Richard pacing the veranda of his house on the hill, apparently reluctant to socialize until the evening meal.

Others who know him well believe his reserve may be a shield for his sensitivity. In a profession where a Ph.D. is practically a minimum requirement for admission, he has not even a Bachelor's degree. Bored by the college curriculum, and having acquired from his parents and from his own reading and field work considerably more knowledge than he felt his instructors could teach him, he dropped out during his first semester.

In other respects, Leakey is a very considerate man. Although it was an inconvenience to him, he flew me from Nairobi to his camp at Koobi Fora in his own plane. In the field a few days later, he noticed my flushed face and recognized the symptoms of incipient heat stroke—an ever-present danger in a region where the thermometer may exceed 120 degrees Fahrenheit, desalinating the body through the skin pores. Rushing me back to the camp kitchen, he forced a spoonful of salt down my throat, which I swallowed with a glass of water, narrowly averting collapse.

The competition between Richard Leakey and Don Johanson shows little sign of abatement. Leakey, who is a citizen of Kenya, and director of the country's National Museum, continues the search around Lake Turkana. In 1978, he and his crew came across a duplicate of the 1,470 *habilis* skull, proving that it was a definite species of man. Later they found most of the skeleton of a *Homo erectus* male almost identical to that of Peking Man, except that it was a million years older and a good deal taller. A big find in 1984 was part of the skeleton of a tall *erectus* boy, who might have grown into a brawny six-footer had he reached manhood.

Since becoming director of the Institute of Human Origins in Berkely, California, Johanson has switched his field work to Olduvai Gorge in Tanzania where, in 1987, he and his team discovered numerous teeth and fossil bones of a 1.8-million-year old female *habilis*. Her height and build were much the same as Lucy's indicating that the human skeleton had not advanced much in a million years, and that the comparatively sudden modernization of the body of her *erectus* descendant, 300,000 years later, may represent an evolutionary spurt or mutation.

Each of these discoveries constitutes a landmark in paleoanthropology. For despite their reputation as "fossil mines," hominid remains are so extremely rare in the African sites that it took Louis Leakey nearly three decades of search to find his first. Vastly more numerous are the bones of weird animals millions of years extinct. Among the beasts found in this primeval Noah's ark are antlered giraffes with short necks, little three-toed horses, short-snouted crocodiles, giant baboons, ostriches, hippos and a species of short-trunked elephants with curling tusks set into their *lower* jaws.

The reason that so many of the ancient bones have been found in the desolate Rift Valley of Africa is due to a slow-motion geologic catastrophe that is still in progress. Eons ago, the area was a vast tropical Eden, filled with meandering rivers, large lakes, woodlands, and grassy prairies teeming with animals—among them a few hominids. As they died, their bones, usually gnawed and scattered by carnivores, were covered by layer after layer of wind-borne dust, silt from the rivers, and ash spewed from volcanoes.

However, several million years ago, the rock plate on which eastern Africa rests began tearing away from the rest of the continent at the rate of about an inch annually, splitting the earth to expose eons of accumulated strata. Thus, while fossils might be found deep in the earth elsewhere, if one knew where to dig, it is only in such open sores as the Rift Valley, where wind and rain keep eroding the earth away, that they appear on the surface.

Fossil hunting in Africa is not a job for faint hearts or flagging muscles, as I discovered during the week I spent at the Koobi Fora camp, followed by several days at Mary Leakey's dig in Tanzania. (Later, I met Johanson and Taieb in Addis Ababa, expecting to accompany them on an expedition to the Afar. But it had to be canceled because war had broken out in the region.)

The work involves weeks of walking and climbing in the intense heat through endless miles of lunar terrain at Lake Turkana in Kenya, or dense thickets at Laetoli in Tanzania, with eyes glued to the ground in the hope of spotting what to the untrained observer often look like nothing more than random bits of whitish rock. Once found, the exact location of the bones are recorded in photographs or sketches, following which they must be eased out with dental picks and brushes. This may require hours or days of stooping under the broiling African sun—it took 4,000 man-hours of work to unearth Lucy. Then the surrounding earth is dug up and sieved through wire mesh to recover any other bits it may secrete, which are picked out with tweezers. Finally, the fragments must be coated with preservatives then fitted together, which is comparable to doing a three-dimensional jigsaw puzzle, with most of the pieces missing, and no picture to guide you.

With the expeditions generally operating on shoestring budgets, meals in the field usually consist of sandwiches made of stale bread and canned fish (shooting game is forbidden by law), washed down with warm beer, when available, or water from holes where animals drink—which even when boiled, filtered, and made into tea, as Louis Leakey complained, may still taste of rhinoceros urine. Baths are taken in rivers or lakes inhabited by crocodiles, and boots are shaken out in the morning to empty them of scorpions which may have crept in. Why do men undergo such hardship and expense to recover a few scraps of bone? "The desire to know where we came from," Don Johanson answers. "We are all searching for roots."

There are great satisfactions in the work, as well—the opportunity to live in intimate contact with ostriches, zebras, gazelles and other game, the possibility of getting one's name into the history books, the joy in camp after a big find has been made, and the good talk around the table in the evenings, presided over by gangling Richard Leakey, wrapped in his after-work sarong, and puffing his curved pipe, or Dr. Mary, smoking cigars and sipping her favorite bourbon.

A popular after-work sport among the younger scientists at Laetoli was throwing at each other dried elephant droppings, which are the size of bowling balls, although much lighter. In an attempt to dodge the flying dung one afternoon in 1976, a participant tripped, fell flat on his face, and found himself staring at the tracks of extinct animals imprinted in the petrified mud. They were partly covered with a layer of volcanic ash which tested out at 3.6 million years old.

The following year, a far more electrifying find was made—two parallel trails of hominid footprints, one set larger than the other. They appear to have been made by a child and two adults, one of whom stepped into the footprints of the first. They had walked together across the damp mudflat just before a volcanic eruption covered their tracks with ash. At one point, the tracks indicate, the smaller hominid made a half turn to the left, as if he or she saw or heard something and turned to look at it before continuing on. The footprints are almost exactly like our own, with a well-shaped modern heel, a strong arch, a good ball in front of the foot, the big toe in line with the others, the toes gripping earth as do ours when we walk barefoot.

"The tracks are of inestimable importance in the story of human evolution," Richard Leakey said. "They demonstrate once and for all that at least 3.5 million years ago, man's direct ancestor walked fully upright with a bipedal, free-striding gait."

The skeletons unearthed by the Leakeys and Johanson have become bones of contention, leaving the experts to argue about who begat whom. Though there are still great gaps and pieces that don't fit, the scenario that most anthropologists accept runs something like this:

On the evidence of the fossil bones found in Pakistan and Iran, as well as Africa, the progenitor of great apes and humans appears to have been one of several species of tree-living primates who lived between 18 and nine million years ago. The next five million years are a blank; no primates of that period have yet been found. During that time, however, world temperatures are known to have cooled, the forests of Africa began to recede, and some of the progenitor's descendants are believed to have left the trees around eight million years ago to make their livings in the grassy savannas and clearings that had appeared. They became hominids. Their cousins who remained in the forest evolved into chimpanzees and gorillas.

The new environment forced radical changes in the hominids' anatomies, through mutation and selective evolution. Perhaps because they needed to see farther on the savannas, they began standing upright on two legs, which freed their hands for other uses. Their big toes moved closer to the other toes, enabling them to stand and walk bipedally. Puny in size, lacking fangs or claws, and no longer able to escape into the trees when attacked by carnivores, they used sticks and stones to defend themselves, and to kill small game. Thus, their hands evolved into a shape better adapted to wielding weapons and tools, and to carrying food. Forced to live by their wits and develop cunning, their brains and intelligence gradually increased.

These physical alterations changed lifestyles, as well. Since using weapons and tools is not an instinctive trait, but must be taught, social organization progressed. These changes did not occur gradually, it should be noted, but in fits and spurts, often separated by eons of time. The first *shaped* stone tools which showed that man could use his head and hands did not appear until almost two million years after he had learned to use his feet. Man walked like a man long before he thought and behaved like a man.

About the actual descent of humans and their near relatives, there is no similar consensus. Some authorities say that too few early hominid specimens have come to light to put them into coherent evolutionary sequence. Others try to squeeze them all into a single lineage. The hypotheses are likely to change with each new hominid discovery. But the geneology that has gained widest *current* acceptance holds that the ancestor of all hominids was *A. afaransis*, which appeared sometime prior to four million years ago. Although its head was still apelike, with a brain scarcely larger than a chimpanzee's, its body had developed along human lines. Its descendants are believed to have split into two branches, one of which evolved into the three australopithecine types described earlier, *africanus*, *robustus* and *boisei*; the other branch became *Homo*. (See chart)

The various species of two-legged creatures lived side by side for almost three million years, all parties agree. But probably because their brains and intelligence never developed sufficiently to adapt to the changing environment, the australos failed in the competition for survival, reaching extinction about a million years ago. And so far as is known, they never left Africa.

The *Homo* line, meanwhile, had developed prodigiously. The heads of the two-million-year old *habilis* were still primitive. But their brains had reached a respectable 800 CC in volume, more than half the size of the average modern adult brain, and their bodies had begun developing into modern form (human knees then were exactly the same as they are today). Although essentially a vegetarian, and only 4½ feet tall, *habilis* and his mates were apparently not afraid to tackle big animals or, more likely, scavenge meat from dead ones, when the opportunity offered. For in the same strata in which their remains lay, were found butchering sites littered with the cracked bones of elephants and hippos, and the stone hand axes and flaked cobble tools that were used to cut the flesh and hides from them.

Habilis, too, appears to have been a homebody. But his bigbrowed, larger-brained (up to 1000 CC), and half-foot taller *erectus* descendants, who appeared in East Africa about 1.6 million

Man's Family Tree

M. Homo sapiens sapiens (modern man). Appeared 150,000 years ago. Average brain size: 1400 cc.

L. Homo sapiens neandertalensis (Neanderthal man). Appeared 150,000 years ago – extinct 30,000 years ago. Average brain size: 1400-plus cc. Average height: 5 feet, 4 inches.

K. Homo sapiens (archaic modern man). Appeared 200,000 years ago. Average brain size: 1150 cc. Average height: 5 feet, 2 inches.

J. Homo erectus. Appeared 1.5 million years ago. Average brain size: 1000 cc. Average height: 5 feet.

I. Homo habilis. Appeared 2 million years ago. Brain size: 642-800 cc. Average height: 4½ feet.

F.G.H. Australopithecus, Robustus, Boisei and Africanus. Appeared 3 million years ago - extinct one million years ago. Brain size: 430-550 cc.

E. Australopithecus afarensis. Appeared 4 million years ago. Brain size: 380-450 cc. Average height: 4 feet.

C.D. Chimpanzees and Gorillas. Appeared 4 million years ago. Average brain size: 380 cc.

B. Hominids separate from great apes. 5 million years ago.

A. Unknown progenitor of hominids and great apes. 8 million years ago.

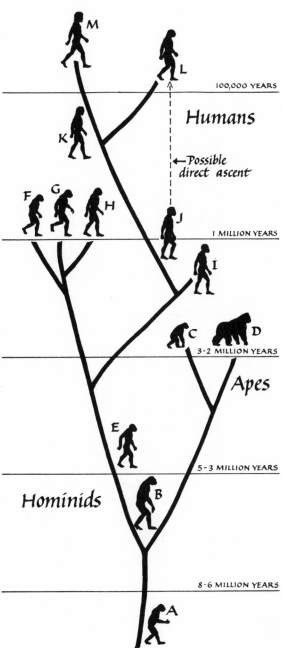

100,000 YEARS

Humans

←Possible direct ascent

1 MILLION YEARS

3-2 MILLION YEARS

Apes

5-3 MILLION YEARS

Hominids

8-6 MILLION YEARS

years back, were confirmed travelers, although slow ones. Heading north, they passed through Ethiopia, Israel and Syria more than one million years ago, leaving a trail of camps and butchering sites behind them. They reached Java 700,000 years ago, got to Peking some 200,000 years later, and were settled in Hungary, the French Riviera, and elsewhere in Europe after 300,000 B.C. Sometime during that long span, as manifested by the more than one-million-year-old blackened hearths and charred bones found in Kenya and South Africa, they had learned the use of fire. Indeed, it may have been this epic discovery that enabled them to leave tropical Africa for colder climes.

Toward the end of his long tenure on earth, around 200,000 years ago, *erectus* had evolved into *Homo sapiens*, an archaic man with a much more modern looking skull, a brain averaging 83 percent the size of our own, and a body almost like ours. Where the species originated cannot be ascertained since transitional skulls, showing a mixture of *erectus* and *sapiens* characteristics, have been found in both Africa and Europe. Like their predecessors, the *sapiens* were nomadic, living in caves or temporary huts made of branches and hides. They were skilled toolmakers with variegated kits of flaked stone implements, some of them small and delicate, which were resharpened when worn. They hunted in sizable bands, using bolas and spears to bring down smaller game. Large animals, such as rhinoceroses and elephants, were often bagged by stampeding them over cliffs or driving them into swamps where they could be more readily killed and butchered.

Sapiens sired two notable lines of descendants, one of which was Neanderthal man who appeared around 125,000 years ago. (An alternative possibility, anthropologists concede, is that Neanderthal evolved from *Homo erectus* directly, rather than through *Homo sapiens*.)

The Neanderthals, whose habitations and skeletal remains have been found throughout Europe, and in Asia as far east as Iran, are much maligned characters. Squat in build (averaging 5′ 4″ for adult males), with large brow ridges, protruding faces, heavily muscled limbs and huge joints, they became the prototypes of the cave men shown in comic strips. Nevertheless, their brains were fully as big as our own—often larger. Their finely fashioned stone tools were more sophisticated than those of their forebears. Some shaped like leaves pointed at both ends have edges sharp enough to slice paper. They buried their dead with reverence, furnishing the bodies with ornaments, food and tools, which betokens a belief in the afterlife. And since such abstract ideas as immortality of the spirit cannot be conveyed by grunts and gestures, they obviously could talk and had a language.

They were also people of sensitivity and emotion. Found in Shanidar Cave in northern Iraq was the body of a Neanderthal infant 60,000 years dead, whose bones were impregnated with wildflower pollen, indicating that the child's body had been covered with the blossoms before burial. Not far from it lay the skeleton of a crippled man whose right arm had been severed in childhood and was evidently blind in one eye. Unable to wield weapons or hunt, he had been protected and provided with food until his death at the age of 40, as the forensic evidence shows.

The last actor, the star of the evolutionary drama, was our own species, *Homo sapiens sapiens* (wise, wise man). Although he arrived on the stage very late in Europe and eastern Asia—a mere 40,000 years ago—he had been waiting in the wings for a long time in Africa.

CHAPTER 2

The Emergence of Modern Man

(200,000 to 15,000 years ago)

The climb to Border Cave, high in the Lebombo Mountains of Swaziland in southern Africa, took an exhausting three hours. Worst of all were the last 20 feet, where we threaded our way across a precipice on a rocky ledge that, in several places, was not quite as wide as the sole of my shoe. It was easy to see why people seeking security would have chosen the cavern as a dwelling. One man could defend it against an army. No animal larger than a squirrel could possible get in. When we finally entered the large grotto, young archeologist Adrian Boshier dropped his pack and said quietly: "Welcome to your ancestral home."

The greeting was not offered in jest but as a statement of literal fact. For based on the discoveries made by Boshier, his associate Peter Beaumont and others, the cave had been continually inhabited by humans for the unimaginable span of 100,000 years. Moreover

the occupants were not the beetle-browed, heavy-legged Neanderthals who occupied the Northern Hemisphere at the time. The
human skull fragments and bones unearthed in the cave—including
the skeleton of a two-month old infant who died more than 90,000
years ago—are those of fully modern men, *Homo sapiens sapiens*
(wise, wise man), the species of which every human being on earth
is a member. They had well-shaped heads, straight bodies, and
brains as large as our own. If dressed in modern clothes they would
probably pass unnoticed in your local supermarket.

Their level of culture was extraordinarily high for an age when
sabre-toothed tigers and giant antlered giraffes still roamed southern Africa. The Border Cave dwellers were expert hunters and
skilled miners. They manufactured a wide variety of sophisticated
tools of stone, bone and wood. They adorned themselves with paint
and cosmetics, and beads made of ostrich eggshells. They could
count and kept primitive records on notched fragments of bone.
They also had strong religious convictions, believed in the afterlife,
and like their Neanderthal cousins, treated their dead with reverence, for the body of the infant in the cave had been carefully and
ceremoniously buried, along with a seashell pendant it had probably worn in life.

Beaumont and Boshier's association with Border Cave began in
1964 when geologists of the Anglo-American Corporation, opening
an iron mine on Bomvu Ridge in Swaziland, came across stone
tools which struck them as being very old. With commendable
foresight, the company engaged the two gangling young archeologists to explore the site before it was clawed up by bulldozers.

What they discovered there has required the rewriting of an
important segment of cultural prehistory. They came across ten
ancient filled-in pits, some as deep as 45 feet, from which a soft
bright-red iron oxide mineral, called hematite, had been dug. There
were also two underground cavities, hacked into the steep slope of
the ridge to a depth of 44 feet, from which glittering black specularite ore had been extracted.

The pits were among the richest deposits of Stone Age relics
ever discovered. In 18 months, the diggers recovered an estimated

half-million mining tools, including cleavers, picks, hammers, wedges and chisels with their edges heavily bruised from usage, as well as mortars and pestles which had been used to pound the ore to powder. They were nearly all made of dolerite, a hard rock foreign to the vicinity which had been hauled up the mountain from the river beds in the valley a mile away. Mingled with them were stone axeheads, beads and bracelets. Although the site, now preserved as a national monument, has been picked over repeatedly in the years since its discovery, the ground was still littered with ancient tools when I visited it.

Exactly how long the mines had been worked is difficult to determine. Charcoal from a hearth fire which the miners lit to roast their meat has been radiocarbon dated to 40,000 B.C.—a date seven times older than the earliest known mines of Europe. But several feet below the dated carbon lie other ash layers estimated to be as much as 80,000 years old.

Yet, the curious fact is that the ancient men had no utilitarian need for the ore they went to such great labor to extract, for it was not until Biblical times, around 1500 B.C., that man first learned the secret of smelting it into iron. The red hematite ("bloodstone" in Greek) was valued entirely for its color. It was used throughout the world—as it still is in some places—as a cosmetic to adorn the body in ceremonies, as a pigment in paintings, as a medicine and, most importantly, in fertility and burial rites. To early man, as to modern primitive tribesmen, blood and life were synonymous. They observed that slaughtered animals and wounded men died when they lost blood, and that when women stopped menstruating they could no longer create new life.

Thus, to assure rebirth in the afterworld, it was necessary to provide the corpse with a substitute for blood, and the red ore—"the blood of mother earth" as African natives describe it—has been used for the purpose throughout human history almost everywhere on earth. The 30,000-year-old bones of the "Red Lady of Paviland" in Wales, and the funerary objects buried with her, were completely encrusted with it, as was the body of a 30-year-old man buried in Bavaria around 20,000 years ago, and human skeletons of

the same era dug out of the permafrost of northern Russia. The
3,000-year-old funeral chambers and sarcophagi of Chinese, Greek
and Etruscan rulers alike were painted in red. Within living memory, American Indians coated their dead with ochre preceding funerals, and Australian aborigines painted their bodies with it during
fertility rites. Indeed, the ground red ore is still sold in witch
doctors' shops in African villages as an antidote for human afflic-
tions, including snake bite, and bloodstones set in rings are still
worn in some parts of Europe for their supposed curative powers.
Few superstitions have been more universal, or more persistent.

The black specularite, often called "looking glass ore," also had
magic significance. Until very recent times, it was powdered,
mixed with animal fat and smeared on the hair and bodies of tribal
chiefs and medicine men to give them unworldly, glittering appear-
ances while performing sacred ceremonies. Thus, it was not physical need, but concern for the spirit, that led to mining, man's first
important industrial enterprise over 70,000 years ago. No more
powerful argument could be advanced to rebut the theory that
economic necessity alone is the motivating force behind all human
advancement.

No human remains were found in the Bomvu mines as it was not
a permanent abode, but a temporary campsite which was abandoned by each party after it had recovered it's quota of ore. To find
out who the miners might have been, Boshier and Beaumont turned
to Border Cave on the southern rim of Swaziland from which
Raymond Dart, in 1934, had brought out stone age artifacts very
similar to those found at Bomvu. Some years later, a local prospec-
tor in search of bat guano dug a pit in the center of the cave from
which he recovered various pieces of a fossilized human skeleton,
obviously old, but difficult to date because of the carelessness with
which he dug. In 1942, archeologists of the University of Witwatersrand revisited the site and found the infant skeleton lying in a
deep stratum. Since scientific dating methods had not yet been
devised, and the bones were so modern looking, it was assumed
they were no more than a few hundred or thousand years old.
Except for occasional picnickers, the grotto had remained undis-

turbed for 30 years when Boshier and Beaumont reentered it in 1971.

The cave proved to be "the most perfect preservation ever recorded at an archeological site extending to such antiquity," Beaumont recalls. In 50 feverish days, before they ran out of the money provided by the mining company to pay the native workers, the archeologists unearthed some 300,000 charred animal bones and stone artifacts. With radiocarbon dating technology now available, they realized the material was very old. Charcoal from an unbroken layer of sediment and ash overlying the body of the buried child proved to have been laid down 90,000 years ago. Stone implements and ground pigments were found in strata down to bedrock, 11 feet below the surface, indicating the cavern had been occupied for 100,000 years.

"Almost everything we found was three times older than the textbooks said it should have been," Boshier observed. The perforated seashell pendant in the child's grave may be the earliest known evidence of human adornment. The recovery of a carefully notched bone from a 35,000 years old level indicates that man may have learned to count at that remote period. The atmosphere of the cave is so dry that layers of twigs, leaves, grass and feathers, brought in as bedding, were found in levels dating more than 50,000 years old.

What the infant burial and other evidence of Border Cave prove, to cite Boshier and Beaumont, is that "as early as 100,000 years ago, man had developed a consciousness and an awareness of happenings and causes beyond the hard everyday needs of survival. This was the ascendancy of reason. No longer was he content to be nature's guest. He began to probe and find out why, to fabricate reasons and explanations. Thus arose an intellect, and here began the growth of religious belief."

Border Cave is not the only repository of early *sapiens sapiens* remains, or even the oldest. Segments of a skull bearing modern *sapiens* features found in the Omo Valley of southern Ethiopia have been dated at 130,000 years. Fragments of anatomically modern skulls and bones estimated to be 115,000 years old have been unearthed from caves and rock shelters at Klasies River Mouth in South Africa. This evidence would indicate that modern man evolved in Africa at about the same time the Neanderthal appeared in Europe, and that it was from Africa that *sapiens sapiens* set out to conquer the world. The oldest known modern human skulls and stone tools outside of that continent, dated 92,000 years old, were found at Qafzeh in Israel, the first country a traveler reaches on leaving Africa by land.

Modern *sapiens* tools found at sites in Greece and Bulgaria show that the migrants entered Europe prior to 40,000 years ago, and within the next 10,000 years, the Neanderthals had vanished. What led to their mysterious disappearance has been argued for well over a century. One long-held belief is that the new breed exterminated the old, but there is not a vestige of proof to support it. Others hold that the two populations interbred, offering as evidence the 60,000-year-old bones of two individuals found in the Skhul cave in Israel who appear to be hybrid types, possessing features inherited from both Neanderthal and modern *sapiens*. But DNA tracings made by geneticists appear to show that the two species did not mate extensively, and certainly Europeans and Near Easterners today look far more *sapiens* than Neanderthal.

The strong possibility is that, though there may have been no violence, the Neanderthals could not compete with their new neighbors in the struggle for survival. The new people were taller and had more agile bodies. They were more proficient foragers, possessing hooks to catch fish. They possessed superior hunting weapons as well, including the spear-thrower and possibly the bow and arrow that could kill animals more accurately, with greater force, at a greater distance. Although the brains of the two groups were the same average size, the newcomers obviously possessed greater creative intelligence. "They knew how to do a lot of things their predecessors didn't," wrote anthropologist Richard Klein of the University of Chicago. "Something quite extraordinary must have happened to the organization of the brain." The results were evident in the superior and esthetically shaped tools, including bone sewing needles, the new men developed or had brought with them, and in the magnificent cave paintings and other art they would soon produce.

The great advances made subsequently by the emigrants in other continents raises a difficult question. If Africa was the incubator of modern man where his intellect, mining skills and spiritual concerns first developed, why did it not retain its cultural lead over the rest of the world, or at least keep pace with it, instead of falling behind? One answer offered by anthropologists is that "nature is conservative," and that animals are not likely to evolve or human populations progress unless forced to do so by a change in environmental circumstances or in the competition for survival. Game was generally abundant in Africa and, except for occasional droughts and wet periods in the past few millenia, the climate remained temperate. The Great Glacier which blanketed much of the northern hemisphere under mile-high sheets of ice as recently as 12,000 years ago never materialized in the southern continent, except for a patch around Mount Kilimanjaro in Tanzania. There was little reason for its inhabitants to change their age-old ways of life since they could live quite comfortably without doing so.

After the Sahara Desert encroached across the northern part of the continent 7,000 years ago, the inhabitants of southern Africa were cut off from the rest of humanity. News of cultural advances elsewhere was slow to reach them. Fearful of upsetting the balance of nature on which their lives depended, the inhabitants came to regard the traditional ways as sacred. Powerful religious taboos were often invoked to forbid even modest improvements—as they still were until recently. Thus, when European explorers and colonists entered southern Africa two centuries ago, they found many of the tribes still living in the Stone Age. They had never left it.

When man trekked north, however, he entered a more hostile environment, which required him to use his brain and hands in ways that had not been necessary before, and to develop skills unknown in his earlier homeland. As game grew scarcer and populations increased, following the last great Ice Age, man had to domesticate and breed the wild pigs, sheep and cattle he formerly hunted, and to keep them and himself alive he eventually learned to sow crops. He abandoned his caves and nomadic campsites to build permanent homes and villages near his fields.

No longer able to forage for all of the necessities of life themselves, communities exchanged goods with each other, which brought with it a fecund cross-fertilization of ideas and knowledge. The intensifying competition for arable land led to development of complex social and governmental structures, and eventually warfare. In their search for better weapons and tools, men adapted their ancient ochre-mining skills, first to the mining of high quality flint, later to copper and iron ores which they learned to smelt into metals. And with the advent of metals came the stupendous cultural explosion that propelled us from the Stone Age to the Space Age in only 5,000 years, a mere minute in man's long history.

Another question that haunts us is how and when racial differences developed among humans. The ancient bones, skulls and teeth, reveal a great deal about the individuals' heights and weights, the size of their muscles and brains, as well as the contour of their faces. But the bones tell us nothing at all about the color of their skins and hair, the shape of their eyes and noses, nor whether their hair was straight or curly. American anthropologist Carleton Coon, 50 years ago, theorized that racial differentiation began far back in time, and that *"Homo erectus evolved into Homo sapiens not once but five times"* in separate parts of the globe. But modern geneticists reject the idea. Analyses of human DNA samples from around the world reveal that regardless of external appearance all people on earth belong to the same genus, *Homo sapiens sapiens.*

Actually, people may be even more closely related than that, a landmark study published in 1987 reveals. Among the constituents of human DNA are mitochondrial genes which can be inherited only from the mother. Tracing the trail of these genes back in time, molecular biologist Douglas Wallace, and his colleagues of the University of California in Berkeley, reached the startling conclusion that all five billion people on earth are descendants of *a single woman* who lived some 200,000 years ago. This primordial "Eve" (tracing genes back to a scientifically derived "Adam" is much more difficult) was not the only woman alive at the time but, the research indicates, she was the sole progenitor of the *sapiens sapiens* species. The family lines of all of her female contemporaries have died out. Thus, roughly calculated, Eve is the 10,000th-great-grandmother of every living person.

This conclusion has raised a storm of controversy, but not among biologists who regard it as a well-established outcome of the laws of genetic probability. The principal arguments revolve around whether the matriarch could have lived as recently as 200,000 years ago, and where her home may have been. Best evidence indicates that the putative "Garden of Eden" lay somewhere in eastern sub-Saharan Africa, and that Eve and her immediate descendants were probably black-skinned. About 180,000 years ago, it is estimated, groups of Eve's progeny left their homeland for other parts of Africa, and by 100,000 years ago had begun fanning out to other continents.

As they entered new environments and were isolated from each other, people began to diverge in appearance, in accordance with the laws of natural selection. Individuals who possessed physical characteristics better adapted to their particular environments lived healthier, longer lives, producing more offspring like themselves, causing the favored characteristics to accentuate. After many generations, the traits dominated the regional gene pool and became common to the entire geographic population. Nevertheless, human bodies have remained alike internally, as have human brains, and physiologists regard the external differences to be trivial variations.

Skin color, for example, is an adaptation to climate—black in Africa for protection from the strong sun, white under the weaker sun of northern Europe to better absorb the ultraviolet radiation that helps produce vitamin D, with various gradations of pigmentation in regions that lie between the two climatic extremes. Similarly, woolly or spiral hair provides an air space around the scalp that insulates the head from the intensity of the sun's rays in the tropics, a protection unnecessary in cooler climes. Noses which serve to modify the temperature and moisture content of air are more prominent, allowing a greater interior surface area of mucous membrane in dry climates, whereas Eskimos in the frigid Arctic have narrow nasal apertures, which can warm and moisten air more efficiently than broad ones. Many more examples might be cited.

Although scientists are not yet prepared to say precisely where each race originated, their common ancestry is "a tremendously important discovery," says Harvard paleontologist Stephen Jay Gould. "It makes us realize that all human beings, despite differences in external appearance, are members of a single entity that had a very recent origin in one place."

The matters discussed in this and the preceding chapter delineate the current extent of our knowledge and theories of man's descent. He evolved in Africa from primordial primates prior to four million years ago; he had several rivals much like himself; and he overcame or outlasted them and all other living species because he walked on two legs, his hands were more efficient, and his brain was bigger and more creative.

Man also had one other characteristic lacking in other species. He was restless and inquisitive, a traveler impelled to find out what lay over the next hill, or on the far shore. *Homo erectus* had left Africa to settle the Old World from the Atlantic to the China Sea. His *sapiens* descendants would people the New World as well, as shall be related in the next chapter.

CHAPTER 3

The Long Walk
to America

(40,000 to 4000 B.C.)

In 1973, young Professor James Adovasio of the University of
Pittsburgh, seeking to train his students in archeological excavation, began to dig into the dirt floor of the Meadowcroft Rockshelter, a large overhanging ledge of rock in the valley of a creek in
southwestern Pennsylvania. It seemed a place where Indians were
likely to have camped in prehistoric times. With luck, Adovasio
hoped, artifacts perhaps one or two thousand years old might be
unearthed.

Peeling back the successive layers of earth, like the pages of a
history book read backwards, the diggers first went through bottle
caps, candy wrappers and other trash left by 20th century picnickers, then 19th century buttons, lead bullets, rusty nails and bits of
hand-blown glass, before the first signs of Indians appeared. Then
came layer after layer of pottery shards, stone tools and arrow-

heads, and refuse dumps and firepits containing burnt animal bones and the charred grains of corn and squash. At the 700-year-old mark, they found a grave containing the skeleton of a dog, and at the 800-year level, the shattered bones and skull of a man who appeared to have been cannibalized.

In the strata dating to the time of Christ, arrowheads vanished, leaving flaked stone spear points and knives as the only hunting weapons. By the 3,000-year-old horizon, corn disappeared. It had not yet reached this part of the New World. Unexpected discovery in a stratum laid down around the time the Egyptian pyramids were built, were the carbonized remains of tightly-woven water baskets, one of which still held the stones which had been heated in a fire and dropped into it to boil the water—one of the methods of cooking food in the pre-pottery age.

For a time, excavation was held up by a slab of rock that geologists estimate had fallen from the roof of the shelter between 10,000 and 12,000 years ago. Was there anything under it? Indeed there was, hearths, roasted animal bones, artifacts, more fragments of basketry, and other evidence of human occupation, right down to bedrock, dating as far back as 19,600 years before the present, give or take a few centuries. While this is not the earliest date ascribed to human relics in America, thanks to the meticulous care with which the radiocarbon dating and the digging was done—some living floors were shaved with razor blades—it seems the oldest *unchallengeable* evidence of man's presence here.

This was the first site I visited in my investigation of man's arrival in the New World. I had expected the task to be easier than researching his appearance in the Old World since it involves a very much shorter span of time—a few thousand years in the Western Hemisphere as compared to millions in the Eastern—and being more recent would appear to be less controversial.

But I was wrong.

To date, the relics of the earliest human ancestors are concentrated in four areas of Africa which are only one-to-four hours of flying time from each other. The evidences of man's earliest appearance in America, however, stretch from Alaska to the Strait of

Magellan, a distance of 12,000 miles, requiring far more stops and days of flying time.

The physical effort required is also greater. In East Africa, a reporter with the proper credentials may be invited to reside in well-appointed, semi-permanent camps established near the digging sites. In the Americas, most of the sites lie in the wilderness, the Arctic, the desert, or deep in the mountains, some of them reachable only on foot, by canoe or helicopter. What camps exist are makeshift and temporary, lasting only during the digging season, weather permitting, or until scarce funds run out.

The nature of the evidence is also different. For reasons that will be explained, very few ancient human remains have been found in the Americas. To a far greater extent, the investigators must rely on questionable evidence—chipped stones that look as though they might have been shaped by man, animal bones with scratches on them that could have been made by a knife, and soot in caves and on firepit stones that may or may not have been kindled by humans.

For these and other reasons, reconstructing the history of early man in America is in some respects a more speculative business than it is in Africa and interpretations are more divergent. Controversies among the anthropologists tend to be more numerous, more spirited, and sometimes downright nasty. The opinions expressed about their colleagues by some of the experts I interviewed verged on insult, and differences of opinion are so bitter that there are those who will not sit at the same table with others. It makes for lively professional meetings.

The quest for the origin of the Americans has been going on ever since Columbus encountered people in the New World and misnamed them Indians. Although the Bible doesn't mention them, the Pope in 1512 officially declared them to be descendants of Adam and Eve. New England Protestant cleric Cotton Mather disagreed; he believed they were brought here by the devil. Others linked them with the "lost ten tribes" of Israel, with ancient Greeks, Trojans, Egyptians, Norwegians and the inhabitants of the mythical continents of Atlantis and Mu. The one thing certain is that man did not evolve in the Western hemisphere. Although there are monkeys in South America, there are no ground-dwelling apes. And no traces of ancient human ancestors, such as *Homo erectus* and Neanderthal, whose remains have been found in Africa, Europe and Asia, have ever been discovered in the New World.

The first arrivals were people of our own species, *Homo sapiens sapiens,* who crossed the Bering Strait into Alaska from northwestern Siberia. It was long believed that this could not have happened earlier than 5,000 years ago because so far as was known boats capable of navigating the open ocean had not been built before that time.

But in 1908, while riding through an arroyo near Folsom, New Mexico, after a flash flood, George McJunkin, a black cowboy, found a pile of bleached bones that were too big to be those of cattle or modern buffalo. When archeologists belatedly got around to investigating the find in 1926, four years after the cowboy's death, they identified them as the bones of 23 extinct giant bison, which had apparently been stampeded over the bank, where they were killed and butchered. Although the species is known to have vanished with the glaciers 10,000 years ago, they obviously had been killed by men. For stuck between their ribs and in their vertebrae were exquisitely fashioned, fluted stone spear points. Also, the tail bones, which hunters usually strip off with the hide when a beast is skinned, were missing from the skeletons. Then in 1932, at another New Mexico kill site near Clovis, the bones of primitive camels, horses and woolly mammoths were unearthed, pierced by larger stone spear points of somewhat more primitive design. Since mammoths disappeared around 12,000 years ago, human occupancy of the New World was pushed back at least that far.

With the development of radiocarbon dating in 1947 (explained in Chapter 5), which can establish the ages of charcoal, bone and other organic material, the dates of man's possible presence leapt progressively backward in time—a 23,000-year-old reading for the burnt animal bones, lying amid stone implements, in Tlapacoya, Mexico; a 27,000 to 30,000-year age for a hide scraper made of a caribou shinbone at Old Crow in the Yukon; and the same age for an assemblage of extinct animal remains, charcoal and stone tools, found near Lewisville, Texas. Even older dates, in excess of 40,000 years, were recorded by the split and burned bones of dwarf mammoths, lying amid tools and charcoal near what looked like U-shaped firepits on Santa Rosa Island off California, and a shell pendant, engraved with the figure of a woolly mammoth, found in Delaware.

Surprising readings came from South America as well. The dung and bones of extinct sloths, camels and horses, lying amid stone tools and charcoal in Pikimachay Cave in Peru, and knife-scarred mastodon bones and stone spearpoints found at El Jobo, Venezuela, are both clocked at 14,000 years before the present. Human remains unearthed in Fell's Cave on the Strait of Magellan prove that Indians had reached the southern tip of the continent prior to 11,000 years ago.

Even more startling, because they were so old, were the discoveries made at a rockshelter in Pedra Furada in northeast Brazil, and in a peat bog at Monte Verde on the Chilean coast, which indicate that the sites had been occupied by humans on and off for 32,000 years. Among the relics found at the Chilean site was a 13,000-year-old footprint of an eight-to-ten-year-old child, and lying in the debris at Pedra Furada were fragments of a wall painting, suggesting that cave art may have been practiced in America at about the same time as it was in Europe.

The search for earlier and earlier dates for man's appearance in America is a never-ending quest. The oldest estimate of man's arrival in the New World was postulated by the late, great paleoanthropologist Louis Leakey, whose discoveries in Olduvai Gorge in East Africa revolutionized our theories of human evolution. In 1963, Leakey visited a site at Calico Hills in the Mojave Desert of California where stones shaped like primitive tools had been found in ancient strata. He adjudged them to be human artifacts over 100,000 years old. Although no bones or other organic traces have been discovered that could be positively dated, the diggers came across a circle of small boulders which they believed to be a man-made hearth.

What makes all of these clues so tantalizing is the inability to prove them beyond question. Having been badly burned in the past by misinterpretations, hoaxes and error, modern archeologists have become cautious, if not downright suspicious. Few are persuaded that the stone "hearth" at Calico Hills is anything more than a random arrangement of rocks, or that the crude stone "tools" are actually artifacts. Although some of them looked genuine to me, they could be "geofacts," created when frost, glaciers, landslides or mountain torrents crack and chip stones into shapes resembling man-made objects. One of the most eloquent archeological documentary scenes ever filmed shows a sweating Louis Leakey arguing his case before an assembly of American paleoanthropologists who make no effort to hide their disbelief.

A few of the early dates for human presence in America have collapsed. The "40,000-year-old" mammoth pendant found in Delaware proved to be a fake. The famous scraper made of a caribou tibia from Old Crow in the Yukon was dated 27,000 years old when the outside of the bone was tested, but later tests of the core reduced its age to a mere 1,350 years. Apparently carbon from campfires or nearby coal deposits had accumulated in the outside layers to give the false reading. Some of the other early dates must also be regarded as equivocal. The 40,000-year-old mammoth bones found on Santa Rosa Island could have been scorched in a fire kindled by lightning or spontaneous combustion, rather than by man. The fact that stone tools lie alongside datable charcoal and animal fossils at Lewisville and elsewhere does not necessarily mean they are contemporaneous, the implements may have been deposited in the stratum later by people, burrowing animals or earth movements.

Yet, American archeologists must rely on age-by-association because ancient human skeletal remains are much rarer in America than in Europe, Africa and Asia. The early population is believed to have been sparser. Caves in which people might live are fewer. Signs of human presence in the open prior to the last great glaciers, which reached their maximum height 18,000 years ago, would have been obliterated by the moving ice, and later by melting glacial waters and high winds that reshaped the landscape in many parts of the continent. The acid American soil also quickly attacks organic materials left in it, and if the ancient Indians exposed their dead, as did many of their recent descendants, there would be little left to preserve.

Despite occasional speculation that early men may have somehow managed to cross the Pacific to reach South America, there is no serious argument about how the first humans got to the New World. They walked here. During glacial times, so much of the world's water was locked up in the ice sheets, which covered almost a third of the earth's land mass, that ocean levels dropped more than 300 feet at times, exposing broad stretches of the continental shelves and creating a land bridge across the shallow Bering Sea between Siberia and Alaska.

So far as can be determined, the bridge existed throughout the last Ice Age, a period extending from 75,000 to 13,000 years ago. Due to low precipitation in the region, both the bridge and the approaches to it—called Beringia—were ice-free, constituting a 1,300-mile-wide stretch of rolling tundra, small lakes, luxuriant grasses and tangles of dwarf birch, willows and alders. The bridge was also open during earlier Ice Ages, and animals had been using it from time immemorial. The ancestors of camels, horses, wolves and other beasts, which had evolved in America, crossed to Asia, while Eurasian mammoths, mastodons, bison, caribou, musk ox and other species migrated to America.

The small bands of human hunters who crossed the bridge could have had no idea they were moving from one continent to another. They were simply following the grazing herds, and the herds were following the grass. Once in Alaska, a few isolated groups of people may have moved down the mountainous Pacific Coast by skin boat. But animals and the great majority of migrants are believed to have made their way south through an ice-free corridor between the towering glaciers, that extended from Alaska through the Yukon, the valley of the McKenzie River and Alberta, into the heartland of the western United States.

The question is when did people begin using the bridge and corridor? Based on the Calico Hills finds, Louis Leakey's supporters are certain that migrations started well before 75,000 years ago. They claim that microscopic examination reveals that the cutting edges of some of the stone "tools" were artificially chipped and worn with use. They also insist the boulders found in a circle had been part of a hearth since tests show that their inner edges had been heated by fire, while the outer edges had not. However, the claims seem unlikely since Russian investigators have found no trace of people in northeastern Siberia until around 40,000 years ago.

At the other extremes are the diehards, headed by anthropologists Paul Martin and Vance Haynes of the University of Arizona. They assert that the Indians arrived in Alaska in a single migration at the end of the Ice Age, approximately 12,000 years ago, headed south soon after, and proliferated rapidly. They base their claim on "overkill," arguing that as the deadliest predator the world had ever known, it was man's wanton slaughter—whole herds stampeded over cliffs or driven into swamps, for example, to obtain the meat and hides of a few—that caused the extinction of mammoths and other species which disappeared between 13,000 and 11,000 years ago. If man had arrived earlier, they reason, the beasts would have been wiped out earlier.

However, the 12,000-year-old date of man's arrival in the New World has a dwindling number of supporters. It conflicts with the almost certain 17,600 B.C. median date of human occupancy in the Pennsylvania rockshelter, and the fairly persuasive 32,000-year ages ascribed to the human evidence found in Brazil and Chile. Besides, anthropologists say, it is unlikely that in a mere thousand years, without knowing where they were going or any known reason for haste, the Indians could have spread throughout the whole of North and South America, exterminating every now-extinct animal enroute. It would have taken far longer, the experts calculate, for the migrants, saddled with household goods and families, to move long distances and resettle. They would have had to acclimate themselves to each new environment they entered, ranging from frozen tundra to steaming jungle; to devise new strategies for hunting and gathering strange animals and plants; and to experiment with unfamiliar raw materials and develop new lifestyles. Although man may have hastened the extermination of the Ice Age beasts, most paleontologists attribute their disappearance to their inability to adapt to the warmer climates that ensued as the glaciers receded. They point out that modern buffalo and deer were hunted just as wastefully, over a longer period of time, yet until Europeans arrived with guns, North America still teemed with them.

The scenario for the peopling of America that most authorities now accept has the first humans trickling across the land bridge from Asia between 45,000 and 40,000 years ago, with migrations continuing in small groups until comparatively recent times. That the new Americans were all of the same stock as the northern Asians they left behind seems certain. Among the distinctive structural traits shared by the majority of individuals in both populations are shovel-shaped indentations on the inside of the incisor teeth, which are rare among southern Asians, and almost non-existent among people of European and African descent.

Based on the analyses of blood types, dental differences, and the similarity of certain words in some of the Indian languages, anthropologists postulate that the migrants arrived in three separate waves. The first groups to arrive from Siberia, called Paleoindians, are held to be the ancestors of the large majority of the populations of both North and South America. Next to arrive were the Na-dene (pronounced nah-*den*-ay) people, ancestors of the present-day tribes of the northwest coast, the Athabaskas of western Canada, and the Navajos and Apaches of the southwestern United States. They may have been the last to cross the bridge before it was inundated 11,000 years ago. The final wave consisted of Eskimos and Aleuts who are believed to have arrived by kayak, or across the ice in winter, between 9,000 and 4,000 years back.

Presumably the people in each of the waves looked much alike and spoke the same or closely related languages. But perhaps due to adaptation to the different environments they entered, or genetic changes caused by isolation in small groups, the Indians began to diverge in both appearance and language. By the time of Columbus, they spoke over 2,000 distinct tongues, more than in all of Europe and Asia combined, some as different from each other as are English, Chinese and Arabic. The dialects of American Eskimos are akin to those of the Chukchi of Siberia, but so far philologists have been unable to trace any clear relationships between American Indian languages and those spoken anywhere else on earth.

The cultural history of the early Americans is better understood. They were hunters who supplemented their meat diet with fish, which they caught with bone hooks, harpoons and nets, and with seeds, roots, berries, mollusks, insects and anything else edible. They had learned to make fire more than a million years earlier and protected their bodies from the Ice Age cold with fur trousers, parkas and foot coverings, sewn with bone needles and animal sinew. Like their contemporaries in Siberia, the first Americans may have lived in frame tents made of sticks or mammoth bones, partially sunk into the ground, draped with furs and skins, weighted at the bottom with stones, dirt and sod. They made utensils of bark, wood, cordage and basketry. They hunted with wooden spears, sharpened at the end or tipped with bone, which could be hurled with considerable velocity by use of a throwing stick, or *atlatl*.

As the artifacts found in the earliest habitation sites prove, the tool kits the immigrants brought with them were highly sophisticated, similar to those of their cousins living in Asia and Europe at the time. In addition to stone choppers, axes, chisels, hide scrapers and awls of various sizes, they had wrenches made of deer antlers that were used to straighten spear shafts, and small implements of considerable delicacy and refinement. Prior to the arrival in America, men had learned that, through controlled percussion and by using antelope or deer antlers to apply pressure to flint and other hard rock, they could flake off thin blades of stone with edges sharp as scalpels. When fitted with wooden or bone handles, the flakes made excellent knives and deadly weapons.

When the Indians got past the glaciers into what is now southern Canada and the United States, however, they found that some of the tools that served them in the Arctic and barren tundra were inadequate in the new environment. The continent they entered, though chilly and moist, was rich in vegetation, forests, lakes and lush meadows. It was a bird hunter's paradise, whose lakes teemed with ducks and geese, which could be seized by hand or trapped with nets during the summer moulting season when the birds were unable to fly. The early adventurers also encountered some of the largest and most remarkable animals ever known—woolly mammoths that stood 14 feet high at the shoulder, with inward-curling tusks twice as long as those of a modern elephant; tree-browsing mastodons and ground sloths that were almost as big; super-bison with six-foot hornspreads; giant moose adorned with antlers eight feet tall; beaver and tapirs the size of modern bears; along with caribou, primitive camels, giant bears, horses three feet high, and a large menagerie of smaller game. There were also nightmarish carnivores, such as huge cave bears, dire wolves twice the size of modern wolves, panthers bigger than African lions, and saber-toothed cats who stabbed their victims to death with eight-inch-long canines.

The opportunity of obtaining meat in huge economy-sized packages from beasts who, through inexperience with men may have had little fear of the puny two-legged intruders, changed the Indians' way of life. By 11,000 years ago, they became highly skilled big-game hunters, developing an array of superbly crafted bifacial (shaped on both sides) hunting and butchering tools and weapons, the most remarkable of which was the Clovis spear point, named for the New Mexican site where it had first been found. It was three to five inches long and fluted, or grooved, on the sides so that it could be lashed firmly into the cleft end of a bone or wooden shaft. When hurled with a spear-thrower, it could penetrate thick hides and reach vital organs of mammoths and other huge beasts with an efficiency that, as noted, may have hastened their extermination. Although hunters in Europe developed stone spear points of different design at about the same time, or a little later, the fluted Clovis points appear to have been an exclusively American invention. They have been found in all 49 continental states of the U.S., throughout Canada, and as far south as Panama, but nowhere else in the world.

As the glaciers vanished around 10,000 years ago, and the climate warmed and grew more arid, the vast lakes of the West evaporated. Deserts, dry prairies and forests appeared, giving America much the same physical appearance it bore when Europeans arrived. With the extinction of the great Ice Age animals, Clovis points were replaced by smaller Folsom spearheads (also named for a New Mexico site) more suitable for hunting smaller game. Edible plants became more important in the human diet, along with nuts, seeds and roots, which were ground to flour on flat stone platters, or *metates*. Forced to adapt to drastically varied regional environments, the once uniform American culture evolved into a dizzying diversity of cultures.

By 5000 B.C., cultivation of squashes, avocados and beans had begun in the highlands of Mexico, followed by cultivation of corn 2,500 years later, which eventually spread throughout the hemisphere. Ultimately the Indians harvested more varieties of plants than were used, or even known, in any other region of the world, including corn, potatoes, tomatoes, peanuts, pineapples, papayas, manioc, chives, chilis, cashews, vanilla beans, cacao for chocolate, along with rubber, chicle, tobacco, a variety of cotton, coca for cocaine and cinchona for quinine. However, except for dogs, which the Indians had brought with them, there were no domestic animals in North America other than turkeys and guinea pigs, plus llamas in the South American Andes. Horses had become extinct in the New World, not to reappear until the Spanish brought them back in the 16th century.

Although agriculture was not always the requisite first step on the road to civilization in Europe and Asia, as shall be seen later in this book, it definitely was in the Americas. Once families were able to harvest enough grain to feed themselves for a year, usually after 12 weeks work in the cornfields, they gave up the nomadic life. Settling down in villages, people had time to devote to the pursuit of art, religion, warfare, and to noting the movements of the sun, moon and planets. As population expanded, irrigation and intensive cultivation and terracing of land developed in Mexico, Yucatan and Peru. Eventually, the food supply in these regions was sufficient to support rich and complex societies, big urban centers, magnificent temples and monuments, businesses, factories, forges, and an export-import trade extending across several thousand miles of land and water. Although agriculture and cities originated earlier in the Old World, there is little possibility that the Indians could have borrowed these ideas since (with two or three exceptions) the plants they cultivated grew nowhere else on earth, and the cities of Middle America and Peru can be traced back to their humblest beginnings.

Historians assume that contact between America and Asia ceased with the disappearance of the land bridge, and that cultural resemblances between the two continents were simply coincidence. Even such advanced technologies as the alloying of tin and copper to make bronze, and the lost-wax technique of casting metal into statues, are believed to have been invented indigenously in America, although they had been employed 2,000 years earlier in the Middle East and Southeast Asia.

However, there are some cultural similarities more difficult to ascribe to coincidence—how, for example, Asians and Mexican Indians could have worked out the same complicated rules for a board game known as *pachisi* in the Old World and *patolli* in the New; why reed panpipes played in the western Pacific not only looked like those of South America, but were tuned to the same pitch, using the same musical scale; why Asians and Amazon Indians half a world apart should both have made bark cloth and used blow guns, which were unknown elsewhere; how South American sweet potatoes, called *kamar*, subsequently came to be grown in Polynesia, where it was called *kumara*; and why the sailing vessels, lodges and totem poles of the coastal Indians of British Columbia and Alaska should so closely resemble those of the Maoris of New Zealand.

While conceding that some trans-Pacific contacts may have occurred, which would explain some of these similarities, historians nevertheless believe such meetings were sporadic and involved small numbers of people, since they had so little influence on American culture. The civilizations developed by the Indians of Middle America and Peru were in several respects superior to that of their European conquerors. They knew more about some aspects of astronomy, and had a more accurate calendar; they were the first to use the decimal system and the concept of zero in arithmetic; some of their cities were richer, and one was larger than any in Europe; they were more sophisticated farmers, who developed crops that now provide over half of the world's food and support many of its industries.

But the Native Americans made one fatal mistake that led to their downfall: they neglected to invent gunpowder.

CHAPTER 4

The Painted Caves: The World's First Great Art

(30,000 to 10,000 B.C.)

It happened on an afternoon in the summer of 1879. Amateur archeologist Marcellino Sanz de Sautuola was on his knees digging into the rubble at the mouth of the recently discovered cave near Altamira on the north coast of Spain. Suddenly, from the depths of a side chamber, less than six feet high, came the muffled scream of his nine-year-old daughter, Maria: "Toros! Toros! Papa, come quickly."

Alarmed, the man dropped his pick and dashed into the grotto where the frantic little girl stood pointing to the ceiling. Raising his lantern, Sautuola looked up and saw not *toros* (bulls) but prehistoric bison, modeled in low relief and magnificently painted on the crystalline limestone in shades of brown, red, yellow and black. In fact, the 60 by 30-foot ceiling was crowded with the shaggy beasts—17 of them in incredibly lifelike poses, standing, pawing the ground, lying down, curled in sleep, bellowing, rolling in the dust or dying of spear wounds—amid stocky little horses, a trembling doe, mountain goats, a wolf, and ferociously charging wild boars. Some of the figures painted on bulges in the rock looked almost three dimensional.

Exploring farther into the labyrinth, Sautuola found dozens of other painted and engraved animals, including great-antlered stags, giant cattle called aurochs, a cave lion and woolly mammoth, along with stenciled outlines of human hands, scores of undecipherable cabalistic signs and meandering lines traced in the clay of the ceiling by men's fingers.

This momentous discovery was to fling open a great door on a totally unsuspected era of human history, add works of unsurpassed genius to the world's art treasures, and present us with unfathomable mysteries. But to the discoverer it brought tragedy. Don Marcellino was 48 years old at the time, a hard-headed civil engineer who had built many of Spain's railroads, not a man to jump to quick conclusions. Yet, from the moment he laid eyes on the murals, he knew they were unimaginably ancient.

The cave, whose mouth had been sealed by a rock fall millenia earlier, had been found by a hunter whose dog had fallen into it through a narrow crevice. Except for a few peasants, no one else had entered it. Most of the animals so vividly depicted were either extinct or had disappeared from Western Europe centuries ago. The artifacts he had dug out of the floor at the entrance on previous visits all dated from the Paleolithic Era, the Old Stone Age, which ended with the melting of the last Great Glacier around 10,000 B.C..

Sautuola presented his findings in a modest pamphlet, together with reproductions of the paintings, to the Congress of Archeology meeting in Lisbon in 1880—which immediately labeled them forgeries. The eminent scientists would not even deign to visit Altamira to look at the paintings for themselves. If works of such antiquity actually existed, they reasoned, they would have been found in one of the historic "cradles" of civilization, Egypt, Mesopotamia, India or China, rather than in the cultural backwater of

The Ancestor Hunters. The famed husband-wife team, Louis and Mary Leakey (*above*), with the jaw of the 2-million-year-old hominid they discovered in Olduvai Gorge, Tanzania, in 1959, contrasted with a modern human jaw below it. Their son, Richard Leakey (*lower left*), with an Australopithicene skull found in Koobi Fora in Kenya. American Donald Johanson (*lower right*) picking out bone fragments of a 3.2-million-year-old *Homo afarensis* found in the Afar desert of Ethiopia.

(Picture credits: Top, Bettman News Service; left, Ronald Schiller; right, Donald Johanson)

Extinct bison (*top*), one of 17 found painted on the ceiling of the cave at Altamira, Spain, discovered in 1879 by amateur archeologist Sanz de Sautuola. Figure called "The Sorcerer" (*below*) found in the Trois Frères cave in Southern France portrays a man dressed for a religious rite wearing a deer mask and antlers on his head, a horse's tail behind, and what appear to be bear paws on his hands. The figures were painted between 30,000 and 10,000 B.C.

(Picture credits: American Museum of Natural History)

northern Spain. Furthermore, it seemed inconceivable that colors could maintain their freshness through so many millenia. Indeed, the pundits had been informed—quite accurately—that some of the painted surfaces still felt tacky to the touch.

But the greatest obstacle to the acceptance of the paintings was the naturalness and modernity of their style, so unlike the stilted, archaic art of ancient civilizations or of modern primitive tribes. They were so sophisticated in concept, executed with such artistic surehandedness and mastery of color, that they resembled the works of the impressionist painters then coming to the fore in Paris. Never, asserted the learned men, could such sensitive art have been created by savages, scarcely emerged from the apes, whom Darwin had described as "completely naked and daubed ... hair tangled ... mouths foaming ... expressions wild and fearful," who "hardly possessed any art at all."

Sautuola was accused of having painted the pictures himself, perhaps as part of a "Jesuit plot" to discredit the new science that challenged the Biblical story of creation, or of having them executed by a deaf and dumb young artist he had befriended—and to clinch matters, the youth actually "confessed" to the deception! With his honor impugned, the proud Spaniard died an object of ridicule in 1888, at the age of 57, his great discovery apparently consigned to oblivion.

Vindication was not long in coming, however. In 1895, more caves were discovered under a potato cellar near La Mouthe in southern France, and in 1901 along the Vezère River. They contained paintings of bison, mammoths, cave lions and bears, hairy rhinoceroses, hippopotami, and other long-extinct animals of the Ice Age, along with outlines of human hands and the faint figures of men wearing animal masks. There were also cryptic signs archeologists call "tectiforms" and meandering lines in the clay they have likened to "macaroni."

These new discoveries shook the skeptics, since some of the figures were half obliterated by stalactite deposits which had taken thousands of years to form or were found behind mounds of earth containing Paleolithic fossils. In one cave, part of a painted mural had fallen to the floor face down where it was covered by the undisturbed dust of ages.

Finally, in 1902, the young archeologist Abbé Henri Breuil, who was to win fame as the "priest of the painted caves," visited Altamira. Beneath a pile of fossil animal bones and antlers, he uncovered more painted and engraved figures almost identical to those on the ceiling. The authenticity of the murals could no longer be doubted. Breuil called on Maria de Sautuola to apologize for the humiliation her father had suffered. The prehistorian Emile Cartailhac, who had led the attack on Sautuola, published an article entitled *Mea Culpa* (I am guilty) in which he humbly confessed his error and hailed Altamira as "the Sistine Chapel of prehistoric art."

In the following decades, over a hundred more grottoes decorated with Old Stone Age paintings and engravings were discovered in Northern Spain, the French Pyrenees and the Dordogne region to the north of it, along with a few in Southern Italy, the Danube basin, the Ukraine and the Urals. Among the more notable in Spain are the four caves of El Castillo, Las Chimeneas, Las Monedas and La Pasiega, which lie side by side in a cliff a few miles from Altamira. In central France are Rouffignac, with its dramatic parades of mammoths and rhinos; Pech Merle, whose dappled horses look as though they came from a toy shop; and the battling reindeer and leaping horse of Font de Gaume. In the French Pyrenees lie Niaux with its superb shaggy ponies; Le Tuc d' Audubert and its modeled clay bison, and Trois Frêres with its eerie figure of "The Sorcerer," half human, half animal.

In none of the newly discovered caves, however, did the paintings look as fresh or compare in grandeur with the masterpieces of Altamira—until 1940, when a band of schoolboys near Lascaux, in France, slid down a rocky chute, into a cavern that proved to be a veritable menagerie of prehistoric beasts. Among the lively figures in this "Louvre" of Paleolithic art are prodigous bulls 13 to 17 feet long; galloping ponies; a magnificent frieze of antlered stags who seem to be swimming across a river; exquisite, yellow and black "Chinese" horses, so-called because they resemble those of the

Tang Dynasty; a leaping cow with twisted horns, who might have come out of the nursery rhyme; megaloceroses (giant elk) with surrealistic antlers; and a mythical monster with the body of a pregnant hippopotomus and a square head which has been called "The Unicorn," although it has *two* long straight horns jutting from its forehead.

Despite a century of intense study, and the use of every technique known to science, archeologists are certain of very little about cave art, or the people who created it. But the few answers they can offer with any confidence are startling.

How old are the paintings? Although they resemble each other so closely in style and feeling as to represent a recognizable "school" of art, radiocarbon dating tests show they were put on the walls at various times between 30,000 and 10,000 B.C., a span four times longer than all of recorded history! Some of the animals of Altamira and those of Lascaux, which look alike enough to have been painted by the same hand, were actually executed by artists who lived thousands of years apart.

This is not to imply that cave art suddenly appeared in full blossom. It took 700 generations to reach its zenith with the masterpieces of Altamira and Lascaux, painted around 12,000 B.C. During earlier eras, many of the depictions were fairly crude, frequently omitting heads and feet, and toward the end, so much attention was paid to detail that zoologists use the figures as anatomical charts. There was even a "cubist" or "Picasso" period, during which the animal's horns were shown front view, although its head was in profile, and its ears might be stuck on its cheek, neck, or wherever else the artist fancied.

There were also differences in the kinds of animals depicted in various periods, for the climate of Europe, although generally cold, varied with the ebb and flow of the Great Glacier. Horses, deer and bison, the cave men's principal sources of meat, predominate throughout the Paleolithic Era. But cave bears vanish during the middle of the period, while mammoths and woolly rhinoceroses disappear from cave walls when the glacier retreated about 22,000

B.C., not to reappear until it returned again some 7,000 years later. During the warm interval, elephants roamed northern Spain.

Who painted the pictures? Western Europe was occupied at the time by Cro-Magnon men, modern people with long limbs and high foreheads, some of the males over six feet tall and powerfully built, the women considerably smaller. They were hunters, fishermen, and gatherers of fruits, berries and shellfish, who had not yet learned to plant crops, domesticate cattle, ride horses or use them as beasts of burden. Even dogs and chickens were unknown, as they had not yet reached Europe from Asia. Their household utensils, often elegantly engraved and ornamented, were made of stone or fired clay, their weapons and tools were of flint, bone, antler, ivory and, presumably, wood which has rotted away. Their clothing was fashioned of furs and hides, sewn together by bone needles threaded with animal sinews, while their personal ornaments and necklaces, of which they were inordinately fond, were made of animal teeth, ivory, small bones and, it is believed, feathers.

Although life in the shadow of the mile-high glaciers was often brutal and short (few men reached 50, or women 35, as the remains indicate), the Cro-Magnons were obviously people of sensitivity and intelligence. Their songs, dances, and culture generally, may have been as remarkable as their visual art. They believed in life after death, placing food and tools in graves to accompany the deceased on their journey. They may have believed animals had souls too. A cave painting in Les Combarelles in France shows a small horse leaping out of a large one, dying of a spear thrust.

Why were the paintings made? They were not done in the spirit of "art for art's sake," archeologists agree, but for serious purposes. Hunting large animals was a formidable task to men of the Old Stone Age. Bows and arrows do not seem to have been in wide use. If they could not kill the beasts by stampeding them over cliffs or into swamps and pits, they had to approach them close enough to cripple them with rocks or run them through with spears, whose range was extended a few yards by use of spear throwers. Judging from the number of broken and mutilated human bones found in prehistoric digs, mortality among Cro-Magnon hunters was high.

The periodic shortage of animals, which threatened tribes with starvation was an even greater peril.

To avert these disasters, the experts surmise, prehistoric man developed a highly complicated religious system based on "sympathetic magic," designed to cast a spell over the beasts. Crude sketches in the grottoes show men and women wearing animal heads, bent forward as though walking on all fours, while other members of the tribe presumably sang magic incantations and launched sham attacks on them with spears, or mated with them. These hunting and fertility rites were perhaps similar to those practiced in recent times by African, Australian and American Indian tribes.

But, as in African voodoo, the most potent magic was to paint or engrave a picture of the beast, for once its likeness was captured on a cave wall, it could no longer resist your power and there were any number of benefits to be derived from it. You might automatically acquire its outstanding physical characteristics, such as speed of foot, if it were a horse or deer, strength, if it were a bison or mammoth, or courage, if it were a wild boar or rhinoceros. You could pray to the spirits to make the animal fecund, and hasten procreation by painting fertility and sexual symbols alongside it. You could transfix it with a painted spear or hurl a real spear at it to assure success in the hunt. Or you might use the figure as an instructional chart to show young hunters the animal's vulnerable points or as a totem symbol to initiate novices into the tribe. There are evidences of all of these practices in the caves.

These motivations may explain why these Paleolithic artists never once showed scenery or plants—there was nothing to be gained by it—and why there are only a few representations of small animals, birds and fish. The magic was too potent to waste on creatures that provided scant danger and little meat.

How were the paintings done? First step, frequently, was to engrave the outline of the figure with a flint burin before coloring it in. The pigments used by the Paleolithic painters may still be bought in art stores today. They had no greens or blues, but they got their black colors from charcoal and lamp carbon, violet from

manganese oxide ore, their brown, red, orange and yellow hues
from ochre (iron oxide) rock, which they ground to powder between stones, then mixed with egg white, animal blood, plant
juices, but mostly animal fat.

The paints were laid on thickly in a variety of ways; by finger;
by brushes made of fur, feathers, or the chewed end of wooden
twigs; by pads of lichen and moss; or—particularly evident in the
silhouettes of hands—by blowing it onto the walls through hollow
reeds or animal bones, as it is still done by Australian aborigines.
Frequently, the ochre was mixed with tallow and rolled into slender
crayons which have been found on ledges in Altamira, laid out in
neat rows with their ends sharpened, alongside 14,000-year-old
shells which held other colors. To light up the stygian blackness of
the caves, the artists used faggots and resinous torches, which left
smudges on the ceilings, and for closer work, roughly hollowed
stone lamps fueled with animal fat, several of which have also been
found, still encrusted with greasy soot.

The loving care and respect with which the animals are portrayed indicate that the artists knew them intimately, admired, and
may even have worshipped them. But this did not prevent them
from showing them upside down, standing on their hind legs or
dying in agony, when it served their purposes. Nor did their sizes
make much difference, a small reindeer might be drawn to a scale
five times larger than a neighboring mammoth. Remarkable three-
dimensional effects were often achieved by taking advantage of the
contours of the cave surface. A small natural hole in the rock might
be converted into a glaring eye, or a larger nick might be lined in
red to represent a wound. Odd-shaped bulges were made into
animal heads, humps or haunches, and stalagmites into legs.

But whether rendered flat or in relief, Paleolithic artists never
niggled at their work. The figures are invariably painted in bold,
sure strokes, a single sweep of the brush often sufficing to outline
an animal's entire head and back. There are no signs of attempted
erasure or correction. Such spontaneity requires careful preparation
and, sure enough, in the strata at the mouths of several caves, flat

stones have been unearthed bearing sketches of the figures that were later painted on the walls inside.

Indeed, the prehistoric artists may have gone to school to learn their craft. In Limeuil, in southwestern France, 137 stone "sketch sheets" were found, many of them poorly executed, with the details often corrected as if by a teacher's hand. A good sketch was highly prized, and may have had commercial value. The drawing of a distinctive, heavy-shouldered bison painted on the wall of the Fon-de-Gaume cavern, the only one of its kind in prehistoric art, was found duplicated on a slab of stone in a rock shelter 200 miles away, leading archeologists to speculate that it may have been sold or traded.

How did the paintings manage to survive for so long? The answer is that the huge majority of them didn't. Most of the painted caves contain only traces of their original art, a carved line here, a patch of color there, the rest of the figures having succumbed to deterioration by frost, heat, water, plant life and other natural forces. Countless other depictions have probably been obliterated without trace. The representations that have survived fairly intact, a tiny remnant of a vanished whole, have been found in pitch black caves in which the temperature and humidity are constant summer and winter, the ventilation good but not excessive, and the moisture content of the air just sufficient to keep the colors from drying out and scaling off. The grease paint applied thousands of years ago to some of the figures can still be smudged by rubbing your finger across them.

Most important of all, rock falls in ages past sealed the entrances of these caves, thus protecting them from people. The perspiration, body heat and microorganisms, brought into the Lascaux cavern by thousands of visitors, along with electric lights and flashing cameras, did more damage to its paintings in 15 years than they suffered in the previous 15,000. With their colors beginning to drip and green algae forming on their surfaces, Lascaux was closed to the public in 1963. No more than five officially approved visitors a day are now admitted to its carefully regulated atmosphere, for 20 minutes, after passing through three air locks and immersing the soles of their shoes in formaldehyde disinfectant.

As a writer on assignment, I was one of the lucky ones. But most people must content themselves with looking at reproductions of the art affixed to the walls of a nearby artificial grotto. Altamira and some other caves have not suffered as much as Lascaux since there is less dampness, and the paintings have been covered in the course of time by a thin, natural limestone glaze, which serves as a protective enamel. Nevertheless, Altamira was closed for many years, although it may now be entered by 40 visitors a day who apply for permission three months in advance.

Before their modern rediscovery, only two important painted caves gave evidence of having been entered since prehistoric times. Las Monedas in Spain, rediscovered in 1952, got its name from the 16th century coins (*monedas*) found on its floor, which appear to have slipped from the pocket of an explorer who lay down for a nap almost 400 years earlier. His hobnailed boot prints were the only ones found in the cave, and he did no damage.

But the cave of Rouffignac, whose "dragons" were listed as a tourist curiosity in a 17th century French guidebook, is filled with names and dates going back to the 15th century, which visitors seared into the ceiling with smoke from their candles or scratched right across the painted rhinos and mammoths. Fortunately, the cave was forgotten some 150 years ago, not to be rediscovered until 1956, or its art might have been ruined beyond recognition.

Actually, much of the credit for the preservation of the figures belongs to the artists, themselves, for *the paintings were never intended to be seen and admired* by the general public, even in prehistoric times. The caves, or at least those parts of them in which the murals appear, were never lived in. They were religious sanctuaries, far from daylight, difficult and often dangerous to reach, into which entrance may very well have been forbidden, except to certain people at certain times and for specific rituals.

Furthermore, the artists often went to inordinate lengths to place the murals in inaccessible places. The splendid friezes of Rouf-fignac lie a mile-and-a-half (two kilometers) from the mouth of the cave. Visitors today reach them on a little electric railway train, whose roadbed is sunk into the cave floor. The ancients had to crawl the entire distance on their hands and knees under a three-foot-high ceiling, across a floor whose length is pitted with the deep nests of hibernating cave bears, 45,000 years old.

In the cave of Las Chimeneas, near Altamira, I followed my guide at a crouch through endless low passages, squeezing sideways between boulders that almost tore the buttons off my jacket. Finally, stretched out in an agonizingly uncomfortable position with my head curled around a stalagmite, I turned my flashlight on an exquisite sketch of a stag, drawn in a dozen bold, black strokes, as glisteningly fresh as if done yesterday. There are murals in Font de Gaume at the end of a twisting tunnel so narrow that they can be seen only by lean men or women pulling themselves forward on their stomachs, one at a time.

Others were placed deep in 14-inch wide crevices, on ceilings that required 20-foot high ladders or scaffolds to reach, on outcroppings where the artists had to cling to the walls with one hand (some of the fingerprints in the clay are still there) and paint with the other. Still another figure in a deep pit in Bedeilhac could only have been done if the painter were held by his feet or suspended from ropes.

Yet in every one of these caves, totally untouched, are great stretches of flat, high-ceilinged walls, where the artists could have stood upright or sat down and worked in comfort. Why? Would the figures lose their potency if they were seen by chance visitors? Was there added advantage to hiding them as deep as possible in the bowels of the caves, to get closer to the spirits that dwelt in the womb of the earth? And if the animal figures were not meant to be seen, why were they rendered in such meticulous, natural detail, when a rough sketch might have sufficed?

Part of the answer undoubtedly lies in the sheer joy of artistic creation, the artists' irresistible impulse to do the best work of which they were capable, for their own satisfaction. But it may have been equally important to inform the spirits beyond the possibility of doubt, exactly which animal the artist intended, or else part of the magic might be lost.

There are other unsolved mysteries. Why did Paleolithic artists have such scant regard for the figures painted by their ancestors? In a few instances faded colors were touched up and outlines retraced after a lapse of centuries. But in the great majority of cases, artists paid no attention whatever to the works already there, painting their own figures right on top or across the older works, as though they did not exist. In some places, there are so many superimpositions that the walls are literal mazes of indecipherable painted and engraved lines.

Again, why? It certainly couldn't have been for lack of space, since cave walls only a few yards away are completely blank. Was it because certain places in the cave were holier than others? Did paintings lose their effectiveness after a certain period? Or did it mean that the magic was not transferable, and the artist derived power only from the figure he painted himself? There are no answers.

Equally puzzling is why there are so very few human representations in the caves, and why they were done so crudely. Painted on the wall of a dry well in Lascaux is the most nakedly savage scene in Paleolithic art. It shows a mortally wounded bison, its entrails hanging out of its slit belly, facing the prone figure of a man wearing a bird mask, who is apparently dead, although his phallus is erect. Beside him lie a spear, spear thrower, and a totemic bird-headed staff. It seems to tell the story of a hunter killed by the beast he had attacked, although interpretations differ widely.

But more significant than the meaning of the picture is the vastly different styles used to depict the two figures. The bison is presented in photographically realistic detail, with threatening head and lashing tail. In contrast, the man is the most rudimentary kind of caricature, his body, limbs and fingers, nothing more than hastily scrawled lines, like a figure drawn by a kindergarten child.

Every other depiction of the human form, save one, is done with equal crudity. It certainly cannot be that the talented cave artists were incapable of depicting the human form accurately, for in the cave of Trois Frères—the single exception—stands one of the live-liest figures in prehistoric art, a dancing man we call "The Sor-cerer," wearing a horse's tail behind, a deer mask and antlers on his head, and what appear to be bear paws on his hands.

The only conclusion that can be reached is that depiction of the human form was banned by a religious taboo so powerful that, in the few instances where the artists dared violate it, they confined themselves to cloddish sketches and never gave the figures recog-nizable faces. The heads are either covered with masks or pre-sented in ghostly outline, with a pumpkin-shaped oval for a head and two dots for eyes. In this respect, prehistoric man acted like certain primitive tribesmen who will not allow themselves to be photographed for fear their souls will be transferred to the likeness, and whatever harm comes to the picture will befall their own bodies.

And what does one make of the "tectiforms," the painted dots, rods, squares, circles, chevrons, abstract designs and other sym-bols, that appear on cave walls by the hundreds? In no area of prehistoric art are the experts in wilder disagreement. A few of the designs, quite obviously, are stylized profiles of the female torso, with buttocks heavily exaggerated in the same manner as the so-called "Venus" figurines found in the Paleolithic strata of other caves, whose presumed function was to promote human fertility.

Other tectiforms resemble the outlines of huts or tents, either for the living or the souls of the dead, or animal stockades and traps (the faint outline of a deer can be seen in one in the cave of La Pasiega). Still others have been variously interpreted as warning signs indicating holes or other dangers in the labyrinth ahead, as traffic directions (no less!) pointing the way to the hidden paint-ings, or as hex symbols warning unauthorized intruders not to proceed any further. They may also be the signatures of the artists, or ideographs which could be read by those initiated to their meaning.

However, Professor André Leroi-Gourhan of the Sorbonne, the most distinguished authority on Cro-Magnon cave art since the death of Abbé Breuil in 1961, insisted that regardless of shape or appearance, every tectiform is a fertility symbol representing either a male or female sexual organ. In fact, reasoning that survival of the race in the face of enormous natural dangers was the strongest instinct of Paleolithic men, as of all men, he holds that even the painted animals in the caves were figures in a prehistoric human fertility drama. He surmises, for example, that all bison, including the bulls among them, represent the female sex, and all horses, mares included, symbolize the male organ. Although this theory seems in stark contradiction to the evidence of our eyes and senses, it has won wide acceptance among modern scholars.

Equally baffling are the "macaroni," the long squiggly lines scratched by human fingers into the soft clay of the ceilings. In some of them you can detect the outlines of animal heads and crudely depicted sexual organs, not dissimilar to the graffiti people today pencil on lavatory walls. Yet, they do not appear to be casual doodles since some of them are so high off the ground that they could only have been reached by ladders or scaffolds.

Some prehistorians have theorized that, like the modern grotto of Lourdes, the cave sanctuaries may also have been places of heal- ing, frequented by invalids in pain who stroked the clay for its soothing, therapeutic effect, and perhaps packed it into their wounds, as was done by some Western physicians in centuries past.

Then there is the enigma of the human hands, silhouetted by red and black paint sprayed on through hollow bones, that fill entire walls of some caves. They are believed to be the oldest designs of all. If they were magic symbols designed to lend strength and cunning to the hands of hunters, why are the majority of them left hands? And why are so many of them mutilated, with joints miss- ing? Were the fingers deliberately chopped off as a sacrifice to the gods, a not uncommon practice among primitive tribes; or were they hands held with their backs against the wall with some fingers bent forward, for some occult reason; or were they, as some physi- cians claim, the crippled hands of muscular dystrophy, rheumatic fever or frostbite victims, who had come to the cave shrines to recuperate or seek a cure?

Even more puzzling is that over half of the hands are those of children, including seven- or eight-month-old infants. Were they sick, carried into the depth of the black caves by frantic parents seeking to save their lives? Or were the stencils put there as part of a tribal initiation rite? Perhaps the latter, for found in the petrified clay of some caves are partial footprints of children walking forward on tiptoe, or on their heels with toes in the air.

Was this strange manner of walking part of the ritual, was it simply a prehistoric game of follow-the-leader, or was it attributable to the youngsters' all-too-human distaste for putting the soles of their feet into the cold, clammy mud? Whatever the reason there is something unutterably poignant in seeing the small footprints, and the blurred outline of the hand of a little girl who evidently winced when the greasy black spray struck her fingers 30,000 years ago.

When the last Great Glacier retreated around 10,000 B.C., prehistoric cave art came to an abrupt end. The bison, mammoths, reindeer and other cold-loving animals, followed the receding ice north and east across Europe, doubtless pursued by many of the tribes who depended on them for food—which may explain the few painted caves found in Central Europe and Southern Russia. As the temperatures in Western Europe steadily rose, the peoples that remained moved out of the warm caverns into reed and wooden shelters along rivers and lakes. They learned to cultivate crops and domesticate animals, gradually losing their dependence on wild beasts for their food. It was no longer necessary to propitiate the spirits of the caves, the dark womb in which many of the animals hibernated. Instead they began to worship the gods of wind, rain and sun, who made crops grow, and lived in the open.

By the time the first Egyptian, Minoan and Phoenician traders reached Spain and France, around 2000 B.C., the last cave paintings were already 8,000 years old, the skills, style and inspiration that created them completely forgotten. The first and one of the greatest eras of artistic expression had passed forever.

It is unfortunate that reproductions do so little justice to the cave paintings. Their fascinating texture, sense of mystery and enormous vitality, do not fully emerge unless seen where the artists placed them, in the dim light of the caves themselves. Lying on my back in a padded niche of the rock platform on my first visit to Altamira, I had been gazing up at the three-dimensional bison for perhaps five minutes, when my tall, white-haired guide murmured in Spanish: "Do you see it yet?"

"See what?" I asked.

"Keep looking," he answered quietly.

I stared at the beasts for another few moments when, suddenly, it hit me. "They're breathing!" I exclaimed. "I can see their muscles twitching!"

"Yes," the old man nodded, with a smile. "Fifteen thousand years old and still alive. That is the miracle of Altamira."

CHAPTER 5

Where and When Did Civilization Begin?

(10,000 to 3000 B.C.)

If you had studied cultural history a generation ago, you would have learned that civilization began in the Middle East some 10,000 years ago when men first turned from a nomadic hunting-gathering economy and settled down in villages to cultivate the native wild wheat and barley and to domesticate animals. This was considered the requisite first step, for by assuring the food supply, agriculture gave men leisure for other pursuits, leading to new cultural advances. Basketry was developed and woven cloth replaced animal skins in clothing. The first pottery was made in Mesopotamia around 7000 B.C., you were informed, and copper smelting began in the Anatolia Peninsula of Turkey a millenium later. By 3000 B.C., brick cities and temples had arisen, and the Sumerians had developed an alphabet and the art of writing. Shortly thereafter, when men learned to alloy soft copper with tin to create durable metal tools and weapons, the Stone Age ended and the Bronze Age began.

From the Middle Eastern "cradle of civilization whose claim to the origination of all the primary inventions is beyond dispute," as one textbook put it, knowledge of the new techniques diffused eastward to India and China, southward to Egypt, whose 4,700-year-old pyramids were considered to be the oldest stone monuments on earth. In the third millenium B.C. they moved to Troy and Crete, reaching Mycenaean Greece about 1600 B.C.

The chronology was based on two principal dating methods. The ages of older objects and sites were determined by stratigraphy, which involved measuring the depth of the strata in which they lay and estimating how long it had taken the layers of earth or rubble about them to accumulate. For "historic" times, meaning the period after men had learned to write, the dating was more reliable. The Sumerians, Assyrians and Egyptians left records of kings and dynasties extending back to a little before 3000 B.C., along with calendars and observations of the positions of the stars during certain important events, which enable modern astronomers to determine accurately the dates they had occurred.

Once the chronology of ancient Egypt had been determined, it was used to establish dates in the lands with which the Egyptians traded. Thus, when stone vases known to have been made in Egypt in the third millenium B.C. were found in tombs on Crete, it established the possibility that the Minoan civilization of the island was at least that old, and so on throughout the Aegean. Unfortunately, such cross-dating was not possible for Western Europe, since no artifacts of provable Egyptian or Aegean manufacture have ever been found in its ancient graves. But on the reasonable assumption that peoples who had not yet learned to read and write must be culturally more primitive than those who had, it was taken for granted that their monuments were built centuries later.

From the Aegean, it thus appeared, the civilized arts spread up the Danube into central Europe and were carried across the Mediterranean by traders and colonists to Malta and the barbarian tribes of the Atlantic coast. The dolmen tombs of Iberia, western France,

Britain, Ireland and Scandinavia, built of massive slabs of uncut rock, were held to be crude native imitations of the more sophisticated stone structures of the east. But, archeologists pointed out, the more elaborate multi-chambered tombs, with their corbelled roofs and wealth of finely wrought copper daggers and gold ornaments, could not have been built on their own initiative by "savages still sunk in the night of illiteracy and barbarism," while such a masterpiece as Stonehenge could only have been erected under the direction of Mycenaean Greek architects. European prehistory, as summed up in 1946 by Gordon Childe, president of the British Association for the Advancement of Science, is the story of "the irradiation of western barbarism by eastern enlightenment."

How civilization reached the New World was a matter of debate. But on the theory that "the important innovations and advances in human culture occurred only once," many held that mummification, sun worship, and the pyramids of Central America and Peru had also been inspired by Egyptian examples.

This orderly sequence of events was so logical, and supported by so much seemingly irrefutable evidence, that it was accepted and taught as fact. Yet, many of the dates and practically all of the assumptions on which it was based were wrong. Recent exploration and more accurate scientific dating methods now reveal that Stone Age humans had settled in permanent villages and devised complex economic and social systems thousands of years before the development of agriculture. Settlements of houses constructed of mammoth bones appeared in central Russia around 20,000 years ago. Elaborate villages of stone houses were occupied by hunter-gatherers nearly 13,000 years ago in Israel.

It is now clear that "agriculture by itself was not the revolutionizing force we thought it was," according to archeologist Douglas Price of the University of Wisconsin. A more likely inducement for foraging bands to settle down in one place was the need to store surplus food for a growing population, as evidenced by the extensive storage pits and facilities that have been found in all of these ancient villages.

The Middle East, Egypt and the Eastern Mediterranean have lost their claims to priority in other accomplishments as well. We now know that the domestication of plants and grain began in Southeast Asia as early as in the Tigris-Euphrates valley. Fishermen in Japan were making pottery 1,000 years before the Mesopotamians, Thailanders were fabricating bronze earlier, and the natives of Romania may have invented a form of writing centuries before the Sumerians. Equally disconcerting was the discovery that some of the megalithic tombs of Western Europe are 2,000 years older than the Egyptian pyramids, and that Mycenaean architects could never have directed the building of Stonehenge, since it was completed centuries before Mycenaean civilization had even begun. If there was a transmission of architectural ideas in Europe, it now appears, it was not from east to west, but the other way around.

The archeological revolution, that made a shambles of the traditional diffusionist theory of prehistory, began in 1949 when nuclear physicist Willard Libby developed radiocarbon dating. It was based on the discovery that when nitrogen in the air is bombarded by cosmic rays from space, some of its atoms are transmuted into radioactive carbon-14, which combines with oxygen just as does ordinary carbon to form carbon dioxide in the atmosphere. This is absorbed by plants during photosynthesis. The animals of the earth eat plants, or eat other animals which eat plants, so that all living things contain the same tiny proportion of carbon-14 atoms as the atmosphere.

When the plant or animal dies, however, it stops absorbing radiocarbon, and what is already in the tissues gradually breaks down, throwing out electrons at a lower and lower rate of discharge, until the radiocarbon eventually disappears. Thus, by measuring the intensity of the radioactivity on Geiger counters, the ages of any dead organic material—wood, ashes, grain, beeswax, cloth, clamshells, antlers or bone—can be determined, give or take a few years or decades.

When the first radiocarbon dates began to roll from the laboratories, archeologists were delighted, since they appeared to confirm the accepted chronologies. But the euphoria vanished when later reports revealed the works of prehistoric man to be hundreds-to-thousands of years older than had been believed. A reverse shock came in the 1960s when carbon-14 readings of Egyptian mummies clocked some of them as being younger than they were unquestionably known to be. The physicists found that they had made an error in assuming that the amount of radiocarbon in the atmosphere was the same in past millenia as it is today.

The discovery was made by analyzing the wood of the oldest living things on earth, the stunted bristlecone pines native to the arid White Mountains of California, some of which have been growing for 5,000 years, as their annual tree rings indicate. Up until about 1200 B.C., the bristlecone rings prior to that date contained progressively more carbon-14, which indicated that the earth in ages past had been subjected to a much heavier bombardment of cosmic rays, perhaps caused by fluctuations in the planet's magnetic field. This meant that dates prior to 1200 B.C. were even more ancient than had initially been reported—ranging from 500 years older for plant and animal remains originally clocked at 2500 B.C., to almost a thousand years earlier for those reading 4000 B.C. This new information explained why the radiocarbon dates for the Egyptian mummies were too young. Today, all carbon-14 readings are corrected, or "calibrated," by adding the bristlecone factor.

However, radiocarbon dating has limitations. It cannot be applied to inorganic matter such as stone tools, pottery or metal objects, which are often the only available traces of early cultures. Nor can it reliably date organic remains much beyond 40,000 years of age—or 100,000 years with a technology employing mass spectrometry—because there is too little radiocarbon left in them to be accurately measured.

To meet these difficulties other scientific "clocks" have been activated. The ages of bones can now be gauged back as far as 500,000 years through a process called aspartic acid racemization, which measures the ratio of D-amino acid to L-amino acid in their tissues. The antiquity of fossils, as well as campsites and artifacts, millions of years old are determined by measuring the extent to which radioactive potassium has decayed into argon gas in the volcanic strata in which they lie.

Methods have also been developed to date inorganic materials. The age of pottery or burnt flint can be determined by means of a process called thermoluminescent dosimetry which measures the intensity of the photon glow emitted by the ground up shards when subjected to high temperatures. Metal objects may sometimes be dated by analysis of the magnetic signature imprinted in them by the earth's magnetic field at the time the molten material hardened. Still other techniques are being perfected to assess the antiquity of glass and obsidian objects, the carvings on stone, and even to map ancient trade routes by determining the origin of the clay in the pottery used as trade goods.

How do prehistorians reconcile and make orderly sense of the spectacularly early dates for human culture that have been popping up in such unexpected places in the world? The answer is that most of them no longer attempt to. The traditional scenario of cultural diffusion from a central source has been largely replaced by the theory of "independent invention," meaning that tools, farming, villages, pottery, metallurgy, writing, cities, kings and states, developed indigenously in several parts of the world independently of each other—and not necessarily in a predictable order.

Although people certainly borrowed ideas from each other when they were useful, each culture developed in a manner dictated by its own needs, resources and ingenuity. The first known potters on earth in Japan were fishermen, not farmers as theory insisted they should have been. Nor did agriculture necessarily tie men to the soil everywhere, leading to a sedentary life in villages. The Mexicans remained nomadic for 3,000 years after they had begun to cultivate corn, as did some early European farmers—probably because their inability to restore nutriments to the soil forced them to move to new fields as the old ones lost their fertility.

The timetables for the arrival of more advanced cultural stages have also been upset. "We once thought of early agriculturalists as peaceful, egalitarian groups, leading simple lives in self-sufficient communities," says anthropologist Mary Voigt of the University of

Pennsylvania. But now the researchers are learning that complex social structures, and sophisticated economic systems involving widespread trade between communities, had developed 3,000 years before the first cities rose or writing had been invented. From the quantity of goods excavated from its ruins, it appears that the 6,000 residents of thriving Catal Huyuk in Turkey, in 6000 B.C., lived on the export of cosmetics (including eye makeup and the wooden sticks to apply it), and obsidian from nearby mines, a highly prized volcanic glass used for knives and mirrors, razors and jewelry.

There seem to be no absolute prerequisites for cultural advancement by a people. The Mayas of Yucatan built great pyramids and developed a written script, but had no unified government, while the later Incas in Peru built grandiose cities and a political empire, without ever learning to write—and neither of them employed the wheel.

As an example of how risky it is to downgrade the capabilities of early men, consider the Stone Age inhabitants of Britain in the third millenium B.C., whom English archeologist Gordon Childe once depicted as "disgusting savages." They were illiterate, sparsely scattered over the land, living without benefit of large towns or kings, so far as can be determined, although they apparently did have local chiefs. Yet somehow they managed to come together in great numbers to design and erect elaborate communal tombs which would dazzled the supposedly more advanced Sumerians and Egyptians of the time.

The building of Stonehenge, their supreme accomplishment, was an incredible undertaking, requiring planning and organization of a very high order. Radiocarbon dating of the antlers and shoulder blades of animals, which were used as picks and shovels, indicates that construction began around 2800 B.C. and continued for over a millenium. The long, flat stones, called "sarsens," weighing up to 50 tons, were cut from a quarry, probably by heating the surface of the rock, then dousing it with cold water until the block split away. Using oxhide ropes, wooden sledges and rollers, it is estimated to have taken 1,100 men seven weeks to haul or ferry each of the larger slabs to the building site 25 miles away. Smoothing down and squaring off the hundreds of blocks with stone hammers would have taken far longer.

To raise each sarsen to upright position the builders are believed to have positioned one end atop an earthern ramp beside the excavation, then jacked up the other end by means of ropes and timbers, higher and higher, until it slid into the hole. To keep the pillar from crashing through the opposite side of the excavation, the far wall was braced with wooden stakes, the vestiges of which can still be found. To make sure the column was properly aligned, its base was chipped to a blunt point so that it could be swiveled into position before the earth and rubble were packed in.

Lifting each seven-ton lintel stone 20 feet into the air was an even more daring feat, requiring the builders to repeatedly lever up one end, then the other, wedging in fresh timbers each time. When the trestle had been raised as high as the tops of the uprights, days later, the "hanging stone" could be tugged across by ropes until the holes bored in its underside fitted snugly over the knobs carved in the uprights, creating a structure firm enough to stand for nearly 5,000 years.

All told, the building of Stonehenge is calculated to have required 18 million man-hours of labor—30 million if one includes the time it took to transport the stones—which meant that the bulk of the working population must have been engaged in the task for years at a time. Why the people should have endured such exhausting toil and sacrifice to build the monument can only be guessed.

It seems unquestionable that Stonehenge was used for religious ceremonies in which the celestial bodies played a key role. For the structure appears to have served as an astronomical observatory, laid out with such geometric precision that on Midsummer Day, when the sun had reached its most northerly point, the rays of the sun rising over the Heel Stone strike into the heart of the circle (although due to a shift in the solar circuit in the past 5,000 years, the sun now rises one degree north). The midwinter sunset on the other end of the axis is also nearly aligned, while other massive stones of the monument's inner horseshoe frame the solstices of the sun and moon.

Carrying the astronomical interpretation even farther, Harvard astronomer Gerald Hawkins, in his controversial 1965 book *Stonehenge Decoded*, claimed that part of the monument served as a computer for predicting lunar and solar eclipses. Although scientists are sharply divided over that claim, they agree that the illiterate early Britons were accomplished astronomic observers, as well as master builders who had employed the principles of angles and circles, triangles and ellipses, 15 centuries before the Greeks. Some "savages"!

The archeological discoveries of the past 30 years have been enormous, and introduction of sophisticated new search devices has quickened the pace. Sonar sounders are locating ancient underwater structures and shipwrecks that were previously unsuspected. Magnetometers have mapped the deeply buried ruins of buildings and streets, ranging from the sixth century B.C. city of Sybaris in Italy, to the camp of George Washington at Valley Forge. Aerial photography discloses the traces of ancient earthworks, roads and villages, beneath ripening grain in the fields. Infra-red satellite photographs make it possible to observe the meandering courses of long-vanished rivers, along whose banks may lie cultures older than any yet known.

No one can foretell just how far back in time man and his civilization may eventually be traced. But the dates are retreating ever further from the innocent days of the 17th century when Irish Archbishop Ussher, using the geneologies of Book of Genesis as his source, calculated that the world had been created in the year 4004 B.C., on the 23rd day of October, at nine o'clock in the morning.

CHAPTER 6

A Newly Discovered Asian Cradle of Civilization

(10,000 to 3000 B.C.)

He was a tall man lying on his side in a flexed position, with his knees drawn up to his chin. Who he was and how he had died over 5,600 years ago are unknown, but his discovery may render obsolete time-honored beliefs about where and when fabrication of metals began. For buried close enough to the man for his skeletal arm to have reached out and seized it, lay a beautifully fashioned bronze spearhead whose wooden shaft had long since crumbled to dust. It is the most ancient bronze object yet unearthed in the world. Six centuries older than anyone suspected bronze had been made. And it was found where archeologists least expected it— beneath a village in northeastern Thailand.

The events that led to the epic discovery began in 1966, when American college student Stephen Young, son of a former U.S. Ambassador to Thailand, tripped over a root near the farming town of Ban Chiang and fell to the ground. As he pushed himself up, he noticed protruding through the soil the tops of broken earthenware pots decorated with bold swirling designs, unlike anything he had ever seen before. Suspecting that the pots might be old, he presented them to the National Museum in Bangkok. Two years later, some of the shards were sent to the University of Pennsylvania's University Museum in Philadelphia to be dated by the new process of thermoluminescent dosimetry. The tests revealed that the vases had been manufactured around 4000 B.C., sensationally old for pottery so sophisticated.

"The readings seemed too old to be credible," recalls the Museum's then director, Froehlich Rainey. But subsequent tests of other Ban Chiang pots, conducted at Philadelphia and Oxford University, produced even older dates. Even more perplexing was the report that the bronze objects had been found in association with the ceramics.

Rainey's bewilderment was understandable, for these were among the first pieces of hard evidence to challenge the traditional view that the earliest civilized arts had originated in the Middle East. China and India were held to be the first beneficiaries of Middle Eastern invention in central and eastern Asia. The cultivation of grains and domestication of animals were thought to have diffused to these areas around 3000 B.C., followed by pottery-making. Bronze manufacture was believed to have reached them about a thousand years later.

Southeastern Asia, where Thailand lies, played no role in this drama. It was regarded as a cultural dead end whose inhabitants, according to archeologist George Coedes, "seem to have been lacking in creative genius and showed little aptitude for making progress without stimulus from outside." The cultivation of rice, which has been the staple food of the region for millenia, was assumed to have been learned from India. Pottery and metallurgy were held to have been imported from far more advanced China not earlier than 800 B.C.

Thus, the archeological world was shaken by the news that pottery of unprecedently early date had been made by people who were believed to have been still squatting in caves. Adding to the consternation were the reports of the excavations made in 1965-66 by the University of Hawaii's Wilhelm Solheim at Non Nok Tha, near Ban Chiang, and at Spirit Cave in far northern Thailand in 1968 by his graduate student Chester Gorman.

In the ancient graves at Non Nok Tha, Solheim and his colleagues found bronze axeheads together with the molds in which they had been cast. They lay in a stratum that was radiocarbon dated to a much earlier period than the first known Middle Eastern or Chinese bronzes. In a 10,000 B.C. layer at Spirit Cave, Gorman unearthed carbonized bits of cucumber, water chestnut, pepper, bottle gourd and other food plants, indicating that the residents may have been growing vegetables 2,000 years before the Mesopotamians. In a 6800 B.C. stratum, he came across shards of pottery of an advanced kind, which signified that they were ahead of them in that art, as well. On the basis of these discoveries, Solheim hypothesized that if there were a single birthplace of civilization, it lay in Southeast Asia rather than the Near East.

Most archeologists at this time regarded the claim as science fiction. Having been taken in many times in the past by premature conclusions and spurious evidence, they have become justifiably cautious. They pointed out that thermoluminescent dating was a new and unproven technique whose validity had not been established; that the radiocarbon dates for the bronze axeheads at Non Nok Tha, too, were suspect because the strata were so jumbled together, with late graves dug into the site of much earlier burials; and that the vegetable fragments found at Spirit Cave could have been picked wild rather than grown by man.

The argument was virulent because archeology is an intensely competitive profession. Authorities who had invested careers and staked reputations on establishing the precedence of the Middle East were not about to relinquish their convictions on the evidence of dubious dates, a few broken shards, and the observations of an unknown graduate student. To account for the presence of the bronze artifacts, some gave serious consideration to a hypothetical migration into Southeast Asia of people from the Black Sea, 6,000 miles away.

In the hope of obtaining more convincing evidence, the Thai government in 1972 authorized an exploratory excavation at Ban Chiang by local archeologists, and a year later, Froehlich Rainey went there to examine what they had found. The hill on which the village lay, 20 feet high and a mile in circumference, was not a natural occurrence. It was a man-made mound built up over the millenia by the people who had lived on it and buried their dead in it. Archeologists dug a hole in the hill and found an amazing quantity of quality bronze, iron and ceramic artifacts, along with ancient plant matter and carefully placed animal bones, suggesting their use as funeral offerings. A number of unexpectedly large human skeletons were also discovered.

Rainey realized that the scientists were in a race. For generations, the villagers had been digging up old pottery with their plows, or in building excavations, using the priceless receptacles to feed dogs and chickens, as storage containers, or grinding them up for cement mix. But since the great antiquity of the pottery had been announced in 1968, dealers had streamed to Ban Chiang to buy up the handsome vessels at prices the villagers regarded as fortunes. The Thai government had banned the digging up, sale and export of the antiquities, even threatening to impose the death sentence on violators. But the regulations were impossible to enforce. The villagers simply draped curtains around the stilts on which their houses are built and dug under them at night—to the point where some of the dwellings collapsed.

In five years, an estimated 30,000 vases and urns had been spirited out of the country, showing up in museums, private collections, and art auctions all over the world. When the real pots began to run out, the villagers manufactured new ones, giving them a patina of antiquity by baking mud over the fresh paint. Some of the fakes were so skillfully made that they have been purchased by museums as the genuine articles.

To archeologists, the digging up of antiquities by amateurs is a tragedy comparable to tearing pages from irreplaceable historic manuscripts. The only way they can reconstruct a picture of ancient societies, in the absence of documents, is to study the artifacts in the strata in which they were found, still surrounded by the other relics of the culture that produced them. The history of prehistoric Thailand was disappearing under the pillagers' pickaxes. With no time to lose, a joint expedition began digging in Ban Chiang in 1974, co-directed by Chester Gorman, who had joined the University Museum staff, and Pisit Charoenwongsa, curator of the National Museum in Bangkok.

"It was the kind of site archeologists dream of, but seldom find," said Gorman. In two seasons of meticulously careful excavation and analysis, the archeologists uncovered six distinct cultural layers, each with its own characteristic types of pottery and other artifacts, all carefully carbon dated, that reached back in time from 250 B.C. to 3600 B.C.—over 3,000 years of human history. They brought out 18 tons of incredibly rich and varied material, layer upon layer of stratified human burials, 126 intact skeletons in all, both adults and children.

One grave held the remains of a young family, man, woman and child, who had apparently died and been buried together. Another contained the 4,000-year-old skeleton of an unusually tall male, whom the diggers named "Nimrod" because he had been buried with deer antlers and hunting weapons. He wore a necklace of tiger claws, with a polished bone pin lying under his skull that had once fastened his long hair. The most important find was the grave at the second lowest, 3600 B.C., level that held the bronze spearhead previously described, the oldest bronze object ever discovered.

Over 400 ceramic vessels came out of the excavations in an endless variety of sizes, shapes and decorations. They ranged from the earliest black pots, incised with geometric patterns; through the handsome red-on-buff vases of the middle period, painted with swirling designed that look like magnified fingerprints (which bear amazing resemblance to the red-on-buff pottery later produced in the Middle East, Egypt and China); to burnished red urns on the topmost levels that are cruder than the earlier specimens, as though the potters had run out of inspiration.

There were also carefully placed animal bones; beads made of stone, ivory, colored glass and blue marble; heaps of clay pellets, believed to be ammunition for pellet bows that modern Thailanders still use to kill birds and small animals; clay figurines of cattle, deer, elephants and human beings; terra cotta spindles for spinning thread; and curious cylindrical rollers with blue, red and ochre, pigments clinging to them that had been used to print designs on cloth—probably silk, since a strand of silk was stuck to one of the rollers. Bronze appeared in profusion through all but the lowest strata, in the form of axes and hunting weapons, bells, ornaments and jewelry, together with the crucibles in which the metal had been smelted. One skeleton had five rings on a single finger, another wore them on every finger and toe. Some had three or four bracelets, another was covered with them from wrist to elbow.

At the 1600 B.C. level, the diggers came across finds that were as important as the discovery of the bronze itself—iron objects, which were as old as those of the Hittites of the Middle East, who heretofore were believed to have been the first to have worked the metal successfully. Its first use was in ornaments and jewelry. One juvenile was buried wearing a wide bronze bracelet with an outside wrapping of iron, which was probably rarer and more valuable at the time than bronze. Later, iron was used in spearheads, knives and other workaday objects.

Evidences of agriculture were numerous at Ban Chiang. Pottery shards down to the lowest levels contained rice husks that had been added to bind and stiffen the clay, and keep it from shrinking and cracking when it was fired. There were also imprints of rice kernels on the surfaces of the pots, and carbonized bits still clinging to ceramic ladles. "This indicated beyond any question to me that the grain had been domestically grown," says botanist Douglas Yen of the University of Hawaii.

Also found in the graves were many cattle and water buffalo bones, the remains of the haunches of meat that had been put there to provide the occupants with food for their journeys. The small size of the bones compared to those of wild cattle and buffalo indicate that they, too, had been domesticated. The large bells that were found are believed to have been cowbells. Other animals remains include pigs, chickens, and a breed of dogs that appear to have descended from wolves, rather than jackals as in the Middle East.

There are still great gaps in our knowledge of events in ancient Thailand, and the significance of much of the evidence is debatable. Nevertheless, by piecing together the findings from Ban Chiang and other sites explored before and since, archeologists have formulated a tentative prehistoric scenario. The earliest known inhabitants of the region were the people who reached Spirit Cave, around 10,000 B.C., which probably served them and later generations as a hunting camp, rather than a permanent habitation. Where they came from is not known. But "they definitely do not seem to be closely related to the present population of Southeast Asia, nor were they typically Mongoloid," states anthropologist Michael Pietrusewsky of the University of Hawaii, who has studied the early Thai remains intensively. They were tall, muscular people, with heavy bones, wide faces, and fairly pronounced brow ridges, quite different from those of the smoothly rounded oriental skull. (Physically, they are more closely related to the Polynesians of the Pacific Islands than to any other people, says Pietrusewsky, which opens up another intriguing vista of possibilities.)

Whatever their origin, the first occupants of the cave were hunter-gatherers and fishermen, living in a Late Stone Age culture. But they made considerably progress. By 7000 B.C., they were producing the earliest known pottery, except for the Jomon pottery of Japan which is 2,000 years older. However, the Spirit Cave pots were already well developed, decorated with a variety of finishes and incised designs, indicating that the art of making them had been acquired millenia earlier. Since pottery is usually made by sedentary agricultural people rather than nomadic hunters, Gorman believed the carbonized food plants found in the cave had been cultivated—and for a considerable period of time.

The presence of two other advanced types of artifacts support his contention—polished stone tools with rectangular horizontal blades that made fine hoes for working the soil (any other use for them is hard to imagine), and slate knives with sharply ground edges similar to those still used to harvest rice in parts of Indonesia. Apparently the people had also begun to domesticate water buffalo, pigs and fowl, whose bones were found in the strata.

Spirit Cave was abandoned around 5500 B.C. The next 2,000 years are still a blank in the record, the "lost millenia," Gorman called them. But by the time we pick up human traces again at Ban Chiang, around 3600 B.C., the people had made enormous cultural, social and economic strides. They had settled down in permanent villages, living in wooden houses whose post holes can be detected in the strata. Though they still hunted, they kept livestock and grew rice in fields that had probably been cleared by slash-and-burn methods. They made splendid pottery, spun thread and wove cloth, wore clothes of silk decorated with printed designs, and embellished themselves with necklaces of many materials, and bracelets and rings fashioned of bronze. They must have learned the use of metals a long time earlier, since the bronze is alloyed in the exact proportions that gives it maximum durability—nine parts copper to one part tin—a bit of information that it had taken Middle Eastern metallurgists 3,000 years to acquire. The presence of seashells in the excavation also indicates that Ban Chiang traded with communities along the coast.

Despite the physical comforts, life must have been hard. From the evidence of the skeletons, the people suffered from anemia, malaria, tuberculosis and dental caries. Often the enamel of their teeth had been worn away, indicating they used them for something besides eating, perhaps chewing animal hides in order to soften them, as the Indians of North America did. Infant mortality was high. Death on the average occurred at 30 years of age, with very few individuals surviving to 45. The dead were entombed with ceremony, accompanied by a rich assortment of grave goods, including jewelry, cloth, religious urns (some decorated on the inside), hunting implements, grain and meat for the journey to the hereafter. Their religion may have been a fertility cult since phalluses and snakes, a common fertility symbol among primitive people, can be seen in some of the pottery designs.

A new social order involving division of labor had arisen since the sophisticated bronzes and the immense amount of pottery, created with such artistry, could not have been made by peasants in their spare time. Mining the ores, melting it into ingots, alloying the metals to exact proportions, and casting it in molds, are full-time occupations for specialists, requiring long apprenticeship and years of experience. Society also appears to have become stratified since there are no humble burials at Ban Chiang. The graves with their pottery and bronzes are those of rulers or the upper class. Social status was probably hereditary, since young children are buried with the same rich assortment of goods as their elders.

Sometime during the second millenium B.C., the economy of Ban Chiang took another leap forward when the people apparently turned from dry-cultivation to more intensive wet-cultivation of rice in flooded paddies—as is done in the Far East today—enabling them to raise crops on a continuous basis rather than once or twice a year. According to anthropologist Charles Higham of the University of New Zealand, the evidence lies in the sudden increase in the number of water buffalo, which would have been needed to pull the plows, and the simultaneous decrease in the deer and other animals that depend on forest habitats for survival. At about this time, objects made of iron also begin to appear. Although the oldest of them are dated from 1600 to 1000 B.C., new discoveries have been made in Lopburi north of Bangkok that may push the beginnings of iron metallurgy back several centuries, giving Southeast Asia a "first" in that technology, as well.

Throughout the nearly 4,000 years of their existence, the people of Ban Chiang appear to have enjoyed prosperity, security and stability. None of the six successive cultures that occupied the site gives evidence of having been destroyed by conflagration or revolt. None of the over 200 bodies unearthed there and at nearby Non Nok Tha appear to have been deaths by violence. No shields or other weapons of war have been found, and there were no fortifications of any kind. Nevertheless, Ban Chiang was abandoned around 250 B.C. for unknown reasons and remained tenantless during most of the next 2,000 years.

"The civilization to which the people belonged was vibrant and sophisticated," Chet Gorman wrote. "In terms of metallurgical skills, it seems to have been unparalleled anywhere in the world at the time," and it remained in the cultural forefront in the Far East until superseded by China in the second millenium B.C.

However, these assertions—indeed, the whole scenario of developments in prehistoric Thailand—are still a long way from being proved conclusively. If the people were so advanced, traditionalists ask, why did they leave no cities, or a written language, both of which have long been held to be hallmarks of civilization? They point out that metallurgy in the Middle East can be traced back to its beginnings, step by step over 3,000 years, whereas in Thailand it appears suddenly, sophisticated and full-blown, with no ancestry at all. They ask where are the more primitive and developmental examples of metal-working? Based on a vague Mesopotamian inscription stating that tin had been imported from "somewhere in the east," they advance the possibility that the arts of metallurgy may have been brought to Thailand by early Near Eastern traders in search of the scarce metal.

The pro-Thai advocates rebut the charges by pointing out that civilizations can flourish without a written language—the highly cultured Incas of Peru, among others, did not have one either—and that unlike the populations of Mesopotamia and Egypt which concentrated along the banks of great rivers, the ancient Thais were spread out over a broad plateau that did not lend itself to the development of cities. As to the sophisticated bronzes, Chester Gorman expressed confidence that evidence of earlier metallurgy would be found in the area indicating "a considerable period of development," although it may not have taken the Thais as long to discover the alloy, since they lived in one of the few places on earth where copper and tin are both plentiful. If there was an interchange of metallurgical ideas, states Thai archeologist Chin Youdi, "they traveled from Thailand to the West."

Few regions on earth hold greater archeological promise, or more likely surprises, than Southeast Asia. Still awaiting investigation in Thailand, as well as in Cambodia and Vietnam when political conditions permit, are huge circular earthworks, up to 20 feet high, that may hide the missing cities of the lost civilization. Strewn across northeast Thailand are 300 other mounds like the one at Ban Chiang, with perhaps as many more to be discovered, that may yield treasures that will revolutionize our knowledge of man's past—provided, of course, that the archeologists get to them before the looters do.

CHAPTER 7

Decoding the Ancient Calendars

(5000 B.C. to the present)

Astronomy is an unimaginably ancient science. While still living in caves, men were recording the days between new moons on animal bones. Before they had learned to write, the Sumerians had mapped the heavens. By 2500 B.C., the Babylonians had traced the rotation of the sun, moon and planets; the Egyptians were forecasting the rising and setting of stars, and had discovered the precision of the equinoxes; and the inhabitants of Britain and northeastern France were calculating the solstices, the shifting courses of the moon, and perhaps predicting eclipses.

Since they lived in the same hemisphere, these ancient people might conceivably have exchanged information. But a thousand years before Europeans crossed the ocean, the Mayas of Mesoamerica, independently, had made astronomic calculations that were even more accurate—so accurate, in fact, that they were not duplicated until comparatively recent times.

Astronomy was vitally important to early people for several reasons: First, because the sun, moon and planets were among their principal gods. Second, because these gods had human passions and appetites, and by knowing their exact positions in the heavens and proximity to each other, one could predict their moods, whether they would bring benefits or catastrophes, good luck or bad (astrology and astronomy were practically interchangeable). Third, and most important, because the calendar is based on the movements of celestial bodies.

The calendar was sacred, the very heart of ancient religions and civilizations, because it helped assure survival. Unless one knew when to plant and when to harvest, and when the annual floods, rains, droughts and frosts were due, the crops might fail and people would starve. Then, as now, calendars were regulated by the rotation of the sun. The most important solar positions that had to be noted were the solstices, when the sun reaches its most northerly and southerly extremities in the sky (usually on June 22 and December 22), which mark the beginnings of summer and winter; and the points midway between the solstices, the equinoxes, when the sun crosses the equator (about March 21 and September 23), which usher in the spring and fall seasons. The phases of the moon, too, had to be watched since they measured the lengths of the seasons and foretold the tides.

Astronomers had also observed that shortly before the crescent moon reappeared in certain years solar eclipses might occur, and that the moon itself might be eclipsed, on occasion, when it was full. Solar eclipses, when the sun would suddenly vanish in broad daylight, perhaps never to reappear, caused indescribable terror in human hearts until fairly recent times. People had to be forewarned of the dreaded event and astronomers who failed to do so are known to have been beheaded.

The sun and moon cannot always be relied on as indicators of the seasons, however, because the sun may be obscured by clouds, rendering it unobservable for days or weeks, and due to the angle of the moon's axis to the earth, its course seems capricious. It does not follow the same set of paths across the sky year after year, but inscribes a north-south circuit, called the Metonic Cycle, that takes 18.6 years to complete. A backup system was needed, therefore, which was provided by the movements of the brighter stars and the five planets visible to the naked eye.

By long observation, astronomers had noted that when the sun reached the solstices or other latitudes in the heavens, or shortly before regularly recurring natural events took place on earth each year, certain stars or planets would coincidentally rise or set on the horizon just before dawn. These "heliacal" risings and settings, as they are called, were carefully watched for. The appearance of Sirius, the "dog star," above the eastern horizon before dawn told Egyptians that the Nile was about to flood, and when the Pleiades set in the west before sunrise ancient Greeks knew it was time to plant their grain.

The horizon was used as a reference point in tracking the movements of celestial bodies because the ancients had no reliable means of determining their positions in the sky. But even with this aid, it is difficult to detect changes in their positions without instruments or observatories, since their courses vary so slightly each day. Moreover, to pinpoint changes in the course of stars and planets with sufficient accuracy to make short-term predictions without instruments seems next to impossible. Yet the ancient astronomers *were* able to make such forecasts, and for centuries scientists wondered how, although the clues lay in plain sight around them.

Among the unusual creations of antiquity are the rough-hewn megalithic (Greek for "great stone") monuments that are scattered across Western Europe from Portugal and Spain to Sweden. Erected in the Late Stone Age, between 6,000 and 4,000 years ago, they range in size from single standing stones, called menhirs, to structures as complex as Stonehenge. The greatest concentration of menhirs is the fantastic array in France near Carnac, in Brittany, where over 3,000 stones, lined up in straight avenues 11 and 12 abreast, stretch across the fields for 2½ miles. At nearby Kerloas stands the tallest stone, 39 feet high, and at Locqumarier lies the largest stone ever used for building purposes anywhere on earth, the fallen 380-ton Grand Menhir Brisé (great broken menhir), now smashed into five pieces, which originally stood 69 feet high.

The purpose of the peculiar objects was so baffling that they were referred to as "the archeologists' nightmare." Historians guessed the stones to be everything from phallic symbols to memorials to fallen warriors, until Alexander Thom, a retired engineering professor from Oxford University, suggested a solution to the mystery in the 1950s. After painstaking investigation, Thom concluded that the stones were arranged to record the changes in the moon's passage across the sky. Using the huge standing stone at Kerloas and the Grand Menhir Brisé as foresights, and other megalithic structures in a 10-mile radius as backsights, the astronomers had clear lines of sight to points on the horizon that marked the widest observable swings of the moon both to the north and south.

The giant array of menhirs at Carnac, in Thom's view, appeared even more remarkable. It was nothing less than a gigantic sheet of stone graph paper that enabled the early Bretons to predict the positions of sunrises and sunsets, moonrises and moonsets, throughout the year. From the way the stones are aligned, Thom believes the builders also knew that the critical periods during which lunar eclipses may take place recur every 173.3 days; that, due to an ellipse in the moon's orbit, the time from the spring equinox to the autumn equinox is slightly longer than the time from autumn back to spring; and that they had discovered the Metonic Cycle that brings both the sun and moon to their northernmost extremities in the sky simultaneously each 18.6 years. The observations permitted by the Carnac array were so precise, says Thom, that "no comparable accuracy was possible until the invention of the telescope" several thousand years later.

Stonehenge, in southern England, is the most impressive, but not the largest, of over 900 similar circular henges scattered throughout the British Isles. As late as the 1940s, history books described the "magic circles" as either corrals for cattle or Druid places of worship, although radiocarbon dating has since revealed they were erected between 2800 and 1900 B.C., up to 2,000 years before the

Druids reached Britain. But in the 1960s, as noted earlier in this book, astronomer Gerald Hawkins demonstrated that the henges, too, were probably astronomic observatories. With the aid of an electronic computer, he calculated that when viewed from the center of the Stonehenge circle on Midsummer Day, the summer solstice, the rays of the rising sun would come in over the outlying "heelstone."

The claim can be verified by visual observation, although due to a shift in the solar circuit in the past 4,000 years, the sun now rises one degree north. Other alignments in the circle recorded sunrises and sunsets, moonrises and moonsets, on other significant dates. These readings, Hawkins postulated, provided the basis of the megalithic calendar, which divided the solar year into eight "months," marked by the two solstices, two equinoxes, and four dates between them. Each period began with a holiday, of which at least one, May Day, is still celebrated.

The ancient British astronomers must have practiced mathematics of a high order, Alexander Thom believes, for to work out the circles and angles of sight so accurately requires the use of geometric theorems whose discovery is attributed to the Greeks 15 centuries later.

But even more startling was Hawkins' conclusion that the Aubrey Circle, a ring of 56 evenly spaced holes inside the periphery of Stonehenge, constituted a computer that enabled the early astronomers to predict solar eclipses, which are governed by the 18.6 year lunar cycle. He was led to investigate the possibility because the number 56 represents approximately three times the number of years in the cycle, which is the closest figure that could be arrived at by people who counted in whole numbers and did not understand the use of fractions. How the eclipse predictor operated involves too much mathematics and technical astronomy to be explained here. But it apparently worked, because Julius Caesar, in the diary he kept during his invasion of Britain in 55 B.C., marveled at the ability of the Druid priests to predict eclipses, which they may have inherited from the builders of Stonehenge.

Hawkins' theories were challenged by astronomers, partly because the purported eclipse computers produced errors, but mainly
because it seemed inconceivable that Stone Age peasants, who had
not yet acquired a written language, were capable of such achievements. But an independent study made by Fred Hoyle, the famed
British astronomer, has confirmed the basic validity of Hawkins'
theories, although revising many of his calculations. He demonstrated that some of the "errors" may have been intentionally built
into the system by the Stonehengers themselves, to enable them to
interpolate the readings in case bad weather prevented them from
making visual observations. "We ourselves could use Stonehenge
to make eclipse predictions without making any substantive
changes in the layout," Hoyle said.

Probably the earliest astronomic observatories, stemming back
6,000 years, were the ziggurats of Mesopotamia, terraced pyrami-
dal towers built by the Sumerians and the later Babylonians to
provide clear views of the horizon. The most famous, and perhaps
largest, may have been the Biblical Tower of Babel dedicated to the
god Marduk (our planet Jupiter), which is estimated to have risen
295 feet (almost 30 modern stories) high. Made of sunbaked brick,
the ziggurats have long since crumbled into featureless mounds.
But the meticulous observations and astronomic timetables, which
the astronomer-priests recorded in cuneiform on tablets of baked
clay, reveal that the Babylonians had acquired a remarkably accurate knowledge of the movements of heavenly bodies.

The Babylonians employed a numeration system which divided
the hour into 60 minutes, and the circle of the sky into 360 degrees
(as is still done today). From their observations, they were able to
calculate the courses and true lengths of the solar and lunar years to
the nearest minute, missing out by less than 10 seconds. They also
worked out the circuits and duration of the revolutions of each of
the visible planets, from the 40-month-long cycle of Mercury to the
29-year circuit of Saturn. This is a remarkable accomplishment for
people using primitive instruments because, unlike the sun and
moon, the planets move erratically when viewed from earth, sometimes appearing to slow down, stop, and even reverse their paths,

during their wanderings. The priests also learned that eclipses were repeated in the same order over 18.6-year periods, and may have been able to predict their likelihood, and perhaps the return of certain comets whose appearance was believed to herald epidemics, military defeats, and the death of kings.

In computing their calendar, the Babylonians were faced with a problem that has plagued calendar-makers from the beginning—the incompatability of the motions of the sun and moon. They solved the dilemma by dividing the year into 12 alternating 29 and 30-day months, coinciding with the 28½ day rotation of the moon, and adding extra months every two to three years, which averaged the years out to the almost correct 356¼ days over a period of 19 years. The system is still employed in the Jewish religious calendar, and by Christians to determine the date of Easter, which is why its advent can vary by as much as a month in the modern calendar.

The Babylonians, and their successors the Chaldeans, 2,600 years ago, were the most ardent astrologers of antiquity. They grouped the stars into constellations named after mythical figures and animals (two of the names, the Lion and Scorpion, have survived) and believed that the sun passed through each of 12 constellations of the zodiac during the year, giving the constellation that housed it control over events on earth during that period. Since only the priests could interpret the constellation's will, no political or military undertaking would be launched without their approval. Living secluded lives in monasteries adjacent to the ziggurats, where they guarded their secrets, the priests were considered so infallible that when a prediction failed, the blame was put not on them, but on the heavens, which for unknown reasons had chosen to deviate from custom.

The ancient Egyptians were not as skillful astronomers as the Babylonians, probably because they did not have to be. With their unchanging climate year after year, the natural event that concerned them most was the annual flooding of the Nile which left the land carpeted with fertile silt in which crops flourished. Their year began when the Nile rose from its banks around June 15, which coincided almost exactly with the pre-dawn rising of Sirius, the "dog star," and continued until Sirius reappeared 365 to 366 days later. The year was divided into twelve 30-day months, with five "unlucky days" added, plus a sixth day on leap year.

Faced with the necessity of redrawing the boundary lines of their flooded fields each year, and of restoring irrigation ditches, dams and temples, the Egyptians became superb surveyors, mathematicians and engineers. The north face of the Great Pyramid of Giza, for example, lies within a miniscule five arc minutes of true north, an accuracy that would be difficult to achieve even with modern instruments for a building that size. The pyramids could not have been employed as observatories since they came to points, and their sides were smooth-surfaced until the Moslem invaders stripped off the marble facings a thousand years ago to build mosques.

However, astronomers had long suspected that the temples erected to the sky gods may have served astronomic functions, and in 1973, Gerald Hawkins, the decoder of Stonehenge, demonstrated that they probably did. His computer calculations revealed that the vast Temple of Amon-Ra (the sun god) at Karnak, whose interior was normally shrouded in darkness, is so aligned that once a year, exactly at dawn on the day of the winter solstice, the rays of the sun glided through the narrow quarter-mile-long central gallery to illuminate the altar at the western end.* Perched atop the temple is a ruined chapel with a single window pointing southeast through which the position of the rising sun could be observed at other times of the year. On its wall, the Pharoah is portrayed facing the window to greet the god. Adjoining temples similarly pointed to the first crescent moonsets, following the solstice.

Other Egyptian temples were oriented to face the pre-dawn rising of certain stars whose appearance marked significant dates in the calendar. However, due to a phenomenon called the "precession of the equinoxes," caused by wobbles in the earth's orbit and

---

*Curiously, the same dramatic trick was used in a 5100 B.C. megalithic tomb at Newgrange, Ireland. It is so designed that on the day of the winter solstice, the rays of the rising sun shine through a slit in the roof down a 60-foot-long corridor to illuminate the spot in the burial chamber where the coffin or body would have lain.

polar axis (similar to the wobbles of a spinning top) on a 26,000-year-long cycle, the constellations slowly alter their position in the skies, rising approximately one degree farther north on the horizon each century. After a few centuries, the temple would no longer precisely align on the star to which it was dedicated and would become useless for religious and astronomic purposes unless it was rebuilt. Thus, a temple at Luxor dedicated to the star Vega was added to four times, each addition deviating slightly from the previous orientation. Another temple, believed to have been devoted to the star Alpha Columbae, consists of two superimposed buildings set at an angle. The first structure, built in the fourth millenium B.C., was aligned to the position of the star at that time, the second erected several centuries later faced the new position of the star, five degrees to the north.

The Egyptians were the first to divide the day into 24 hours, which they measured during daylight hours by means of water clocks indoors, and with sun dials outdoors which ranged in size from small portable devices to giant obelisks. The hours of the night were measured by "star clocks," which were diagrams that indicate the names of the stars or star-groups that rise above the horizon on each date at a particular time and hour of the night. Keeping track of time was so important to the Egyptians that they painted water clocks and star diagrams on the inside of coffin lids as a convenience to the deceased in the afterlife.

Unlike the Egyptians, the astronomers of ancient Mexico and Yucatan could use their pyramids as observatories since their tops were flat, and were raised high enough to provide a clear view of the horizon over the obstructing jungle. Mayan bas reliefs show priests using cross-stick sighting devices and plumb lines to make fixes on Venus, whose steady circuit they regarded as a more reliable timepiece than the sun.

The Middle Americans also built specialized observatories, of which two—the circular Caracol at Chichen-Itza in Yucatan, and the arrow-shaped building at Monte Alban near Oaxaca, Mexico—have survived. The seemingly randomly-placed windows and apertures of the Caracol are so arranged that, when viewed from doorways in the interior, they framed the rising and setting moon and sun on the days of solstices and equinoxes, as well as the extreme positions of Venus. To correlate the findings of the major observatories, astronomic congresses were apparently held at Copan in Honduras in the seventh century A.D., and at Xochicalco in Mexico some time later. The portraits of the astronomers attending, and the symbols of the cities from which they came, may be seen engraved on the walls.

The skill of these early American observers was phenomenal. They calculated the solar year to within 12 seconds of its true length, and estimated the revolution of Venus with an error of only seven seconds in 50 years, figures not improved upon until modern times. A Codex now in the Dresden Museum in Germany, one of only three Mayan books that escaped destruction by Christian missionaries, is filled with detailed hieroglyphic tables forecasting the likelihood of solar eclipses for several centuries, by relating them to the periodic reappearance of Venus and the new moon. There is also a page of corrections that adapt the charts for future use.

"The Codex was a work of genius," states U.S. astronomer Charles Smiley. "It predicted eclipses visible not only in Central America, but all over the world. The authors couldn't have known how good they were." He found that in one 33-year period, the table successfully predicted every eclipse that occurred on earth, without a miss, and that it would be just as accurate in the 25th century A.D.

The Mayans were obsessed with time, calculating it as far back as 400 million years into the past. They inscribed dates on everything, in terms of days, months, years, 20-year *katuns* and 400-year *baktuns*, using numbering systems which have been deciphered. By correlating these dates with those of our own calendar, archeologists can tell almost to the exact year when a particular temple, pyramid or stone monument, was erected. Their calendar, which began in our 3113 B.C., was enormously complicated, comprising 260-day, 13-month religious years, with five extra bad-luck days, during which work stopped and people cowered in their homes praying for survival. Each 52nd year, when the two calendars coincided, was a time of great dread for the Mesoamericans. They believed the world had been created and destroyed four times in the past, and that this world too would be destroyed at the end of one of the 52-year cycles.

Astrology was as important to Mayans as it was to the Mesopotamians, although their mythology was totally different. Each day was ruled by four separate gods, who carried time on their backs in tumplines suspended from their foreheads. Some of these deities were well disposed to men, some were not, and to foresee the future and offset the bad influences with the good, it was vital to know which of the gods would be marching together on any given day. "It was an involved computation on whose successful solution depended the fate of mankind," observed Mayan scholar Eric Thompson.

From Mesoamerica, the knowledge of astronomy apparently filtered north to the now vanished Anasazi of the Southwestern United States, who left behind observatories built of adobe that are similar in function and design to those of the Mayas. However, the nomadic tribes to the north of them developed their own unique devices for keeping a calendar—stone-marked, spoked circles, that have been found on hilltops and in forest clearings across the western United States and Canada. White settlers called them "medicine wheels" in the belief that they had been used by medicine men to make magic. Their true purpose was not revealed until 1972 when U.S. government astronomer John Eddy investigated the medicine wheel in the Big Horn Mountains of Wyoming. More elaborate than most wheels, it forms an irregular circle 25 yards in diameter, with a large stone cairn at its hub, six smaller cairns on the periphery, and 28 uneven spokes of stone radiating out to its rim.

Employing some of the same techniques used at Stonehenge, Eddy demonstrated that the Big Horn Circle, too, was an astronomic observatory. When viewed from the center cairn, one of the outlying cairns lines up almost exactly with the rising sun at summer solstice, while another set of cairns, probably used as a backup in case the morning was cloudy, pointed to the setting sun on the same day. Other alignments marked the rising of the three brightest stars of the summer dawn in the years between 1400 and 1700 B.C., when the wheel was believed to have been in use: Aldabaran, which appeared a few days before the solstice, alerting medicine men to the coming event; Rigel, which rose a month later, perhaps marking the beginning of the warmest month of the year when the corn grew best; and Sirius, whose ascension another month later may have signaled the end of the short summer season, warning the people it was time to leave the mountains and move south. The 28 spokes of the wheel, Eddy speculates, may have been used to mark the days between new moons.

Equally remarkable is the "calendar stick" of the Winnebago Indians. It was a square, 53-inch-long, hickory rod etched on four sides with vertical notches which precisely denoted the months of both the lunar and longer solar years, with a special marking for a leap-year adjustment. "That's very sophisticated stuff for a people who didn't have writing or high arithmetic," observes archeologist Alexander Marshak of Harvard's Peabody Museum. That the Indians should have abandoned their calendar sticks and medicine wheels is ironic, because the sticks and wheels provided them with calendars that were probably more accurate than the one they adopted from the white man at the time.

Our present-day system of recording time is a hodgepodge inherited from a variety of sources. We got our 60-minute hours from the Babylonians, our 24-hour days from the Egyptians, and the seven-day week from the biblical Hebrews—although they are named for pagan gods. Our months came from the ancient Greeks, via the Romans who made such a hash of them that most of us still have to recite the nursery rhyme "Thirty days hath November, etc." to figure out how many days there are in each.

The problems began in the seventh century B.C. when the Romans decided to begin the year with January, instead of March. This moved the months from September through December to the 9th, 10th, 11th and 12th positions, although their names in Latin mean Seventh, Eighth, Ninth and Tenth Months. Some centuries later, Julius Caesar and his successor, the Emperor Augustus, re-

A street in Herculaneum (*top*). Buried under 66 feet of rock-hard tephra by the eruption of Vesuvius in 79 A.D., the city was acidentally rediscovered in 1709. What happened to its people, however, was not known until 1980. Protected by the tephra, this private villa (*below*) remains largely intact after 2000 years, as do most of the other buildings and elegant houses of the city. Only one-quarter of ancient Herculaneum has been unearthed. The rest lies under the modern city of Ercolano, whose buildings may be seen in the background, above the ancient ruins.

The Inca city of Machu Picchu. Built on a mountain peak and abandoned in the 14th century before the Spanish arrived, the city lay forgotten for nearly 600 years until rediscovered in 1911. Because no skeletons of males under 60 years of age were found in its cemetery, Machu Picchu is believed to have been a cloister for the Inca Virgins of the Sun and the aged enuchs who served them.

(Picture credit: George Holton/Photo Researchers, Inc.)

The Great Temple of the Aztecs in Mexico City. Chief archeologist Matos Moctezuma (*top*) inspects a carved wall of human skulls unearthed in the excavation of the temple in 1978. It is a replica of the racks holding 136,000 real skulls of sacrificed men which the Spanish saw in the courtyard in 1519. The author (*lower left*) examines a carved eagle head that adorns the second pyramid built in 1390, which was later covered over by four more pyramids. The statue of the Aztec earth goddess, Coatlicue (*lower right*), is one of the most hideous ever conceived. Her face is formed of the heads of two serpents, her toes are ferocious claws, she wears a skirt of writhing rattlesnakes, and a necklace of human hearts, chopped off hands, and a skull.

(Picture credits: Top and lower left, Ronald Schiller; lower right, Andrew Rakocsy/Woodfin Camp & Assocs.)

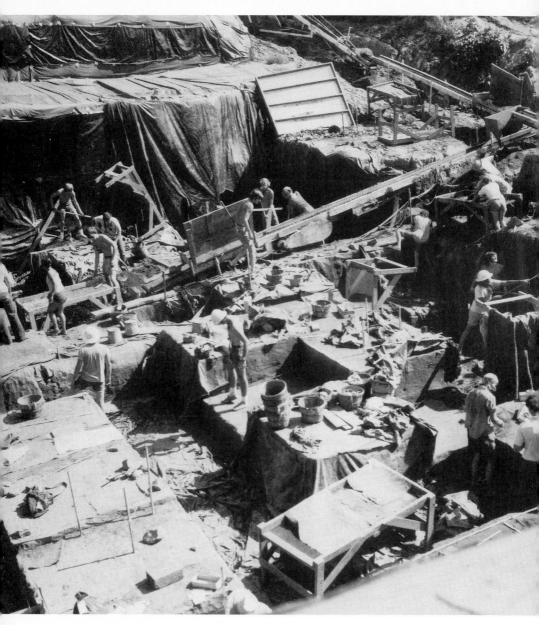

The Koster excavation began with the discovery of ancient Indian artifacts in a cornfield belonging to farmer Theodore Koster near Kampsville, Illinois, in 1968, and continued until 1978. The excavation eventually reached a depth of 38 feet, revealing that people had been living at the site for almost 10,000 years. This was one of the first archeological projects in which the work was done by students and volunteers of both sexes, who paid for the privilege. The practice has since become common in Western countries.

(Picture credit: Ronald Schiller)

named two summer months "July" and "August" in their own honor, and to increase the prestige of their creations, each stole a day from February to make their months 31 days long. To account for the extra quarter-day of the solar year, Julius added an extra day to February every four years.

This Julian Calendar served Europe for the next 1,600 years. But it had a flaw in it. The length of the solar year is actually nine minutes and 9.539 seconds longer than 365¼ days, which meant that the calendar kept getting farther and farther out of step with the seasons. In 1582, Pope Gregory XIII corrected the error by omitting 10 days from the calendar, declaring what would have been October 5 to be October 15. Roman Catholic countries quickly installed the new Gregorian Calendar, but Protestant nations were slow to adopt it, and Orthodox Catholics of eastern Europe never did. By the time Britain got around to making the change on behalf of itself and its American colonies, 180 years later, the error amounted to 11 days. The correction was made by dropping all the dates between September 2 and September 13, 1752. They do not exist in American and British history books.

To average out the year to its almost exact length of 365.2422 days, Gregory added an extra day (February 29) to years that are evenly divisibly by four, but not to centennial years unless they are exactly divisible by 400. This is why the years 1800 and 1900 were not leap years, but the year 2000 will be—in case you were wondering.

CHAPTER 8

The Riddles of the Egyptian Pyramids

(2700 to 2300 B.C.)

No monuments on earth have inspired greater awe and admiration, more avid curiosity or wilder speculation, than the pyramids of Giza in Egypt—particularly the Great Pyramid of the pharaoh Khufu, whom the Greeks called Cheops. Although built 4,500 years ago, it is the most massive solid stone structure ever erected, with room in its 13-acre base to enclose the six largest cathedrals of Europe. Its 2,300,000 blocks of stone, weighing from 2½ to 5 tons, soar to a peak 450 feet above the desert, the height of a 45-story skyscraper. Napoleon calculated this was enough masonry to raise a wall 10 feet high and a yard wide around the whole of France.

When completed and sheathed in 22 acres of polished white limestone that "gleamed like a mirror," as ancient writers describe it, the pyramid was a dazzling sight. But over the millenia, tourists managed to scale the slippery slopes to carve their names and other graffiti into the limestone. Before the Arabs stripped off the facing to build the mosques and palaces of Cairo seven centuries ago, there were reportedly enough inscriptions on the sides to fill 18,000 pages of manuscript.

Yet even in its present denuded state, the pyramid embodies architectural skills that have rarely been equaled and in some respects never surpassed. So accurately were the stones cut and fitted together that a sheet of paper can scarcely be inserted in the joints between the few remaining facing blocks. The southeast corner of the structure stands only half an inch higher than the northwest corner. The difference between its longest and shortest sides is less than eight inches, a discrepancy of less than .09 percent. The faces lie within a miniscule five arc minutes of perfect alignment with true north—and this may be attributable not to the architects' error but to the continent of Africa, which has twisted $1\frac{1}{4}$ feet westward in the past 4,500 years, carrying the man-made mountain with it. Even with sophisticated modern instruments, such figures would be phenomenal in a structure that size.

This achievement has led some investigators to suggest, quite seriously, that the pyramid could only have been erected with the aid of computers, perhaps by superminds from another planet, who used laser beams to cut the blocks and anti-gravity devices to raise them. Mathematicians have claimed that its geometry incorporates mathematical principles which were not supposedly discovered until 2,000 years later. Others have held it to be a place where the major events of history, both past and future, are prophesied; a memorial to a planetary cataclysm; a celestial observatory and geodetic marker on which the geography of the earth and stars have been brilliantly charted; or the repository of a universal system of weights and measures, which record the length of the year, the speed of light and the orbit of the planets, with absolute accuracy.

Early Freemasons venerated the pyramid as a shrine where such sages as Moses, St. Paul, Plato and Pythagoras, were initiated into the secrets of their order. The Freemasons, who were well represented in the early American congresses, succeeded in having its likeness incorporated in the Great Seal of the United States. Among the more recent claims is that the pyramid effuses an unidentifiable radiation that cures colds, prevents meat and milk from spoiling, and resharpens dull razor blades.

Modern Egyptologists, needless to say, treat such occult notions as romantic rubbish. There is not a vestige of evidence to show that the building was intended as anything but a tomb. Yet, though it has been intensively measured, probed, X-rayed, studied and re-studied, with the aid of every device known to science, it poses fundamental and disturbing questions that have never been satisfactorily answered.

How was it built? This is one of the most perplexing engineering puzzles in history. Builders ask how a people who did not use the wheel or draft animals in construction, who had no knowledge of pulleys, block and tackle, winches or derricks, could erect such an enormous and almost perfectly proportioned structure with nothing more than copper tools, crude surveying instruments, and their own muscles?

Part of the answer we know from archeological evidence. The stone for the central core was cut from the coarse red sandstone of the Giza plateau itself. The limestone facing came from the East bank of the Nile and the granite for the galleries and chambers from Aswan, 600 miles south on the Egyptian frontier where the quarries can still be seen. Since copper tools cannot cut granite, the quarrymen used mallets of ultra-hard stone called dolerite, to chip slots in the face of the rock. They then inserted wedges of wood into the slots and soaked them with water, causing the wood to expand until the block was split away from the matrix. Masons then hammered the blocks to shape, using quartz abrasives to obtain a smooth surface, and painted them with a variety of quarry marks, some indicating the distination of the stones, others the names of the crews that had produced them, the "Vigorous Gang" and the "Enduring Gang," among others.

When finished, the blocks were levered onto sledges with wooden crowbars, tied down with ropes made of papyrus reeds and hauled by gangs of sweating laborers to the Nile, where they were put on barges. To get the stones as close as possible to the building site, the transportation was done in spring when the Nile overflowed its banks to become a great lake. But there was so much rough ground between the water's edge and the pyramid, that a causeway, half a mile long and 60 feet wide, was built to bridge the distance. The causeway has long since disappeared, but the Greek historian Herodotus, who visited Giza in 480 B.C., reported it to be a magnificent structure almost as impressive as the Great Pyramid itself.

At this point, hard fact ends and the riddles begin. According to Herodotus, who got his information from temple priests, it took 10 years to build the causeway and another 20 years to erect the pyramid. He states that 100,000 men labored on the project constantly, being relieved by a fresh lot every three months. But Egyptologists challenge the figures, pointing out that Khufu reigned only 23 years, and that if he had died before the structure was completed, it would probably have remained unfinished—as happened to the pyramids of other pharaohs who expired prematurely. They also doubt that so many workers could have been employed, since they would have constituted a major share of the manpower of Egypt, whose population at the time is estimated at between 1.5 and two million. Besides "the logistics of sustaining 100,000 people, of supplying the necessary foodstuff, are beyond the organizational capacities of the third millenium B.C.," says Egyptologist Hans Goedicke of Johns Hopkins University.

A more baffling problem is how the heavy stones could be raised to such great heights by brute strength alone. According to Herodotus—who, it must be remembered, wrote of the event 2,000 years later—the blocks were lifted from one step to the next by "machines" formed of short wooden planks. But engineers have estimated that 3,500 such hoists—if that's what they were—would have been needed to build the pyramid, which would have been difficult for treeless Egypt to supply. It would have taken the cumbersome devices considerably longer than 20 years to lift the more than two million blocks, and though they might have been able to manage the 2½-ton stones used in the core, they could never have handled the 50-ton granite slabs that line some of the pyramid's chambers.

Most authorities are convinced that the blocks were hauled up manually by means of a vast ramp built of brick, earth and rubble, similar to the ones whose ruins can still be seen alongside the pyramids of Medum, Lisht, and a smaller one at Giza. But this feat would have been as phenomenal as the construction of the pyramid itself. To drag the massive stones up an incline without power equipment, even with the aid of wooden rollers, sledges and greased skidways, would have required a gradient of not more than 15 degrees. Moreover, the ramp would have to be raised and lengthened each time a new layer of stone was added to the growing pile. By the time the final blocks were put in place on the 201st step atop the Great Pyramid, the ramp would have been a mile long, with a volume of masonry four times greater than the building it served. Engineers have calculated that there was not enough manpower in the whole country to construct such a ramp beyond the halfway mark. A height of 50 feet or so is the practical limit.

In addition, the ramp would have narrowed in width until it was only three yards wide at the pyramid's apex. Where did the hauling crews put their feet when they were dragging the last blocks to the pinnacle, 40 stories in the air? It seems unlikely they could have pushed them the last few yards, since there would be room at the summit for only six men abreast. Even with the aid of platforms and scaffolding, engineers say, the builders could not have placed enough workers at the top of the pyramid to heave the 15-ton capstone into place.

In an effort to solve the riddle, researchers have suggested several alternate solutions. Some speculate that instead of a single monstrous ramp extending outward from the face of the pyramid, there may have been four smaller ones corkscrewing around the sides of the pyramid—much like the spiral ramps that lead cars to the tops of some parking garages. Since such ramps need not have been more than 10 feet wide, they could have been built with much less effort.

American engineer Olaf Tellefsen, who has studied the pyramid for years, theorizes that instead of using a ramp, the haulers stood atop the working level of the pyramid and pulled the blocks up its sides on greased wooden runways. He further postulates that when the pyramid had grown to the point where the working space had become too narrow to accommodate sufficient men for the purpose, the last stones were raised into position by a device with balance arms of unequal length, operating on the see-saw principle, that would enable a few laborers to do the work of many. By these means he estimates the pyramids could have been built by only 3,000 men, instead of the assumed 100,000.

But archeologists reject these explanations on the ground that there is no evidence to support them. The Egyptians were inordinately proud of their technical achievements, depicting them in minute detail in their tomb paintings and in hieroglyphic manuscripts. Although there are numerous drawings showing armies of men dragging colossal monoliths, and straight, giant ramps being used in construction—as well as the remains of the ramps themselves—there is not a single picture, written mention or archeological trace of spiral ramps, skidways up the sides of buildings, balance arms, or the machines Herodotus describes.

Nevertheless, the researchers are far from satisfied with their own answers. Famed British Egyptologist Sir Flinders Petrie pointed out that in the pyramid of Khafre (Chephren), which adjoins that of his father Khufu, there is a two-ton granite portcullis, which would require a force of at least 40 men to put into place. Yet it lies in a narrow passage with room enough for no more than eight men to work on it at once. Dr. I.E.S. Edwards, former Keeper of Egyptian Antiquities of the British Museum, added that the Great Pyramid could never have been built unless "technical advances" had been developed to enable the masons to handle the bulky stones. But what they may have been, he does not say.

Why was the pyramid built? To the ancient Egyptians, life on earth was a transitory phase of existence to be followed by life in the hereafter which lasted for eternity. However, they did not conceive of resurrection as a mere spiritual rebirth, but as an actual corporeal existence in which the deceased enjoyed all of the fleshly pleasures and prerogatives they had known on earth. To achieve this desirable goal, several things were necessary. First, it was mandatory that the body be preserved from decay, and to this end the Egyptians developed embalming techniques which have rarely been excelled. Second, should anything happen to the body, it was essential to have substitutes available in the form of statues and likenesses—26 was the prescribed number—which could be brought to life in the afterworld through magic incantations which were inscribed on coffin lids and elsewhere.

Third, the departed had to be provided with all of the material possessions he or she might need or desire. They included actual clothing, jewelry, weapons and furniture, usually gilded or made of solid gold; reserves of food, beer and wine, sufficient to last for centuries; statuettes and models representing soldiers and servants, boats and workshops, along with their entire personnel; and pictures on the wall depicting all of the dead man's estates and the activities that went on in them, as well as his wives, children, retainers, conquests, and even the sports he enjoyed. Finally, the body, statues, regalia and representations must all be locked in an impenetrable tomb, surrounded by temples dedicated to the deceased and guarded by priests. And to make sure the priests would provide the dead rulers with their daily quotas of fresh food and drink, and offer prayers for their well-being forever, the pharoahs endowed the temples with rich estates until they eventually owned most of the best lands of the Nile.

Undoubtedly the sepulchers, and the wealth that went into them, constituted heavy drains on the economy of the country, taking men and materials away from more productive pursuits, and none were more costly than the pyramids of Giza. Some scholars claim that the peasants engaged in the gruelling labor willingly, both as a religious duty to the god-kings and because it provided them with employment during the annual floods when their fields were under water.

But ancient writers describe Khufu and Khafre as tyrants who enslaved the population to build the gargantuan monuments to their vanity, and many Egyptologists agree they may well have been megalomaniacs. To help raise funds for his pyramid, Herodotus relates, Khufu actually forced his favorite daughter into prostitution. She was a wily girl. In addition to the fees she charged on the king's behalf, according to legend, she also demanded that her suitors provide her with building stones, eventually accumulating enough to build her own small pyramid.

Apparently Khufu did not initially plan to build so huge an edifice for his body, for the first burial crypt was cut into the bedrock beneath what was a comparatively modest structure. It was connected to the outside by a passage less than four feet square, sloping downward at an angle of 26 degrees (see diagram), just high and wide enough to slide the mummy case through. But as the king's building mania grew, he expanded the pyramid, constructing a larger granite-lined vault, erroneously called the Queen's Chamber, with a 16-foot-high niche for a statue set into its walls, then a third and still larger granite hall, the King's Chamber, at a height of 140 feet above the ground almost in the heart of the pyramid.

To reinforce this last resting place against the enormous weight above it, the architects built a five-tier structure of heavy granite slabs above it, surmounted by a gabled roof. It served its purpose well, for there is evidence that the pyramid was severely shaken by an earthquake a few years after it was built. Though the granite walls, ceilings, and the slabs above them were badly cracked, the chamber did not collapse. Narrow channels extend from the two rooms to the surface of the pyramid. They were installed either to provide air, or to allow the *ka*, or soul, of the king to come and go at will.

The Queen's Chamber is reached through a slanting Ascending Passage, 40 inches high. Beyond it, leading to the King's Chamber, is the sloping Grand Gallery, an architectural masterpiece, 17 feet wide at the base and 19 feet high, whose walls taper inward. Three six-foot-long plugs of granite and numerous limestone blocks were stored in the Grand Gallery when it was built. They rested on temporary wooden supports, the holes for which can still be seen. After the king's servants placed his body in the chamber and the

Interior Plan of the Great Pyramid

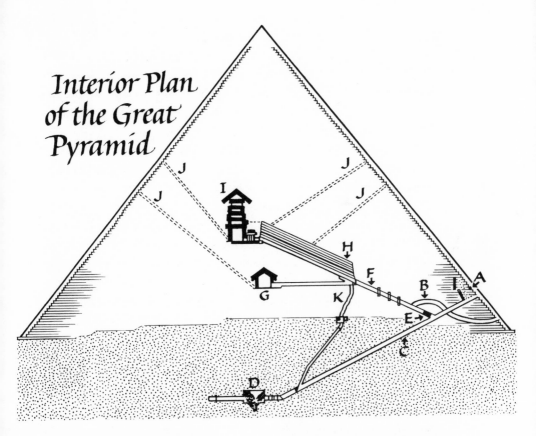

A. Original entrance, concealed by an undetectable stone door set into the limestone facing.

B. Tunnel dug by Caliph Abdulla Al Mamun, circa 820 A.D., when he was unable to find the entrance.

C. Descending Passage, a little less than 4-feet square.

D. Subterranean crypt, the original burial vault carved in the bedrock when the pyramid was planned as a much smaller structure.

E. Three 6-foot-long granite plugs, intended to seal the interior of the pyramid forever after the pharoah was interred.

F. Ascending Passage, same dimensions as the Descending Passage.

G. Second burial room, erroneously called the Queen's Chamber, built when the pyramid was enlarged.

H. The Grand Gallery in which were stored the granite and limestone plugs which were slid down the passage after the king's death.

I. The King's Chamber, third and final burial vault, surmounted by a four-tier structure and roof of granite slabs, designed to relieve the weight on the room.

J. Narrow ducts leading to the surface of the pyramid, installed either to admit air to the burial chamber or permit the dead king's KA (soul) to leave it.

K. Rough-hewn vertical bore, 3-feet wide not discovered until 1837. Obviously not part of the architect's plan, it could have been dug to allow workers to escape after lowering the granite plugs into place, by priests anxious to inspect the interior of the pyramid after the severe earthquake, or by thieves.

funeral procession had departed, the wooden supports were removed, allowing the granite and limestone plugs to slide down into
the Ascending Passage, thus sealing the tomb for what its occupant
hoped would be forever.

The only entrance built into the pyramid lay on the 13th step of
the north slope, 51 feet above the ground and about halfway between the sides. According to the geographer Strabo, who toured
Egypt in 24 B.C., it was concealed by a hinged flap door of limestone so cunningly set in the face of the wall, that when closed it
could not be detected. Only the priests knew where the door was
and how to open it. When the last Egyptian priest died in early
Christian times, the location of the entrance was forgotten, not to
be rediscovered until the limestone facing was removed from the
pyramid more than a thousand years later.

Was pharaoh actually buried in the pyramid? The question is not
as strange as it may seem. In the year 820 A.D., the Moslem Caliph
of Egypt, Abdullah Al Mamun, decided to break into the Great
Pyramid, less for the treasure it presumably contained than for the
scientific and astrological manuscripts believed to have been deposited in it, along with such other wonders as "strange metals that
would not rust" and "malleable glass which could be bent without
breaking." Unable to find the secret entrance in the steep polished
surface of the structure, the search party simply burrowed into it a
few feet above the sand, cracking the stones by heating them in
fires and dousing them with cold vinegar, then knocking out the
fragments with battering rams. After tunneling into the solid rock
for 100 feet, they were about to give up, when a workman heard
the muffled sound of something heavy falling within the building
east of the tunnel. Renewing their efforts the diggers finally broke
through to the Ascending Passage. It is the Caliph's tunnel that
visitors use when entering the pyramid today.

Groping their way down the low, slippery incline, the Caliph
and his men reached the unfinished subterranean crypt. However, it
contained nothing but dust, debris, and inscriptions written in the
ceiling with the carbon from burning torches by Greek and Roman
visitors centuries earlier, who had probably bribed the priests for

admission. Halfway up the passage, however, the searchers had noticed the end of one of the granite blocks which plugged the entrance to the Ascending Passage. The stone covering it had fallen to the floor, which is probably the sound they had heard on the outside. Unable to make a dent in the granite with their iron tools, the men cut around them through the softer limestone of the surrounding walls. Beyond the third granite plug they found the passage filled with limestone blocks, which they cracked with chisels and removed piece by piece, eventually reaching the lateral passage leading to the Queen's Chamber. But it, too, was empty.

Retracing their steps, the searchers scrambled up the steep incline of the Grand Gallery to the King's Chamber in the heart of the Pyramid. But here again they found nothing except a huge lidless sarcophagus of dark, polished granite. Since it was wider than the passages leading to the chamber, it must have been placed there while the pyramid was being built. In a fury of disappointment, the Arabs ripped up parts of the floors of the chambers and burrowed tunnels into the walls seeking hidden rooms, but nothing of value or interest was ever found.

This is incredible. Considering the immense treasure found in the tomb of Tutankhamen, an unimportant ruler who died at the age of 19 after only nine years on the throne, the burial treasure which the mighty Khufu assembled during his 23-year reign must have been several times as great. And to be of any use to him, according to Egyptian ritual, it had to be interred with his body. How had it been removed?

Unknown to the Caliph, another passage existed that was not discovered until 150 years ago. It is a meandering, roughly hewn vertical shaft, 200 feet long and just wide enough to allow a man to worm his way through, which leads from the bottom of the Descending Passage to the entrance of the Grand Gallery. Obviously not part of the architect's plan, archeologists speculate that it may have been dug either by workers, without the king's knowledge, to enable them to escape after sliding the granite plugs into position in the Ascending Passage; by priests anxious to inspect the damage done to the interior of the pyramid after it was shaken by the earthquake; or by grave robbers.

The robbers could have dropped the smaller valuables down the shaft, and the larger ones by breaking them up, along with Khufu's dismembered mummy, which was probably encased in gold, with precious stones wrapped in the bandages. But where are the thousands of vases of food which still fill the passages of other rifled pyramids from floor to ceiling? And what happened to the missing granite cover of the great sarcophagus in the King's Chamber and the large statue which presumably stood in the niche of the Queen's Chamber? They could never have been forced down the crawl hole. Perhaps the thieves smashed them. But if so, why would they go to the immense labor of removing the worthless shards instead of leaving them where they were, as they did in other plundered tombs?

Some Egyptologists theorize, without much conviction, that the missing objects were taken out through Al Mamun's tunnel which had actually been bored centuries earlier, although Arab accounts leave little doubt that it was dug at the Caliph's order.

But the more intriguing possibility is that Khufu had never been buried in the Pyramid. It was not uncommon for pharaohs to erect duplicate tombs for themselves. Khufu's father, Senefru, had two pyramids, another ruler built three. Adding weight to the argument was the discovery in 1926 of the tomb of Khufu's mother, Hetepheres, a few yards from her son's pyramid. Situated at the bottom of a vertical shaft cut into rock, 85 feet deep and solidly packed with masonry, it had never been opened since it was sealed. Found in it were gold vases and food vessels, cosmetics, jewelry, a gold manicure instrument, a bed, and other personal objects and pieces of furniture belonging to the queen. But when the alabaster sarcophagus was opened, the mummy was missing.

Thus, it may be that the Great Pyramid was intended as a decoy to lure thieves and that, like his mother, Khufu and his treasure were secretly interred in a less conspicuous sepulcher that has not been located.

Could there be undiscovered rooms in the pyramid? There well may be. The stepped pyramid of Zoser at Sakkara, built a century earlier, is literally honeycombed with chambers, connected by over a mile of passages. Yet only a few passages and three chambers have been found in Khufu's pyramid, and only one passage and a single small burial crypt in Khafre's—and they lie not in the pyramid itself, but underneath it. It seemed inconceivable to Nobel Prize-winning physicist Dr. Luis Alvarez, of the University of California's Lawrence Radiation Laboratory, "that Khafre, who had watched his father's slaves build the Great Pyramid, with its intricate internal structure, would then erect a pile of rocks almost as large with no internal structure at all." He believed the more plausible explanation was that Khafre's architects were cleverer than Khufu's in hiding the chambers, and that they have escaped discovery.

British treasure hunters 150 years ago blasted holes in both pyramids with gunpowder in an effort to locate secret rooms, but Professor Alvarez and his co-workers used less destructive methods. In 1966, in cooperation with the Egyptian government, they installed a cosmic ray detector in the chamber beneath Khafre's pyramid. By recording the direction and speed of the cosmic rays which penetrate through the stonework from space, and feeding the readings through a computer, an X-ray picture of the pyramid's interior was produced. But except for some small irregularly shaped gaps in the masonry, no hidden orifices were found in the upper part of the building. This does not preclude the possibility that rooms may exist in the lower half of the structure beneath the reach of the detector, and the game of hide-and-seek still goes on.

The search in the area surrounding the pyramids, however, has produced spectacular results. In 1954, a magnificent, 36-foot-long cedar boat, complete with gilded cabin, doors, oars, coils of rope and copper hardware, was discovered in a crypt under the sands on the south side of the Great Pyramid. Carefully disassembled and laid out in a pit covered with granite slabs, many of the pieces had hieroglyphs painted on their sides—which turned out to be do-it-yourself instructions for putting them together! The reassembled vessel, which now stands in a museum alongside the pyramid, is believed to be Khufu's "Sun Boat," which he would use to sail the heavens during the hours of daylight. A similar "Moon Boat" lies on the east side of the pyramid. Although its crypt has been punctured and the contents televised, the boat has not yet been excavated.

"What's the hurry?" asked Egypt's Director of Antiquities. "It's lain untouched for 45 centuries, so another few decades won't make much difference. And—who knows?—the old man may still need it."

CHAPTER 9

The Explosion That Changed the Course of Civilization

(1550 to 1450 B.C.)

It was a peaceful summer's day in the Aegean. The wind blew from the northwest. The beautiful island of Santorini lay basking in the sun. Its harbor and circular canals were crowded with ships. Its terraced vineyards and orchards were heavy with fruit. In the warm springs that gushed from the sacred mountain in the center of the island, people bathed, and in the steam fissures on its slopes, they consulted the oracles.

Suddenly, without warning, the mountain heaved, roared, then exploded in a volcanic eruption of unimaginable violence. Later, two thirds of the island dropped into a deep hole in the sea. The pieces that remained were buried under volcanic ash.

The eruption, collapse, and the gigantic tidal waves it created, changed the course of human history. They snuffed out an estimated one million lives in the eastern Mediterranean, obliterated the magnificent Minoan civilization of Crete, may have drowned the fabled realm of "Atlantis," brought great woe to Egypt, and could have set the Israelite slaves on their epic migration to the Promised Land. The cataclysms, out of which Western civilization eventually emerged, occurred between 1450 and 1550 B.C.

This picture of ancient events, pieced together by scientists and historians over the years, was largely speculation until recently. There was archeological evidence to indicate that the historic events described had taken place around the 15th century B.C., and geological proof educed by Swedish and American expeditions that the island of Santorini had erupted some four millenia ago. But there was no certainty that the eruption actually had occurred at the precise time, or was of sufficient magnitude, to have produced the effects attributed to it.

In 1956, both questions were dramatically answered through an accidental discovery made by geologist Angelos Galanopulos of the Athens Seismological Institute. While on a trip to the island of Thera, one of the shreds of land that survived the Santorini disaster, he was invited to visit a mine from which volcanic ash was removed for use as cement. At the bottom of the mine shaft, he discovered the fire-blackened ruins of a stone house. In the house he found two small pieces of charred wood and a handful of human teeth. Medical examination disclosed that the teeth had belonged to an adult man and woman. Radiocarbon analysis disclosed that they had died in the 15th century. B.C. The volcanic ash that covered them was 100 feet thick, proving it had been laid down by what had to have been the greatest volcanic eruption in human history.

To measure the violence of the Santorini explosion, scientists turned to the records of the Krakatoa eruption in the East Indies, in 1883 A.D. Krakatoa was an island built up from the sea by volcanic outpourings over the centuries, to a height of 1,400 feet. An earthquake or tremor cracked the island at its base, causing an inrush of cold sea water, which mingled with the hot lava, filling the subterranean passages with expanding steam and gas. The irresistible pressure blew off the top of the mountain, shot a fiery column of steam and dust 33 miles into the air, blanketed the surrounding territory with burning ash a foot thick, and hurled stones and blocks of pumice, big as a man's head, to a distance of 50 miles.

The dust and sulphurous vapors plunged the islands of Java and Sumatra into total darkness for two days. The accompanying roar cracked walls and broke windows 100 miles away, shook houses to a distance of 480 miles, overturning lamps and setting fires. The detonation sounded like gunfire to ships 2,000 miles away. The fine dust spewed into the stratosphere circled the earth, turning sunsets so red that fire departments were called out in Connecticut and New York weeks later.

When the eruption had spent its force after several days, the empty shell of the volcano, 13 square miles in area, collapsed into a 600-foot-deep crater in the sea, called a caldera. The sudden displacement of water created 100-foot tidal waves, which destroyed 295 towns, drowned 36,000 people, and hurled ships two miles inland. Spreading around the globe, the waves had enough force left to pull ships from their moorings in the harbors of Chile, 10,000 miles across the Pacific.

The explosion of Santorini followed the same pattern as the Krakatoa disaster, geologists say, except that it was many times greater and more violent. The energy released was equivalent to the simultaneous explosion of 430 hydrogen bombs, according to Galanopulos. The blast might have been heard over one-third of the earth's surface, from Lapland to South Africa, and from Portugal to India. It blew up a mountainous island, estimated to have been 4,900 feet high, which the ancients called Stronghyli, meaning "round" in Greek. It buried what remained of the island under 100 feet of ash, as compared to only one foot deposited by Krakatoa. The prevailing summer wind spread the ash over a 120,000 square mile area to the southwest, where it still lies on the sea bed, from several inches to many feet deep.

How many days or weeks the fiery rain continued, no one can say. Some time after the volcano had emptied itself—it could have been as much as 30 years later—the hollowed-out mountain, 35 square miles in area, dropped into its crater 1,200 feet below sea level, creating tidal waves estimated to have been one mile high at the vortex. Roaring outward in all directions at a speed of more than 200 miles per hour, the waves swept over the island of Anaphi, 18 miles away, to a height of 800 feet, smashed the coast of Crete, 70 miles distant, with successive walls of water over 100 feet high, engulfed the Egyptian delta three hours later, and still had enough force left to deposit floating volcanic ash 26 feet up the sides of the hills of Israel, a thousand miles from Santorini, where it still lies.

These are the physical facts and surmises about the Santorini explosion, derived from geological evidence and mathematical calculations. The historical effects of the catastrophe were equally profound.

Western civilization traces its ancestry back to two principal sources. The first is the esthetic, intellectual, democratic tradition inherited from classical Greece. The second is the religious, monotheistic, moral codes derived from early Judaism. At the times of the Santorini explosion, Greece was inhabited by primitive Helladic tribes whose level of culture was little higher than that of the less advanced tribes of America when Columbus made his landing. The great culture that later flowered in Greece actually owes its origin to an unidentified non-Greek people, whom we call Minoans, on the island of Crete.

The Minoans were a populous race for those times, estimated to have been from 800,000 to one million strong. They lived in a dozen cities built around huge stone palaces on the coasts and plains of Crete, with an outpost on Santorini. Their civilization, the first that is recognizable "western" in spirit and appearance, was the most brilliant and attractive of the ancient world. They employed a sophisticated form of writing, called Linear A, which has not yet been deciphered. They enjoyed a variety of sports, including boxing, wrestling, and bull games in which young men and women vaulted over the horns of the charging animals. They used flush toilets, and air conditioned their houses by means of screens and passages that channeled in cool breezes. They created superb vases, ornaments and wall paintings, so modern in appearance that they would be high fashion in our living rooms today.

Minoa's prosperity was based partly on agriculture and lumbering, but principally on their great merchant fleets which ranged the oceans of the ancient world. They brought back amber from the Baltic for jewelry, tin from Britain to smelt into bronze, and apes from Ethiopia, which they used as pets. Pictures of wasp-waisted Cretan ambassadors, similar in appearance to the figures on the wall paintings of the Minoan palaces, have been found in Egyptian tombs. The vases they bore as tribute are identical in appearance to those unearthed in Crete and Santorini.

In the middle of the 15th century B.C., at the height of its strength and prosperity, this brilliant civilization abruptly ended. Excavations indicate that all of the Minoan cities were wiped out within a short time of each other, all of the great palaces were destroyed, their huge building stones tossed around like matchsticks.

Until the recent geologic discoveries, the destruction of Minoa was an intriguing mystery, variously attributed to internal revolution or enemy invasion, although no one could imagine where so vast a seaborne expedition could have come from, or why the rebels or invaders did not remain to enjoy their conquest. However, most historians now recognize that the destruction was related to the eruption of Santorini, 70 miles to the north. The palaces were devastated by the same earthquake that caused the eruption, by the serial shock waves, and by the 100-foot tidal waves that struck at a speed of 200 miles per hour, roaring miles inland and up the slopes of the mountains to a height of 500 feet. The heavy fallout of volcanic ash blanketed the fertile valleys, destroyed the crops, and rendered agriculture impossible perhaps for decades.

The probable fate of the people was graphically described in a study made by geologists Dragoslav Ninkovich and Bruce Heezen of Columbia University. "The initial cloud, composed of volcanic ash, dust, gas and vapors, covered the whole area. . . causing total darkness for several consecutive days after which the tidal wave destroyed the coastal areas, quenched lamps and may have caused the burning of cities, while the gas and vapors poisoned the population."

The frantic haste with which the people fled was evident in the Minoan excavations. In one palace, six big cross-cut saws were left scattered on the floors of the state rooms, as if the carpenters were interrupted while making repairs. In another, a little ivory butterfly and silver cream jug were found in the corridor, as though dropped in flight. In a third palace, people did not stop to retrieve tools or valuables, the workshops and treasure rooms were found intact. But there was no escape. Those that were not killed in the first holocaust were drowned in the tidal waves, or died of starvation and disease later. If archeologists' estimates are accurate, close to a million inhabitants perished. As a people, the Minoans disappear from the pages of history.

There were scattered survivors, however, among those who managed to reach the high mountains, or who may have been on voyages at the time of the tragedy. Some are believed to have gone to the Balearic Islands and east coast of Spain, where they introduced their pottery and bull games, which persist in a different form to this day. Others may have settled on the coast of Palestine, where the Bible records them as "Philistines from Caphtor (Crete)." Their influence may have been felt in Egypt a few years later, during the reign of the remarkable monotheistic Pharaoh Ikhnaton (1375-1358 B.C.), who replaced the rigid, stylized art forms traditional to Egypt, with more natural, graceful paintings and statuary, evocative of Minoa.

These are speculations. But there is actual archaeological evidence to prove that most of the Minoan survivors fled to the wild country of western Crete and from there northward to Mycenae on the nearby shores of Greece. Although mainland Greece had been battered by Santorini's tidal waves, it had not suffered from its volcanic fallout, thanks to the strong northwest wind.

The results of the Minoan migration were quickly apparent in the flowering of Mycenaean civilization, about 1400 B.C., when the written history of Greece begins. The refugees introduced the Greeks to their script, art, frescoes, bull games and archery, all of which were hitherto unknown on the mainland. They taught them to work in bronze and gold and may have helped them build the magnificent Treasure of Atreus, the tombs of Agamemnon and Clytemnestra, and the great palaces that are the glory of Mycenaean culture.

Archeologist Spyridon Marinatos believes the Minoans also taught the Greeks to keep their slaves under more humane conditions, founded music and poetry, and developed new legal codes. "As for the (Greek) religion," adds Marinatos, "it has already been proved that most of its elements are derived from the Minoans... No break in the cult is perceptible from the height of Minoan times to the last days of Greco-Roman antiquity."

Later, when the soil of Crete had regained its fertility, Greeks from the mainland rebuilt the Minoan capital of Knossos, under King Minos, whose name was mistakenly applied by modern historians to the whole Cretan civilization. Actually, Ninkovich and Heezen point out, "Minos apparently had as little knowledge of the ancient Cretan civilization before the eruption of Santorini as did the Greeks of later days."

But Greeks of the "Golden Age" did not entirely forget the vanished civilization, nor the catastrophe, to which they owed so much of their own great culture. It lived on in the legend of Deucalian and Pirrha, king and queen of Thessaly, ancestors of the Hellenic race, said to be the only survivors of a great deluge sent by Zeus. They floated on a ship for nine days, landing on Mount Parnassus. The Greeks did not regard the Deucalian tale as a myth, but as literal history. Even Aristotle, who was a skeptic and scientist, accepts it as fact. Historians, using geneological records and monuments, ascribe the deluge to the year 1430 B.C., which is well within the time range established for the tidal wave caused by the Santorini eruption.

Even more significant is the story of Atlantis, related to Solon, the Athenian lawmaker and poet, on his visit to Egypt in 590 B.C. According to Plato, who recorded the incident in his dialogues, *Timaeus* and *Critias*, 200 years later, the Egyptian priests told Solon that the Greeks were mere babes with no knowledge of the ancient past: "You do not know there dwelt in your land the fairest and noblest race of men which ever lived of whom you and your

whole city are only a seed or remnant. . . But afterwards there
occurred violent earthquakes and floods, and in a single day and
night of rain all your warlike men in a body sank into the earth, and
the island of Atlantis in like manner disappeared beneath the
sea . . . the consequence is that, in comparison of what then was,
there are remaining in small islets only the bones of the wasted
body, all of the richer and softer parts of the soil having fallen away
and the mere skeleton of the country being left. And this was
unknown to you, because for many generations the survivors of
that destruction died and made no sign.

"This is no invented fable but genuine history," Plato added.

Atlantis, according to Plato's account, consisted of one large
island, and a nearby small one sacred to Poseidon, which was the
religious center of the federation of kingdoms of which Atlantis
was comprised. The main island was of near continental size,
800,000 square miles in area, too big to fit into the Mediterranean.
Plato placed it in the ocean beyond the Pillars of Hercules (the
Straits of Gibraltar), thereby giving the Atlantic its name. It was
destroyed, according to Plato, 9,000 years before Solon's time.

Archeologists, who believe there is a historical base to all folk
traditions, point out many impossibilities in Plato's account. Atlantis must have flourished much more recently since the people used
bronze, which was unknown in the Mediterranean until around
3000 B.C., and it was at war with Athens, which had not yet been
founded. It could not have been located in the Atlantic since geologists have found no trace of a sunken continent in that ocean, and
the distance would have been too great to have caused a fountain in
Athens to run dry when it disappeared, as Plato states. Besides, its
patron gods were Poseidon and Hercules, whose names were unknown until millenia later. Even Plato doubted the size of Atlantis,
noting "it seems incredible that it should be so large as the account
states. . . but we must report what we heard."

Galanopulos believes the discrepancies are due to a simple
error by Solon, who misread the Egyptian symbol for "100," as
"1,000," thereby multiplying all figures tenfold. Eliminate the extra zero and the destruction took place 900 years before Solon, in

the 15 century B.C., which coincides with the destruction of Santorini. Its size would have been 80,000 square miles, which accords nicely with the dimensions of the islands of the Eastern Mediterranean. Galanopulos notes that there are two promontories in the southern coast of Greece near Crete which were also called "Pillars of Hercules," that the Atlantans lived in 10 cities, built huge palaces, had a great navy, hunted bulls without weapons, and resembled the Minoans in many other ways.

Even more remarkable are the descriptions of the plain on which the "Royal City" of Atlantis was located, which closely resembles the Plain of Messara in Crete on which the Minoan capital of Knossos stood, and of the nearby "sacred island," with its steam fissures, hot springs and concentric circular canals. According to geologist Angelos Galanopulos, "the description . . . is quite the same as that of a volcanic island after a long period of quiescence. It fits perfectly the features and especially the shape and size of the island of Santorini before the eruption. Traces of the canals and harbors are discernible even now on the floor of the caldera (undersea crater)." Hydrographic maps of the U.S. Navy bear out the last assertion.

These and other parallels, too close to be coincidences, have induced some historians to declare that the riddle of Atlantis has been solved. Atlantis was Minoan Crete. The island that disappeared in the sea was Santorini.

The second great historic consequence of the Santorini cataclysm is the effect it may have had on northern Egypt, less than 600 miles away, where the children of Israel labored as slaves at the time. The extent to which the meteorological and geological aftereffects of the eruption may have contributed to the Biblical Ten Plagues, the Exodus of the Israelites and the Miracle of the Red Sea are explored in the next chapter.

The theories about the Exodus stand on shakier ground than those concerning the destruction of Minoa and the disappearance of Atlantis. Nevertheless, these events, together with others that have not been related here, seem to have occurred too closely together in time to be ascribed to mere chance. "They fit together like parts of an incomplete jigsaw puzzle," says Galanopulos. Scientists and historians are working to find the missing pieces that will prove the contention that Western civilization was born in the flame and ashes of a volcanic eruption in the Aegean during a windy summer, 3,500 years ago.

CHAPTER 10

The Biblical Exodus: Fact or Fiction?

(1500 to 1200 B.C)

One of the most dramatic stories in the Bible deals with the flight of the ancient Israelites from Egypt and the events surrounding it. It is also fundamental to the faiths of Christians, Jews and Moslems, alike. So it is not surprising that Egyptologist Hans Goedicke, of Johns Hopkins University in Baltimore, drew worldwide headlines in 1980, when he contended in a speech that the flight of the Israelites occurred in the 15th century B.C., and that the miraculous drowning of Pharoah's pursuing army was an actual historical event.

The lecture triggered a battle royal among Biblical scholars whose findings are at wide variance with Goedicke's and, often, with the Old Testament accounts as well. The large majority of these experts were convinced that the Exodus, if it occurred at all, took place more than two centuries later, in the 13th century B.C., and that the Miracle of the Red Sea was fictional. "It is a master-piece of literary composition, but has very little to do with history," stated Israeli archeologist Eliezer Oren.

The debate provides a fascinating glimpse into the complicated detective work often involved in archeological research. Goedicke bases his thesis on three primary pieces of evidence: a set of Egyptian hieroglyphs, a verse from the Bible, and the eruption of the volcanic island of Santorini in the Aegean Sea.

The hieroglyphs are taken from an inscription left by the female pharaoh Hatshepsut who reigned from 1490 to 1468 B.C. Scholars have puzzled for more than a century over its meaning. As Goedicke translates the text, it tells of a people called the *Amu* (an Egyptian term for Canaanites), among whom was a group of aliens called the *shemau* (semites?) who had enjoyed special privileges which Hatshepsut had annulled, and had "disregarded the tasks assigned to them." After she allowed these "abominations of the gods" to depart, the "father of fathers (whom Goedicke identifies with the primeval water god Nun) came unexpectedly" and "the earth swallowed their footsteps." To Goedicke, this is nothing less than an Egyptian version of the Exodus, which has the aliens drowning instead of pharaoh's forces.

The second clue Goedicke relies on is the Biblical verse (I Kings 6:11) which states that the temple of Solomon was built 480 years after the departure from Egypt. Since the temple is known to have been erected around 970 B.C., the Exodus, by this reckoning, would have occurred in the 15th century B.C.

The third event he cites was the eruption and explosion of the volcanic island of Santorini in the Aegean in the 15th century B.C., the greatest natural catastrophe in human history (see previous chapter), whose role in the drama will be described subsequently.

There is additional evidence to support the 15th century date for the migration from Egypt. Letters from Canaanite rulers to the Pharaoh in the 14th century B.C., preserved in the Amarna tablets, complain of wandering marauders called the *habiru,* which some scholars equate with "Hebrews." Excavations at ancient Jericho indicate that the city was destroyed around 1400 B.C., which is when Joshua would have attacked it if the Israelites left in the mid-15th century and spent 40 years in the desert.

There is also a famous stele recording the military conquests in Palestine made by the pharaoh Merneptah in the fifth year of his reign (1219 B.C.) which boasts that "Israel is laid to waste, his seed is not." If the Israelites left late in the 13th century, Goedicke argues, they could not have coalesced into a nation important enough to warrant Egyptian attack by the year 1219, especially if they had spent 40 years in the desert before entering Canaan. The Old Testament appears to support the contention. It relates that the Israelite tribes were disunited, and often at war with each other, for a long period after their arrival, and lists 18 generations between the time of Korah of the Exodus, and Heman the singer in the time of Solomon's father, David (I Chronicles 6:33- 37), who united the nation.

The events of the Exodus, as Goedicke reconstructs them from the biblical and archeological evidence, run as follows: The ancestors of the people who later became the Israelites were sedentary pastoralists who lived in Canaan. Sometime during the first half of the second millenium B.C., they were officially invited to settle in Goshen in the eastern Nile Delta, perhaps by Joseph, one of their number who had risen to high office under the Hyksos, a mixed horde of invaders who had conquered and ruled Egypt, or parts of it, between 1720 and 1540 B.C. Allowed to live as an independent people, the Israelites supported themselves by raising sheep and cattle. Goedicke believes they also served as military auxiliaries, guarding the eastern frontier of Egypt.

With the overthrow of the Hyksos in 1540 B.C. and the ascension of a new dynasty of pharaohs "who did not know Joseph" (Exodus 1:8), their situation changed abruptly for the worse. Against their will they were set to work building the cities of Pithom and Raamezez (Exodus 1:11). Seeking to escape from bondage, they decided to return to their ancestral homes in Canaan and asked the pharaoh for permission to leave. However, the request was not granted until God had inflicted the Egyptians with Ten Plagues. They included: thick darkness that descended on the land for three days; the turning of the waters of the Nile and lakes into blood, killing the fish; hailstorms, accompanied by severe thunder and lightning, that destroyed the crops; successive infestations of frogs, mosquitoes, locusts and flies; an epidemic of boils that afflicted men and animals alike, followed by disease that carried away much of the livestock; and finally a mysterious plague that killed the firstborn of all Egyptian families and cattle.

Geologists have long noted the resemblance between the Ten Plagues and the physical and meteorological disturbances that accompany eruptions—particularly in the Eastern Mediterranean, where volcanos may spew iron oxide particles that turn the surrounding waters red, poison the fish, and often engender high winds, torrential rains and swamps.

Taken in this context, the Plagues could be plausible natural events. The immense clouds of thick volcanic dust blown from Santorini might easily have plunged northern Egypt into darkness for three days. With the sun blotted out, the temperature dropped causing the precipitation to fall as hailstones, which destroyed the standing grain. The fallout of iron oxide from the volcanic clouds turned the waters red (as blood), killing the fish and driving frogs on shore. The high winds carried in locusts which devoured what crops remained, leaving the animals to starve. Infestation of flies and mosquitoes, which bred in the rotting carcasses and swamps, infected both humans and livestock with diseases that caused skin eruptions (boils). Death was so rampant as to amount to the killing of the "firstborn" of every Egyptian family, in the hyperbole of the Biblical narrators.

That the fallout reached Egypt is confirmed by the discovery of pieces of pumice in a tomb and a stratum of volcanic ash underlying the Egyptian Delta, both of which are identical in chemical composition to the tefra left on Santorini by the great eruption. Egyptian documents of the era also lend credence to the disasters.

"The land is utterly perished . . . the sun is veiled and shines not in the sight of men," says one papyrus. "There was no stepping out from the palace for a period of nine days . . . Those nine days were in violence and tempest; none . . . could see the face of his fellow."

"O that the earth would cease from noise, and tumult be no more!" laments another papyrus. "There are none whose clothes are white . . . the river is blood . . . trees are destroyed, no fruit nor herbs are found . . . lower Egypt weeps . . . hunger all animals, cattle moan . . . plague stalketh the land and blood is everywhere . . . many dead men are buried in the river."

(The same papyrus mentions the disruption of trade with Crete. "What shall we do for cedar for our mummies?" asks the scribe. "And with the oil of which chiefs are embalmed as far as Keftiu [Crete]? They come no more." Simultaneous to the Santorini eruption, frescoes of Minoan ambassadors bringing tribute disappeared from Egyptian tombs.)

The last Plague finally induced the reluctant pharaoh to allow the Israelites to leave, the Bible relates. Led by Moses, they set off across the desert guided by "a pillar of cloud by day" and "a pillar of fire by night" (Exodus 14:21). These phenomena, too, may be related to the Santorini event. Volcanologists have calculated that the eruption shot fiery billows of ash, burning lava and steam, 33 miles in the air, which could have been seen on the horizon from the Egyptian Delta, 500 miles away, as a cloud of smoke in daylight and a fiery glow at night. (Fumes from the far smaller 1980 eruption of Mt. St. Helens, in Washington, were visible for 600 miles.)

Goedicke is certain that the point of the Israelites' departure was the city later known as Pithom, which he identifies as the ancient ruins of Tell el Rataba, where remains of an early Canaanite settlement have been found. From here two roads led across the Delta into Sinai, a direct northern route along the seacoast, which the Bible refers to as "the way of the Philistines," and a more circuitous southern route, "the way of the wilderness" (Exodus 13:17-18), that lay on higher ground.

The Exodus apparently started out on the northern route. However, pharaoh repented his decision and sent a force of 600 chariots to bring the Israelites back. Learning of the pursuit and hoping to evade the Egyptians, according to Goedicke's reconstruction, Moses decided to "turn back and encamp" between Migdol and the sea, before Baal-Zephon (Exodus 14:2), which lay south of the

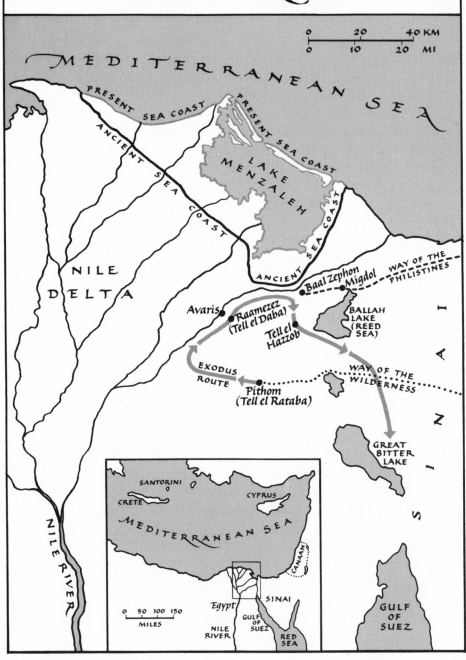

route taken. But the feint did not work and the Egyptians came hot on the fugitives' trail.

The Hebrew words *yam suf* can mean either "red sea" or "reed sea," and scholars almost unanimously agree that it was the latter the Bible refers to. Goedicke identifies this reed sea as Ballah Lake (see map), known to the Egyptians as the Papyrus Swamp, which lies a few miles south of Lake Menzaleh, a large coastal lagoon just west of the present Suez Canal. Seeking to make a stand against their enemies, Goedicke postulates, the Israelites encamped on the only defensible position in the area, a 40-foot-high mound called Tell el Hazzob, with the Egyptian chariots arrayed on the low-lying ground beneath them. It was here, says Goedicke, "in the early hours of a spring morning in 1477 B.C." that the flood came which drowned the Egyptians while sparing the rejoicing Israelites.

This so-called "Miracle of the Red Sea," Goedicke believes— as do several geologists who preceded him—was caused by the tidal wave, or tsunami, that was created when the hollowed-out shell of Santorini, 4,900 feet high and 35 square miles in area, had emptied itself and collapsed into the sea. As the preceding chapter relates, the towering wave engulfed the coasts of the entire Eastern Mediterranean. Gathering height as it approached the shoaling beaches of northern Egypt, it swept across shallow Lake Menzaleh and flooded the plain to the south to the edge of the desert plateau, overwhelming the Egyptian charioteers as they prepared to attack the Israelites on Tell el Hazzob. (Others agree with the account, but place the location at Lake Bardawil, farther east on the Mediterranean coast.)

"The event was not a miracle," says Goedicke. "It was a natural happening, although a rare one. The miracle lies in the coincidence that the tidal wave arrived at the critical moment, and in the exact place that it did." In confirmation he cites an Egyptian papyrus written a few years later that invokes the god Seth to stop the spread of a plague "as he had stopped the sea before Avaris"—a town in the Egyptian Delta that stood 80 miles from the coast.

But the coincidence seems too far-fetched for most Biblical scholars to accept, as is much of the rest of Goedicke's scenario.

Those who do not dismiss the drowning of the Egyptians as entirely mythical believe it might have been caused by a violent storm at sea, or a flash flood on the easternmost branch of the Nile. Although conceding Goedicke's expertise as an Egyptologist, his critics accuse him of taking unwarranted liberties with the Hatshepsut inscription. As they read the text, there is no mention of the annulment of the former privileges enjoyed by the aliens, nothing about them disregarding their assigned tasks, and no reason to assume that the "abominations of the gods" who were allowed to depart were the people of the Exodus, since a great many other Asians lived in Egypt at the time. The "father of fathers," they say, refers not to the water god, but to the sun god Amon-re, and the phrase "the earth swallowed their footsteps" simply means that the migrants disappeared, with no inference of a flood.

Biblical scholars are also highly suspicious of the accuracy of the figures in the Old Testament, some of which are contradictory, and particularly of the "480 years" that purportedly elapsed between the Exodus and Solomon's temple. Some postulate that the number actually refers to 12 generations, which the Bible calculates as lasting 40 years each, and that if the more realistic figure of 25 years per generation were used, the departure would have occurred only 300 years earlier than the building of the Temple.

The argument for a 13th B.C. century date also rests on three pieces of evidence. The first revolves around the building of the city of Raamezez by the Israelites, which has long been taken to mean the capital erected by the great builder Ramesses II who reigned from 1290 to 1224 B.C. (*Note:* the difference in the spellings of the two names is intentional.)

The second proof lies in the excavation of the ruins of several of the cities listed in the Bible as having been destroyed by the Israelites during their conquest of Canaan. The artifacts found in them indicate they fell during the late 13th and early 12th centuries B.C. (except for Jericho which, unaccountably, was destroyed considerably earlier).

The third exhibit is the Biblical report (Numbers 20 and 21) that the Israelites had to travel *around* the kingdoms of Edom and Moab because they were refused permission to cross them. From the historical evidence, these kingdoms had not even formed until the beginning of the 13th century. "If the Israelites came before that time," American Biblical archeologist Nelson Glueck noted, "they would have found no kingdoms to deny them the right of transit."

But these arguments are all open to rebuttal. The meaning of the Hatshepsut inscription depends on whose version one accepts, and Goedicke's qualifications as an interpreter of hieroglyphs are recognized to be among the highest. The 480-year figure may not be exact, but the long history of events and the Biblical recital of geneologies between the flight from Egypt and the building of the temple, lends credence to its general accuracy.

Unquestionably, several of the Canaanite cities attacked by the Israelites during the conquest *were* reduced to ruins during the 13th and 12th centuries, but not necessarily by the Israelites, for that was an era of continuous warfare in Palestine. Many of these places had been destroyed and rebuilt several times, British archeologist John Bimson reminds his colleagues. After providing what he considers to be more logical dates for the bronzes and pottery found in their ruins, Bimson concludes that, of the nine identifiable cities the Bible states were destroyed by the Israelites, eight fell in the 15th century B.C. and only four could have been overthrown again in the 13th. And of all the cities mentioned in the conquest narratives, Jericho and five others no longer existed in the 13th century.

The assumption that the city referred to as Raamezez was the one built for the pharaoh Ramesses has also been challenged. Despite their similarity, Canadian Egyptologist Donald Redford has shown the names derive from different sources and have different meanings. And the only city widely identified as Pithom in antiquity was not built until the sixth century B.C. Thus, the names may be among the many anachronisms which crept into the Old Testament before it was edited into final form nearly a thousand years after the events we are talking about.

The Book of Genesis, for example, recounts dealings between Abraham and "Abimelech, king of the Philistines." But Abraham lived five centuries before the Philistines had arrived in Palestine.

Camels are mentioned in Egypt during the time of Abraham's grandson Jacob. Yet it is known for a certainty that they did not reach Egypt until the 12th century B.C. That the Israelites built two cities is not doubted. But the names Pithom and Raamezez were apparently applied to them much later. Jacob, too, is described as settling in "the land of Raamezez" (Genesis 47:11), centuries before the appearance of the first pharaoh of similar name.

The surprising possibility is that the 15th and 13th century dates may both be right. From their researches, modern biblical scholars are almost unanimous in their conviction that the Israelites neither arrived in Egypt all at once, nor left in a single body. "Just as there were several entrances into Egypt, there were several exoduses," states leading Biblical historian Roland de Vaux. He and many other experts surmise there may have been two major departures from Egypt, for the Bible presents two conflicting itineraries for the journey to Canaan. They hold that one migration, involving the tribes descended from Jacob's wife, Leah, perhaps led by Joshua (a member of the Leah-tribe of Ephraim), took the direct route to Canaan, passing through the territories of Edom and Moab without hindrance, as described in Numbers, Chapter 33. The second migration, involving the tribes descended from Jacob's wife Rachel, led by Moses (a member of the Rachel-tribe of Levi), took the more circuitous route around Edom and Moab. described in Numbers, Chapter 31. (The four tribes descended from Jacob's two concubines could not have participated in the Exodus, these scholars believe, because contrary to the Bible they had never left Canaan.)

If the Exodus was, indeed, a long drawn out affair, it is conceivable that the first large departure occurred in the 15th century, following the Santorini eruption and collapse, and the second occurred two centuries later. This would explain why the first group had no trouble passing through the territories later occupied by Edom and Moab, while the second group was denied permission to cross after those kingdoms had been established.

This still leaves the question of the miraculous events surrounding the Exodus. Many authorities consider them moralistic tales, devised by later Hebrew theologians to provide proof of Jehovah's special concern for his Chosen People. Father Dennis McCarthy, of the Pontifical Bible Institute in Rome, characterizes the Ten Plagues as "a highly sophisticated literary construction." Historian Benjamin Mazar of Hebrew University regards even Moses as "a synthetic character who never lived."

But some cultural anthropologists would disagree. They hold that there is "a kernel of factual truth underlying nearly all folk traditions," which become garbled and enhanced in the telling and retelling. If such a kernel of truth does underlie the Biblical accounts of the Ten Plagues, the pillars of cloud and fire, and the Miracle of the Sea, then credence must be given to the 15th century date for at least one phase of the Exodus, since no cataclysm is known to have occurred in the region after the eruption of Santorini that could account for them.

CHAPTER 11

The Fascinating, Disturbing Pyramids of Mesoamerica

(600 B.C. to 1400 A.D.)

Teotihuacan, 25 miles northwest of Mexico City, is the site of a battle that changed the course of history. It was there that Hernan de Cortés and a few dozen Spaniards defeated 50,000 Aztec warriors, in the year 1520. At the time, the place was described as "a gentle valley lying between two high hills." What the invading Spaniards did not know, and the Aztecs only half suspected, is that the hills were man-made. Two magnificent stone pyramids that had been abandoned almost a thousand years earlier were hidden beneath the earth, shrubs and trees. The larger, the Pyramid of the Sun, is three to four times the size of the Great Pyramid of Giza in Egypt, although not as tall. The other, the Pyramid of the Moon, is about one-third smaller.

Digging through the earth and rubble that filled the valley around them in the early 20th century, excavators uncovered an incredible forgotten city, a geometrically laid out maze of great courtyards, temples, roadways, dwellings and patios, stretching over 13 square miles, larger in area than imperial Rome, and almost as populous. But this was not all. Probing into the side of the smaller Pyramid of Quetzalcoatl* in 1919, Mexican archeologist Manuel Gamio discovered another, and far more elaborate, pyramid lying intact beneath it. Emblazoned from top to bottom with superb sculptured heads of feathered serpents and rain gods, it is one of the showpieces of pre-Columbian art.

We have no idea who built the great city and its pyramids, or what the people called themselves. Teotihuacan (pronounced tay-o-ti-*kwan)* is a later Aztec term meaning "abode of the gods." Nor do we know why the city was abandoned around 700 A.D., nor whether the earth that buried the structures was blown in by the winds over the centuries or carried in by people intent on obliterating all trace of their existence. We do know that when construction began around the time of Christ, the art of pyramid building in Mesoamerica was already ancient.

The pre-Columbian history of the region comprises not one, but several, distinct cultures, developed by peoples who spoke widely different languages, and bore little resemblance to each other either facially or physically. First to arrive around 1200 B.C. was an unknown folk referred to as the Olmecs (people of the rubber country), who settled along the southern coast of the Gulf of Mexico. They erected pyramids of sun-baked brick, 120 feet tall, and carved colossal stone heads, six to 10 feet high, of crying babies, with the snarling mouths of jaguars, wearing the helmets of ball players (explained later). Amazingly talented, they also devised a system of hieroglyphic writing, an elaborate calendar based on the movements of the sun, moon and planet Venus, and a decimal system of arithmetic based on multiples of 20, which employed the concept of zero 2,000 years before it was used in Europe.

*The Mesoamerican god of life and much else. The name combines the *quetzal*, a bird of jewel-like beauty whose plumes were worn by priests and nobles, and the serpent or rattlesnake, *coatl*, whose growth of a new skin every year symbolized rebirth.

The Olmecs disappeared without trace around 400 B.C., probably in a revolution which left the statues of their gods decapitated, altars smashed, and the colossal heads mutilated and buried. But their culture passed on to the builders of Teotihuacan in Central Mexico, the Zapotecs in Oaxaca along the Pacific coast, and the Mayas of southern Mexico, Guatemala, Belize and Western Honduras. These civilizations similarly flourished for a few centuries only to vanish in turn as mysteriously as had that of the Olmecs.

All of these cultures were theocratic in nature, built around city-states dominated by priestly rulers. But around 900 A.D, the marauding Toltecs swept down from the north to build their capital Tollan (now called Tula), ruled by kings. The invaders conquered an empire extending from Central Mexico to Yucatan, which lasted for two centuries. Lastly, in 1325, came the upstart Aztecs, an even more savage warrior tribe from the north. From their magnificent island-city of Tenochtitlan (which now underlies the heart of Mexico City), they ruled an even greater empire, comprising 38 provinces. With their conquest by the Spanish in 1521, the native civilization of America was snuffed out forever.

Although the glyphic writings, symbols carved in stone, employed by each of these cultures differed, their religions, calendars and systems of numeration, were similar. In all of them, pyramids dominated religious, civic and cultural life. There are literally thousands of them in Middle America still covered with earth, only a fraction of which have even been investigated. The handful that have been actually uncovered and restored in whole or in part are among the finest examples of ancient architecture in existence. And in welcome contrast to the monotonous sameness of the buildings in other civilizations, no two Mesoamerican pyramids are alike.

Pictures rarely do them justice. Among those that must be seen to be appreciated (we use the names given to them by the Indians, Spanish or archeologists — no one knows the real ones) are Teotihuacan's Great Pyramid of the Sun; the Pyramid of the Niches at El Tajin near Vera Cruz, on the Gulf of Mexico, which looks like a seven-tiered wedding cake; the grim Pyramid of the Warriors at Tula, north of Mexico City, with its wall of carved skulls, surmounted by 15-feet columnar figures of armed fighting men; the ruins of Xochicalco, south of Mexico City, which seem touched by magic; Monte Alban near the city of Oaxaca, with its eerie dancing figures, perched on a mountain top that was leveled flat by the Zapotecs 2,300 years ago; and the temples of nearby Mitla, covered with intricate geometric designs. Its stone slabs are laid without mortar on rows of recessed small stones, like ball bearings, so as to ride out the shock of earthquakes. (The great pyramid-temple at Mexico City, rediscovered in 1978, is discussed in a later chapter.)

Even more elegant than these monuments are the pyramids of the Mayas in the south; the dreamlike Temple of the Inscriptions nestled in the jungle at Palenque, to me the loveliest ancient site in Mesoamerica; the forbidding elliptical Pyramid of the Sorcerer at Uxmal in Yucatan; the temples of neighboring Kabah, covered from top to bottom with a lacework of long-nosed Chacs (Mayan gods of rain); and nearby Chichen Itza, whose palaces and pyramids have been declared "second only to the Acropolis of Athens" in grandeur. Equally unforgettable is the Hieroglyphics Staircase of Copan, in Honduras, encrusted with 2,500 undeciphered glyphs, guarded by figures more grotesque than the gargoyles of Notre Dame. Most spectacular of all, perhaps, is the 255-foot-high skyscraper pyramid of Tikal in Guatemala, whose ornate roof soars above the green jungle like a lighthouse at sea.

To raise the gigantic edifices required enormous labor and monumental faith. For the Mesoamericans did not employ the wheel, except in toys, and had no draft animals, pulleys nor metal tools of any kind. The blocks of limestone, weighing up to 45 tons, had to be extracted from the quarries with chisels of harder stone, ground smooth with abrasives of sand and obsidian, dragged many miles to the building site by armies of men, then hauled aloft by earthen ramps, with the aid of fiber ropes. Archaeologists estimate that it took two centuries to complete the great pyramid at Teotihuacan, and 1,000 years to raise the pyramids of Tikal in Guatemala to their ultimate heights.

Actually, a pyramid was never completed. It was continually being added to, or covered over by a larger structure, either to honor the accession of a new high priest or king, to commemorate a victory or, most often, to thank the gods for survival at the end of each 52-year-long "century." Thus, almost every large pyramid contains smaller pyramids nested inside it. The pyramid of Cholula near Mexico City, held to be the most massive man-made building on earth, consists of seven superimposed pyramids, with a later Spanish church perched on top.

Perhaps to avoid arousing the wrath of the god to whom the pyramid was dedicated, the builders apparently made no effort to salvage anything from a structure before covering it over. Like the pyramid of Quetzalcoatl in Teotihuacan, with its marvelous carvings, it was buried intact. The pyramid of El Castillo at Chichen-Itza in Yucatan was erected by the Toltecs in the 11th century. Inside of it, you may walk through an archeologist's tunnel and up a narrow flight of lighted stairs to the temple atop a pyramid built by the Mayas centuries earlier. It still houses a magnificent jaguar throne encrusted in jade, guarded by a supine stone idol called a *chacmool*. How many similar treasures lie in the dark hearts of other pyramids, no one knows.

Archeologists reject the idea that the Mesoamerican pyramids could have been inspired by those of Egypt, since they can be traced back to their primitive beginnings in this continent, and because they are so utterly different in appearance, design and function. The Egyptian pyramids, with their pointed tops, were built exclusively as tombs, located far from population centers. The American pyramids stood in the busy centers of cities and were all surmounted by temples resting on flat platforms.

Primarily, the pyramids were places of worship, raised high either to bring the priests closer to the celestial deities, overawe the populace, or enhance the city's prestige. Their height also provided a vantage point from which priests could observe the positions of the sun, moon and planets, whose movements were of supreme religious importance to these early Americans. The Mesoamericans also had astronomic observatories, two of which survive at Monte

Alban and Chichen Itza, and astronomers apparently correlated their findings at congresses held at Copan, in the seventh century A.D. and at Xochicalco sometime later. The likenesses of the astronomers attending and the symbols of the cities from which they came can still be seen on the walls. The skill of these early observers astounds modern astronomers. They predicted the exact time of solar and lunar eclipses, calculated the solar year to be 365.2420 days long, only 17 seconds off, and estimated the revolution of Venus with an error of only seven seconds in 50 years—figures that were not improved upon until recent times.

The Mesoamericans were obsessed with time, calculating it as far back as 400 million years into the past. They inscribed dates on everything, in terms of days, months, years, 20-year *katuns* and 400-year *baktuns,* using numbering systems which have been deciphered. By correlating these dates with those of our own calendar, archeologists can tell, almost to the exact month and year, when a particular pyramid, temple or stele (stone monument) was erected. (Toward the end they grew sloppy, however, leaving out some of the first ciphers, making it more difficult to fix the date, just as a future historian might have trouble determining in which century the Gold Rush of '49 occurred.)

The Mesoamerican calendar, which begins in our year 3113 B.C., was enormously complicated, comprising 260-day, 13-month religious years, and 360-day, 18-month civil years, based on the revolution of the sun, with five extra "bad luck" days, during which work stopped and people cowered in their houses praying for survival. Each 52nd year, when the two calendars coincided, was a time of particular dread for the Mesoamericans. They believed the world had been created and destroyed four times in the past, and that this world, too, would be destroyed at the end of one of the 52-year cycles.

The experts were long certain that the American pyramids were never used as tombs. The belief persisted until 1949 when Alberto Ruz-Lhuillier, Director of Mexico's National Institute of Archeology, discovered a stairway leading down into the center of the Temple of Inscriptions at Palenque. It was found beneath a stone slab in the shrine atop the pyramid. The stairway had been deliberately blocked by dirt and rubble, which took Ruz and his men four years to clear. On reaching ground level, they drilled through a stone wall several yards thick into a chamber in which lay the skeletons of six young men, who had probably been slain to serve their master in the afterlife. Breaking through the last stone barrier, Ruz stepped into a vaulted room, from whose ceiling hung thousand-year-old stalactites.

In the center lay a womb-shaped sarcophagus, covered by a six-ton sculptured stone slab. The room was guarded by painted stucco reliefs on the wall portraying the nine Maya gods of darkness. Since the sarcophagus cover was too big to have been carried down the passageway, it had obviously been installed in the early days of the pyramid's construction. Beneath it lay the skeleton of a six-foot man, exceptionally tall for a Maya, ornamented with nearly a thousand pieces of jade jewelry, including a magnificent jade portrait mask, with inlaid eyes of shell and obsidian, and a pearl in his mouth to pay his passage to the underworld. From inscriptions on stelae in front of the pyramid, archeologists have identified him as the high priest Pacal, who died in 673 A.D. at the age of 80.

Since that discovery, burial chambers have been found beneath several other Mayan pyramids, indicating that, like the pharaohs of Egypt, high priests and rulers of that area probably began building their tombs almost from the day they acceded to power, sometimes covering the pyramids and defacing the effigies of their predecessors in the process. Although interred bodies of notables have also been found in some of the pyramids to the east of Palenque, they lie in holes dug into the floors of the platforms long after the pyramids had been built.

A mystery about the pyramids still being argued is why the risers of the steps leading to the tops of many of them are so high—close to three feet, in some cases—while the treads are so narrow that even the small-statured Mesoamericans could have climbed them only on tiptoe, or by planting their feet on them sideways. One speculation is that they were built in this fashion so that a line of priests ascending the pyramid, in their brilliant quetzal-feather headdresses, would have to weave back and forth across the stairway like a crawling snake, thus replicating the movement of the feathered serpent god, Quetzalcoatl.

Another puzzle is that the pyramid stairways are often set at such steep angles that the guards have had to install chains to enable visitors to climb up and down them. Tourists who do not cling to the chain have sometimes fallen to their deaths. Some archeologists theorize that the steepness is an architectural trick, designed to enhance the illusion of the pyramids' height.

But there is a grimmer, more plausible, explanation. The gods of Mesoamerica were innumerable, implacable and voracious. Unless they were fed, they would not permit the rains to fall, the crops to grow or life to continue—and the food they lived on was human blood and human hearts. To assure survival, human sacrifice was practiced from the earliest times. Indeed, it may have been considered the principal reason for man's existence. Favored victims were hunchbacks and other deformed people, who were believed to possess magic powers, and children, whose tears were particularly precious to the rain gods. The Colossal Heads of the Olmecs are believed to represent those of decapitated babies. The bodies of slain children were buried at the corners of the pyramids of Teotihuacan. Lying beneath an altar at Cholula, archeologists found the skeletons of boys six to eight years old, with artificially deformed heads, who may have been reared for sacrifice.

Girls and women were also sacrificed, usually by strangulation, decapitation or drowning. But only grown men could be offered to the gods of war and the sun. Flung on their backs across altars atop the pyramids, their arms and legs were held down by four priests, while a fifth priest sliced open their chests below the ribcage with a razor-sharp flint knife and tore out their throbbing hearts. The lifeless bodies were then flung over the sides of the pyramid. Thus, the stairways were built steep, according to this explanation, to allow the cadavers to roll down unimpeded. In compensation, the victims' souls were wafted straight to paradise, without having to cross the nine rivers of hell.

Considering the thousands of pyramids that existed, and the necessity of feeding the gods *every day,* the slaughter is believed to have been enormous. Usually the victims were slaves or captives of war, but no one was actually immune. The rewards for dying for the gods were so great that captives who were offered their lives, sometimes chose death, and even the nobles offered themselves or their children to the knife on critical occasions. The common people, on arising, would prick their ears and those of their children, including babies, to draw blood for the Morning Star. Priests contributed their daily quotas of heavenly nutriment by piercing their cheeks, calves and penises, with stingray spines, and drawing cords threaded with cactus thorns through their tongues. The scenes are graphically depicted on vases and in bas reliefs on the walls of the ancient cities.

A pleasanter aspect of life in Mesoamerica—at least for spectators—was the sacred ball game. Although its religious significance is unknown, one or more playing courts can be found near every major pyramid. The rules varied widely, depending on time and place. The courts, usually shaped like a capital I, ranged in size from small enclosures to fields 500 feet long. The solid rubber balls might be as small as a softball or as large as a medicine ball. With from two to seven players on a side, the game might resemble anything from American football, field hockey or soccer, to volley ball or basketball. Scores were made by sending the ball through a vertical stone ring set high on the wall.

However played, it was a rough and strenuous sport. The ball could not be struck with the hand, only with the arms, thighs or body, and players are depicted falling on their hands, knees and backs, to prevent the ball from hitting the ground. Though the participants were protected by visored helmets, gloves, and heavy padding on arms, knees, hips and chest, as shown in the carvings, they were often maimed or killed when struck by the hard, rocketing sphere, or died of exhaustion.

The games were enormously popular, and betting on them was heavy. On certain occasions, the victors could strip spectators of everything they had, including their clothing, provided they could catch them. Pictures exist that depict spectators fleeing, with the winning players in hot pursuit. The losers might be executed. One unforgettable scene carved on the wall of the ball court at Chichen Itza in Yucatan portrays the kneeling figure of the decapitated captain of the losing team, with streams of blood spurting from his neck in the form of serpents. The winning captain stands opposite him with the knife in one hand, the severed head in the other. Since the victim automatically attained divinity, however, some archeologists surmise that it might have been the winning captain who surrendered his head, and the loser who cut it off.

The most baffling question of all about the pyramids and the cities in which they lay is why they were abandoned. In only a few cases do we know the reason. The Zapotecs left Monte Alban near Oaxaca around 1000 A.D. when defeated by the Mixtecs, who later used it as a royal burial ground. The Toltecs fled Tula in about 1165 A.D. in the face of the invading Chichimecs. Other cities, such as Tenochtitlan and Cholula, were razed by the Spanish, who built their own cities on the ruins.

But though neither conquered nor destroyed, life in mighty Teotihuacan flickered out around 750 A.D., to be followed by other cities in the north. The southern Mayan cities of the Classic Era abruptly closed up shop one after another during the ninth century A.D., leaving temples unfinished and engravings half done. And within another four centuries, grass grew in the once-crowded marketplaces and palaces of the later Toltec-Mayan centers of northern Yucatan. Their inhabitants simply walked away leaving the cities empty, but largely intact. The damage they subsequently suffered was wreaked by the elements or the jungle, and by early untrained archeologists, modern vandals and art smugglers, who picked the cities apart in search of information, amusement or treasure.

Many reasons have been suggested for the mysterious exodus— seismic upheavals, epidemic diseases, cultural exhaustion, over-population, an unbalanced sex ratio, as well as power struggles among the elite, a shift in trade routes, and insurmountable urban problems similar to those that threaten modern cities. More plausible explanations for the abandonment may lie in the exhaustion of the soil and decline in food production caused by slash-and-burn, single-crop farming, and the lack of animal fertilizer in the north; and in the south, by the cutting down of forests for lumber and firewood, leading to a change in climate and drought that dried up the irrigation canals on which Mayan agriculture depended.

Though some of these factors may have contributed, most archeologists believe that the collapse of the Mesoamerican cities was triggered by popular revolts against the ruling elite, similar to the one that may have finished the Olmecs centuries earlier. They point out that, with no sign of invasion, the populace had apparently burned the wooden buildings and temples of Teotihuacan before its abandonment, and that sacred monoliths in the Mayan cities were overturned, defaced or battered to bits.

The real question, perhaps, is why the revolt was so long in coming, considering the tyranny under which the great majority lived in the rigidly stratified society. Medical examination of skeletons unearthed at Tikal reveal that the common people suffered severe malnutrition, while the upper classes ate extremely well. The rulers had also grown degenerate. Contemporary Mayan vase paintings portray them as obese and haughty, besotted with alcohol, and addicted to narcotics, which they injected into their bodies with anal syringes made of animal bladders and hollow bones. They also smoked cigars believed to have been manufactured from the leaves of the weed *Nicotinia rustica,* a potent hallucinogen.

So long as the priestly rulers and their gods provided livelihood and food, the people held them in awe, tolerating their excesses, submitting to the never-ending labor of building pyramids, and the pain of yielding their children to sacrifice. But when priests and deities failed to provide, bringing drought and hunger, the pent-up fury of the populace exploded. "In city after city," states archeologist Eric Thompson, "the ruling group was driven out, or more probably massacred, and the gods overthrown."

The revolts were a catastrophe. With their world in shambles, people fled to other areas in Mesoamerica. The population of the Mayan region is estimated to have dropped from over three million to 450,000 in less than a century. For a time, a few survivors stayed on, camping in the palaces and temples—where the ashes of their cooking fires have been found—clumsily attempting to re-erect the sacred monuments, including one they stood on its head. But eventually they too departed, leaving the great cities to be strangled by the jungle from which they had been wrested a millenium earlier. They were so completely forgotten that even the inhabitants of the region did not know of their existence when the Spanish arrived. The story appears to have been much the same everywhere.

So, the Mesoamerican world ended with a whimper. Leaderless, and beset with anarchy in the south, obsessed with hatred of their brutal Aztec overlords in the north, the Mesoamericans fell easy prey to the invading Spaniards. Yet, as the pyramids attest, the civilization they created was one of the most brilliant the world has known. And it lasted for 2,000 years.

CHAPTER 12

China's Great "Wall of Tears"

(250 B.C. to 1550 A.D.)

No picture ever taken—in fact, not even a visit to any one section of it—can convey more than a hint of the magnificence and immensity of the Great Wall of China. Stretching across one-twentieth of the earth's circumference, from the shores of the Pacific to the edge of the Gobi Desert, it is the most stupendous engineering feat ever undertaken by man. In its 3,700-mile-length, the Wall contains enough building materials to girdle the globe at the equator with a barrier eight feet high and three feet thick.

The Wall is also one of the strangest structures ever erected. Begun in the third century B.C. and added to several times in the next 1,300 years, it snakes, loops and doubles back on itself, meandering across plains and valleys, scaling mountains, plunging into deep gorges, skirting precipices and leaping raging rivers. If straightened out it would span the United States from New York to

San Francisco, and back to Salt Lake City. No one knows why the rampart takes such an eccentric course, or why it was extended to guard mountain peaks over which an invading army could not possibly pass. One ancient belief is that it was laid out to follow the wanderings of the emperor's sacred horse, or the contortions of a celestial dragon.

We do know from the ancient accounts of the terrible suffering of the million men who were conscripted to build the fortification. Many were the intellectual elite of China, whose soft hands had never handled a tool heavier than a writing brush. Toiling with little shelter or clothing in brutal cold and heat, kept on short rations, and driven to the extremities of exhaustion by the whips of overseers, 300,000 are reported to have perished. Their bodies buried in the foundations, together with those of men who were bricked up alive for failing to work hard enough, have earned the Wall the grim appelations of "the Wall of Tears" and "the longest cemetery on earth."

One can obtain some idea of the incredible labor involved by taking a trip to the Wall in Badalang Pass near Beijing, the section which most tourists visit. When first viewed from a distance, with its crenelated battlements shimmering in the summer haze, it seems almost ephemeral, an illustration from a child's story book. But as you approach, the Wall gradually turns into a masterpiece of military architecture. A massive fortification, 15 to 30 feet wide at its base, it is constructed of beautifully dressed, gray granite blocks to an average height of 20 feet, surmounted by five-foot-high parapets, between which runs a paved roadway wide enough for five horses to gallop abreast.

But the Wall was not built for horses, or tourists either, for the roadway climbs at angles so steep that you may find it a hard struggle to reach the crest on the slippery cobbles, if you make it at all. In the mountains, where the Wall passes over peaks nearly a mile high, explorers have had to be pulled up on ropes, or make the climb hanging onto a mule's tail. How two-ton granite blocks were transported to such heights without machinery is a mystery. The Chinese say they were dragged up by giant mountain goats.

However, the Wall does not present the same appearance everywhere, since the architects used the materials at hand. In rolling country and the plains, they built it of clay, packed down between log walls, or carved it out of natural hills, then faced and topped it with stone. In the deserts, they used adobe bricks, which over the centuries have crumbled into shapeless mounds hundreds of miles long, many covered by the drifting sands. Elsewhere the Wall has almost disappeared, its stones carted away to build houses.

Still standing, even in areas where the Wall itself has disappeared, are many of the 25,000 projecting towers, 40 feet high, that sheltered the garrisons. Constructed at intervals of 700 feet, exactly two bowshots apart, they were surmounted by blockhouses from which soldiers armed with powerful crossbows fired steel-tipped arrows that could pierce the metal armor of invaders, or stone pellets that killed like bullets. Relaying smoke signals by day and flares at night, from one watchtower to another, they could transmit a message across the empire in 24 hours. At strategic passes, great forts were erected, and here and there throughout the Wall's length stand fanciful, multi-roofed pagodas where the defenders worshipped. In the Great Wall's glory days, Chinese historians tell us, an army of a million men was needed to garrison the mighty rampart. Their ancient graffiti still cover the stones in places. One centuries-old inscription warns: "Beware of the Russians."

The Chinese did not originate the idea of protective walls. They are among the earliest relics of civilization, appearing in the Middle East shortly after the development of cities 8,000 years ago. But China had a particularly urgent need for them. The massive country lies on the edge of the great plateau of central Asia called by historians "the cradle of races." During glacial times, bands of Mongoloid hunters followed the mammoths and deer from this heartland across the land bridge connecting Siberia with Alaska to settle the New World.

In early historic times, wave after wave of nomadic tribesmen left the bleak steppes seeking better lives for themselves in the more congenial parts of the Eurasian continent. Celts, Persians, Germans, Slavs, Finns, Magyars and Turks moved westward to conquer and destroy the empires and civilizations of the Middle East and Europe, and eventually set up kingdoms of their own. Huns, Khitans, Tanguts, Nuchens, Mongols, Tartars and Manchus, pushed east and south into the fertile valleys of the Yellow River, slaughtering as they traveled. Practically all of the two-score dynasties that ruled China, or parts of it, for 4,000 years were descended from one or another tribe of bandy-legged nomads who lived on horseback and subsisted on a diet of mare's milk and rancid cheese.

But China, with its teeming population and its vastness, had the ability to swallow invaders almost without trace. Within a generation or two, all of the savage hordes succumbed to the civilization they sought to destroy and became Chinese themselves, only to be overrun in their turn by new waves of barbarians from Siberia. Warns an old Chinese proverb: "Fear not the tiger from the south, but beware of even a rooster from the north."

The constant incursions kept China in political turmoil for almost 2,000 years. In the third century B.C., it was divided into a dozen warring feudal states, each surrounded by a protective wall. Had the situation continued, the region might have developed, as did Europe later, into a conglomerate of independent nations, inhabited by different ethnic groups, speaking different languages.

But China's destiny changed in 234 B.C. when a 13-year-old boy acceded to the throne of the half-civilized Ch'in (the Chinese now spell it Qin) kingdom on the western edge of China. He was the son of a dancing girl, some said a prostitute, who was already pregnant by another man when she became the king's favorite. His enemies described him as having a "high pointed nose, slit eyes, pigeon breast, wolf voice and tiger heart." He was also a political and military genius. Launching a war of unprecedented savagery against his neighbors—his generals reportedly slaughtered 400,000 soldiers of one rival kingdom after their surrender—he conquered, or terrorized into submission, the whole of civilized China in 12 years, to become absolute master of an area almost as large as Europe.

Assuming the title of Ch'in Shih Huang-ti (literally: First Sovereign Emperor of Ch'in), the monarch set about to unite the country into a cohesive national entity, through a series of farsighted acts that influence the lives of a billion Chinese to this day. He abolished feudalism, organizing the country into 41 provinces under a centralized administration that persisted until the establishment of the Chinese Republic in 1912. He decreed a single written script for the nation, which has enabled Chinese speaking different languages to understand each other's writing ever since. He unified customs laws, codified legal statutes, and standardized weights and measures for the whole of China. He forced a uniform width for roads throughout the empire by ordering that the axles of all wheeled vehicles be exactly the same length. He also drained swamps, built huge irrigation systems, dug canals connecting rivers for transportation, constructed tree-lined highways linking the major cities, and much else. To make sure his decrees were being carried out, the emperor worked tirelessly, "reading 120 pounds of reports each day," according to the chroniclers, and frequently made inspections in disguise.

One of Ch'in's most inspired decisions was to tear down the walls that divided the country, except those facing north, the direction from which the enemy would come. These he linked together, enlarging and fortifying them with stone, and extended them east and west for 1,800 miles across the entire border of the empire. This became the Great Wall, which was completed in an incredibly short 18 years. Whether the extensive fortification was successful in repelling invasion is questionable, as we shall see. But none of the monarch's actions served more effectively to weld the various ethnic groups of the empire together and give them a sense of national identity. From that time forward, everything north of the Wall was considered barbarian territory, everything south of it became "China" which took its name from the emperor's Ch'in dynasty.

In view of these accomplishments, it might be imagined that the First Emperor would be venerated as the father of his country. Instead, his name has been execrated for 2,000 years. For in addi-

tion to his admirable qualities, he was a paranoid and megalomaniac, who enforced his laws with unprecedented brutality, with
death meted out for the slightest infraction. During his reign, practically every able-bodied man in the empire, along with a great
many women, were forced to work on his building projects or to
serve in his three-million-man army.

He sought to destroy the humanizing influence of Confucianists
and other scholars, whose ethical teachings threatened to under-
mine his dictatorial regime. And he ruthlessly suppressed philo-
sophic debate and the teaching of morals and religion, ordering all
books to be burned except those devoted to medicine, soothsaying,
agriculture, and his own glory. Those who resisted were branded
on the face and sent to labor on the Great Wall. In the year 212 B.C.,
he had 460 scholars in the capital buried alive for "spreading
heretical ideas to confuse the public." For centuries, Chinese parents curbed unruly children by threatening that Ch'in would return
to punish them unless they behaved.

But the Emperor's moods were unpredictable. Rather than kill or
imprison the feudal lords and their families, he transported 120,000
of them to his capital, where he built them luxurious palaces identical to those they had been forced to abandon. In retaliation for
being buffeted by the wind on a visit to Hsiang Mountain, he
ordered every tree on it cut down and had the whole mountain
painted red, the color worn by criminals. He would disappear for
weeks at a time in search of magic mushrooms that guaranteed
eternal life. He sent 600 youths and maidens into the Pacific on a
fleet of ships in search of islands on which they were said to grow.
They were never heard from again, although legend said they
became ancestors of the Japanese. Ch'in also had a grim sense of
humor. When an oracle predicted that the Great Wall could not be
completed without the sacrifice of a *wan* (10,000) of men, he found
an individual with the name of Wan and had him killed instead.

The emperor lived in unbelievable splendor. His gargantuan
palace, a mile and a half long and a half-mile wide, contained
thousands of rooms, including a brocade-hung auditorium seating
10,000, and quarters for a harem selected from the most beautiful

women in the empire. They were so numerous that, according to legend, it would have taken the monarch 36 years to spend a night with each. But Ch'in did not frequent the palace often. Fearful of assassination—at least two attempts were made on his life—he built 270 lesser imperial residences in a radius of 60 miles, linked by covered tunnels, sleeping in a different one each night. It was an offense punishable by death to reveal his whereabouts.

The mad emperor's tomb, near Xian, which took six years to build, was as spectacular as his palaces. It was covered after its completion by a man-made hill of earth, two miles in area and 150 feet high, that so closely resembles the natural hills around it that it escaped detection for 22 centuries.

One of its subterranean vaults, accidentally discovered in 1974, has deservedly become a world-class archeological sensation. Lined up in battle array in the vast chamber, 700 feet long and 200 feet wide—an expanse equivalent to 28 football fields—stands a life-sized army of 6,000 armed soldiers and archers, along with chariots and horses, all cast in fired and painted terra cotta. The faces of the men, no two of which are alike, are believed to be actual portraits of the emperor's bodyguard.

Two other life-sized pottery regiments stand in equally large chambers nearby which have not yet been excavated, although two chariots and drivers, drawn by four horses cast in bronze, were dug out in 1981. The emperor's burial place, itself, has recently been located. Not yet known is whether it is walled in bronze, surrounded by rivers of quicksilver, and protected by arrow-firing booby traps, as the chronicles relate. Chinese archeologists say it will take decades to excavate the entire tomb.

The labor required for Ch'in's undertakings was staggering. The emperor conscripted 700,000 men to build the palace. An equal number toiled on the tomb. Millions more were rounded up by press gangs to construct roads, canals and the countless other public works. But no project consumed more men, caused more suffering, or took a larger toll of life than the Great Wall. The chroniclers tell us the workers were housed in vermin-infested, makeshift camps. They toiled naked in summer, clad in skins and rags in winter, and died by the tens of thousands from exposure, disease, exhaustion and hunger. They were kept on starvation rations because the porters bringing food often would not approach the Wall for fear of being drafted themselves. One account says that of 182 loads of grain sent from the Shantung peninsula to the Wall, only one arrived. Ballads lamenting the fate of the scholars who died and the heartbreak of their wives are still sung in China.

The Wall, and the countless other monuments to the insatiable emperor's mania, drained China of its manpower and bankrupted the country. Rebellion seethed when peasants could not raise enough grain to pay their exorbitant taxes and were forced to sell their children to meet the emperor's need for funds. Ch'in died while on a fortnight's journey from his capital in 204 B.C. at the age of 49. His body had to be spirited across China in a carriage by night, with a cart of rotten fish hooked on behind to disguise the odor of the decomposing corpse. It was interred secretly.

Ch'in boasted his dynasty would last for 10,000 generations. It was overthrown just three years after his death, the shortest in China's imperial history. His magnificent palaces were looted and torn down by rioting mobs. His monuments were destroyed, and one of the great chambers that housed his pottery army was broken into, the weapons stolen, and its wooden roof burned. However, the pillagers never found the entrance to his tomb.

The one thing the people did not attack was the venerated Great Wall. Emperors of the succeeding Han Dynasty preserved and extended it. Later rulers added nearly 2,000 miles of fortifications, spurs and secondary walls, to the 1,800 miles that Ch'in had left. It achieved its final form under the Ming Dynasty in the 16th century A.D.

Was the great rampart worth the blood, treasure and suffering it cost? Some Chinese argue that it was, saying that "though one generation was sacrificed to build it, it saved the hundred that followed." But some modern historians doubt that the Wall was seriously intended for defense. They point out that it was too extensive, too costly to maintain and wasteful of military manpower, and that it guarded too many impossible invasion routes such as mountain peaks and raging rivers. They believe that, like the pyramids of Egypt, it was built by the megalomaniac emperor and those that succeeded him as a symbol of their might. History supports the contention. Although the Wall doubtless prevented sporadic raids by small bands of marauders, it was penetrated time and again by invading armies, most notably in 1260 A.D. when Genghis Khan and his hordes swept across it to conquer China, and in 1644 A.D. when the Manchus came through it from the north to establish a dynasty that lasted until 1912.

Nevertheless, as a political and cultural symbol, the Great Wall served its purpose. By preserving the idea of the unity of all peoples "within the wall," it kept China intact during the long periods of government breakdown and foreign incursion that threatened to dismember the country time and again throughout its history. The Wall became a favorite theme of poets and artists and a source of magic to the common people, who believed its ground-up cement would cure everything from cuts and disease to stomach disorders. The Great Wall also created a psychological barrier, turning Chinese thoughts inward, giving them a sense of isolation, of cultural superiority, and a contempt for all things foreign that caused them to fall farther and farther behind in the arts of civilization and war.

The stupendous monument to China's past greatness no longer protects the country's frontier, since its borders now extend far beyond it. But its symbolism is as potent as ever. In 1899, a fictitious item in the *Denver Post,* cooked up by bored reporters, stated that American engineers were on their way to demolish the Wall. It triggered riots throughout China and helped to ignite the Boxer Rebellion in which thousands of lives were lost. Even the present Communist regime, which initially condemned the Wall as a relic of "the evil imperial past," now praises it as a monument to "the wisdom and creative power of the working masses." The government has expended great effort to restore it.

The Great Wall no longer keeps out foreigners. Rather, it lures them, in ever increasing numbers. It has become one of China's most prolific sources of foreign exchange, a windfall attributable entirely to a mad emperor's vanity.

CHAPTER 13

The Life and Death of an Elegant City

(79 A.D.)

The morning of August 24, 79 A.D., was clear and sunny along the Bay of Naples. But some of the residents of the fashionable resort town of Herculaneum were uneasy, for the earth had been trembling beneath their feet for days. Since such tremors are frequent in that highly seismic region of Italy, however—and these were mild compared to the earthquake that had damaged the city 16 years earlier—the citizens went about their business.

In his bakeshop, Sextus Patulcus set out the loaves of bread, pizzas and pastries, imprinted with his initials. Greengrocer Aulus Fuferus watered the fruits and vegetables on his stand. A gem-cutter rushed to finish the delicate cameo he was carving. The bronze caster worked on a candelabrum and small statue that had been brought in for repair. Tailors, cloth dyers, artists and tavern keepers, were equally busy, as was probably the lady believed to

161

have been a prostitute, whom we know as Portia. For the town was crowded with visitors come to enjoy the festivities and the contests in the Palestra, the athletic field, which were being held to commemorate the birthday of the dead Augustus, the first emperor of Rome. Among the visitors was a soldier with a good deal of money to spend.

There would be other entertainments, as well. On the stone stage of the 2,500-seat open-air amphitheater, actors rehearsed for the afternoon performance. In the two elaborate public baths, one in town, the other near the beach, slaves stoked water boilers in preparation for the expected rush of business. A patrician lady put on her gemmed rings, gold bracelets and other finery, for a social event she would attend. In another sumptuous villa, a servant began unpacking a crate of delicate glass goblets embedded in straw, that may have been bought for a party.

Not everyone was in a festive mood, however. Locked in a room with barred windows in the Shrine to Augustus on the Forum lived a high-born or priestly prisoner whose crime is unknown. In the back room of the gem-cutter's shop, a sick boy lay on a wooden bed, watched over by a woman who wove cloth on a small loom nearby. In a boatyard near the marina, a stocky slave braced his aching muscles to heave yet another heavy load onto his back. In a nearby mansion, a 14-year-old nursemaid tended a 10-month-old infant girl, who wore gold and pearl earrings.

Toward noon, activities tapered off as the Herculaneans retired to their homes for lunch, and visitors to the numerous snack bars of the city where they could buy bread, cheese, hard-boiled eggs and wine, or hot meals served from urns embedded in the marble counters. In the gem-cutter's shop, someone brought the sick boy a piece of chicken, which he had no time to eat. For just as the diners were biting into their rolls and cracking their eggs, they felt a shock and heard a violent explosion, followed by a continuous rumbling noise as of nearby thunder. Forgetting their half-eaten lunches (which lay untouched for 17 centuries), the people rushed into the streets and saw a pillar of roiling white ash and pumice rocketing up from the cone of Mount Vesuvius, four miles to the east. As they watched, the column soared rapidly to a height of 16 miles, mushrooming out at the top like an umbrella which partly obscured the sun turning the day into ominous twilight.

The Herculaneans were as goggle-eyed with wonder as was the writer Pliny the Younger, who witnessed the phenomenon from his family home in Misenum, 20 miles to the north. Although a few Roman scientists, Vitruvius, Strabo and others, had suspected as much, the inhabitants were unaware that their beautiful, verdant Vesuvius was a dormant volcano, or that their homes and fertile vineyards were built on the debris left by its previous eruption 1,200 years earlier.

Dogs, cats and rats probably fled the city, since none of their remains have ever been reported. But scientist Haraldur Sigurdson of the University of Rhode Island, who has made an intensive study of the eruption, doubts that the people would have felt much alarm at this point. Though the air was filled with the smell of sulfur and the earth continued to tremble, the winds were blowing from the north so that only a sprinkling of ash fell on Herculaneum. However, the onlookers could see a huge, dense cloud of the stuff drifting toward the city of Pompeii, seven miles to the south.

By mid-afternoon, it is conjectured, Pompeiian refugees began passing through Herculaneum on their way north with terrible tales to tell. They reported that ash and pumice were raining down on the city at the rate of several inches an hour, along with stones as large as bocce balls that smashed through houses, forcing people to protect their heads with pillows. The ash fall had plunged Pompeii in darkness, making breathing difficult, and the buildings were beginning to collapse under its weight. Fearing that a shift in the wind might cause a similar ash fall on Herculaneum, some of the residents apparently joined the trek north to Naples where they camped in a section of the city still known as the Herculaneum Quarter. (There was next to no fallout on Naples.) However, most people stayed to protect their homes and property.

Night fell, but few Herculaneans went to bed. For though the fallout was still light, never reaching more than one-half inch in depth, the eruption continued unabated, made more ominous by the burning gases spewing from the crater, its upper part rent with flashes of lightning. Terrified by the sight, more residents may have left. But, as we know now, many others went down to the beach, doubtless planning to move up the coast road or to flee by boat, if the situation got any worse. Some people, rich, poor, young, old, free and slave, as well as a horse, found shelter under the stone arches that supported the terraces and buildings on the bluff over-looking the sea, which were normally used as stables, or to store fishing boats.

The eruption continued for 13 hours. Suddenly, shortly after midnight on August 25th, Sigurdson calculates, the towering erup-tion column collapsed, and the horrified Herculaneans saw a ground-hugging, fiery avalanche—volcanologists call it a "pyro-clastic surge"—of turbulent, superheated ash and pumice, mixed with air and volcanic gases, cascading down the slopes of Vesuvius toward the city. It flowed at a velocity of over 60 miles per hour, its temperature is estimated to have been as high as 400 degrees Celsius (750 degrees Fahrenheit).

With only minutes to save themselves before the fiery avalanche reached their walls, Herculaneans still in the city raced to the beach. In the panic, the sick boy in the gem shop, a baby in its crib, the prisoner in the Shrine of Augustus, and a few other individuals were forgotten or, like the six men and women found in the public bath, did not flee because they were indoors and unaware of what was happening, or felt safe where they were. The fiery tide swept over the entire city and onto the beach, pouring into the houses, shops, and the archways along the shore in which people had taken refuge.

Some people on the beach may have managed to set sail in the few boats available, but it is doubtful they escaped, for the water had receded leaving fish and squid flopping on the sand. The underground magma chambers which lay near the coast had been emptied by the eruption, and collapsed, creating waves so violent, that the young Pliny's uncle, Pliny the Elder, who had set sail in a large vessel to rescue his friends, could not reach them and had to land at another port.

Following the first surge by a few minutes came a second, more devastating, pyroclastic flow that knocked down walls and colonnades, tore statues in the Forum from their pedestals, leaving behind only the bronze hooves of horses and the feet of men. It also blew off the roofs and upper stories of some houses, carrying the debris with it to the coast and into the sea. During the next 10 hours, four more surges and flows poured down from Vesuvius, killing the 2,000 people still left in Pompeii.

The people who remained in Herculaneum were unaware of these later events, however. They had all died in the first surge that overwhelmed them around midnight. Choked by the fine ash that plugged their windpipes, "they lived for as long as they could hold their breaths," says Sigurdsson.

When the eruption ended 17 hours after it had started, the sites of the two cities were deserts. Pompeii was buried under 20 feet of gray ash. Herculaneum lay under 66 feet of black, rock-hard tephra that extended its coastline a half-kilometer farther out to sea. As the centuries passed, even the locations of the cities were forgotten.

Herculaneum was rediscovered 16 centuries later by chance. In the year 1709, workmen digging a water well reached the stage of the theater and began bringing out blocks of dressed marble and valuable Greek and Roman statues. The discoveries triggered a frenzied treasure hunt. More shafts were sunk, with tunnels radiating in all directions, and for the next half-century, the excavation became an "art mine" yielding masterpieces of statuary, and of mosaics and other priceless objects that are now displayed in museums in Naples and elsewhere. The find that caused particular excitement was the cache of over 800 charred, but still legible, papyrus manuscripts found in the library of a great palace, now called the Villa of the Papyri,* that had belonged to the father-in-law of Julius Caesar. Scholars hoped to find among them some of the famous plays, poems, and other Greek and Roman literary works that have been lost. Disappointingly, the documents were nearly all dull essays by a minor philosopher.

*A replica of the villa built in California now houses the Getty Museum.

The early excavators did incalculable damage. Looters, with little knowledge of, and less interest in, the civilization they were unearthing, undermined buildings, smashed through walls, destroying the murals and mosaics on them, discarding anything that did not command a ready price in the art market. Fortunately, the cement-hard volcanic tefra covering Herculaneum was extremely difficult to penetrate with hand tools, and as the tunnels lengthened, they became increasingly dangerous to work in. In 1765, the excavations were abandoned as interest turned to the newly-found treasure trove at Pompeii where no tunnels were needed. The loose ash covering the city could be removed with picks, shovels and wheelbarrows.

The incredible discoveries made in the two cities created a sensation throughout Europe and America. They led to the neoclassical revival of the late 18th and early 19th centuries that influenced the shape of everything from paintings, sculpture and architecture, to the design of clothing, furniture, tableware and household objects. Monticello, the home built by Thomas Jefferson on his return from Italy, was modeled on classical lines, as was the Capitol in Washington, whose halls were soon filled with statues of U. S. senators clad in Roman togas.

Although excavation was renewed sporadically at Herculaneum over the decades, it was not resumed in earnest until 1927 when compressed air-drills, electric tools, bulldozers, dumptrucks and other modern equipment were available. This time the work was directed by trained archeologists who sought to restore the city rather than loot it. To date, four square blocks have been uncovered down to their cobblestoned streets, together with sections of other blocks, as well as the Forum, part of the Basilica which housed the administrative offices and law courts, and about half of the spacious Palestra, the athletic field. They reveal that though Herculaneum was small, with a population that could not have exceeded 5,000, as compared to the 20,000 in Pompeii, it was a rich community indeed. Built on a bluff overlooking the sparkling bay, it was a summer home for the Roman elite, including emperors and their relatives.

Visiting the city is like passing through a time warp into the ancient past. Unlike Pompeii, where many buildings had collapsed under the weight of the fallout, most of the buildings of Herculaneum and their contents were miraculously preserved by the pyroclastic material that filled them, although much of the wood and other organic substances are carbonized and many of the frescoes were damaged. The upper stories of some of the houses are intact, their staircases still usable. Doors and shutters still swing in their sockets. Cabinets can still be opened. Bronze water faucets can be turned on and off. Fragments of the ancient panes of glass are visible in a few of the windows. In one place, a sagging roof is still supported by a temporary wooden scaffold installed 1,900 years ago.

Before most of the household objects were removed or locked in glass cases to protect them from souvenir hunters, the rooms looked as though the occupants had just stepped out. The crate of glassware in the sumptuous villa was still unpacked. On a plate next to the sick boy's bed lay the charred chicken leg he had not eaten. Found in other homes were dressing tables strewn with combs, hairpins, cosmetics, tiny perfume bottles and silver-backed mirrors; jewel cases filled with rings, bracelets and brooches; sewing kits holding thimbles, needles and the remains of thread; wooden cabinets containing dice and board games similar to checkers and backgammon. In the kitchens, shelves were stacked with plates, colanders, porringers and chafing dishes; pots and pans rested on charcoal stoves. Graffiti added to the sense of living presence. Scribbled on the wall of one house is a memorandum in Latin of wine deliveries and their dates, on another is a list of spelling words to be learned by a schoolboy, near the entrance to a third is the announcement: "Portumnous loves Amphianda."

Time had also stopped in the stores and craftsmen's shops. Lying on the workbench where the gem-cutter had left them to go to lunch, were the half-finished cameo and an uncut aquamarine. The bronze candelabrum and small statute still awaited repair in the tinker's shop. The oven in Sextus Patulcus' bakery held 80 loaves of bread in their pans. Cafes and grocery stores were stocked with glass jars of jam and marinated vegetables, mounds of carbonized grain, olives, eggs, walnuts and pistachios, figs, dates and other comestibles, along with bronze scales to weigh them. Discovered in a lawyer's office was a file of waxed writing tablets inscribed with legal notes of a case he was working on.

The villas of the rich patricians, with their airy atriums, gardens, colonnades, pergolas and solariums, are dazzling. Those that escaped the attentions of the early tunnelers are adorned with their original statuary, portrait busts, bronze lampstands, finely crafted furniture, and couches used for dining. The floors are covered with polychrome marble and tiles in intricate designs, the walls with superb mosaics and vivid frescoes painted by artists who knew the use of perspective. A few of the great houses whose owners had apparently fallen on hard times had been divided into apartments, offices and shops, which were rented out, and at least one appears to have been converted into a hotel for transient guests. Tradespeople also lived well in the rooms above or behind their shops. The quality of some of their furniture and decorations rival those of the patricians. The only people who did not enjoy the general prosperity were the numerous slaves, who slept in tiny, airless rooms, usually in the upper stories of the houses.

Herculaneum boasted some surprisingly modern facilities. It had an efficient sewer system. Pipes molded of lead or terracotta carried water from the mountains to public fountains and horse troughs, and into kitchens and lavatories of homes and shops. The two public baths are luxurious, their rooms lit by skylights, their temperatures regulated by warm air flowing through ducts between the walls and under the floors.

The baths served as social meeting places for men, with separate sections for women. They offered airy, mosaiced dressing rooms with individual cubicles for the bathers' clothes, exercise courts where games similar to bocce and handball were played, as well as steam rooms, saunas, and sculptured pools kept at three different temperatures, hot, warm and cold. The athletes in the Palestra were provided with a much larger pool, fed by water flowing from the five heads of a giant copper serpent.

The Herculaneans were a religious people. Although no temples other than the one devoted to Augustus have yet been unearthed, shrines to the household gods are found in almost every home and shop in the city. Alien gods were also worshipped. There are depictions of oriental and Egyptian deities and their priests, and among the numerous graffiti scratched on the walls appears the unmistakably Jewish name, David. More controversial is the cross-shaped indentation in the plaster of a wall of a second floor bedroom which could have been left when a wooden cross attached to it was ripped down by a fleeing resident, or it could have been left by a book shelf or cabinet.* It is possible that Christianity may have reached the city, since St. Paul had landed at nearby Possuoli 17 years before the eruption to preach the new gospel.

By far the most common symbol, however, is the male phallus, which was regarded as a good luck charm. Erect phalli appear everywhere—on brazier legs carved in the shape of satyrs, molded on the plaster walls of baker's ovens to ward off the evil spirits that might prevent the dough from rising. Cast in bronze, they were used as door handles, bell pulls, and chimes.

Although no brothels have yet been identified in Herculaneum, as at Pompeii, prostitutes were readily available, particularly in the public baths as indicated by the explicit notices scratched on the walls of their back rooms. The Romans regarded sex as a normal aspect of life and saw no need to hide it. Sexual acts in all of their variety are portrayed in murals and statuary in homes throughout Herculaneum, along with numerous depictions of the god Priapus whose penis was a large as his torso. There is also a good deal of bawdy humor. Adorning a room of one mansion is a statue depicting Hercules, the god for whom the city was named, as an aging giant, staggeringly drunk, caught in the act of urinating.

Only the people are missing from the Herculaneum time capsule. Since only nine human skeletons were discovered during the first 250 years of excavation, it was long assumed that the population had managed to escape. But this theory posed a puzzle. Unless they

*The latter is more likely as the earliest Christian symbol was not a cross but a fish.

had made no preparations, and waited until the last possible moment to flee, why would shopkeepers leave behind the cash in their tills, or householders fail to take with them the gold coins, jewelry, precious gems, gold cups and other easily portable valuables found in homes throughout the city? Surely they would need them to support themselves in their flight to they knew not whither.

Like the discovery of Herculaneum, itself, this mystery too was solved by chance. In 1980, while installing a pump to remove the groundwater that was undermining the ancient suburban bath, workmen uncovered two human skeletons lying on the sands of the ancient beach. One, a stocky male, was called the Helmsman, because he was found next to an oar near an overturned boat and was assumed to have been a member of the crew, a mistake as it later turned out, since the skeleton and the boat lay in different volcanic strata. The other skeleton was that of a woman who became known as the Pretty Lady. Clearing more of the beach two years later, the archeologists encountered 13 more skeletons, writhed in unnatural positions, indicating the agony of their deaths. Among them was the Soldier, identifiable by the military sword, scabbard and belt he wore. Still unspent in his purse was some silver and three gold coins, one bearing the image of the Emperor Nero, which were worth a good deal.

But greater shocks awaited the excavators when they drilled through the rock plugging the entrances to the deep stone arches under the wall. Huddled together in one were the remains of six adults, four children, and the 14-year-old Nursemaid cradling the infant in her arms. In a second arch, skeletons of 48 people and the horse lay in rows, like souls "floating down the river Styx," one archeologist observed. Heaped up in the third chamber of horrors were the tangled skeletons of 19 humans. The Patrician Lady who had put on her jewelry and gemmed rings earlier in the day had not managed to squeeze into the crowded refuge. Her body was found at its entrance.

The scene was "a masterpiece of pathos," recalls archeologist Giuseppe Maggi who directed the excavation. The victims had not died quietly, as their contorted jaws and flailing arms and legs reveal. Some lay or sat with hands clasped over their noses and mouths, others with head flung back and mouths wide open as though screaming, and a few with fingers clawed as though trying to dig themselves out of the hellish brew that engulfed them. Many appear more concerned for others than for themselves. A mother crouched over a child trying to protect it with one hand, cuddling a baby against her cheek with the other. A husband and wife clung to each other, shielding a child between their bodies.

Mingled with the people were some of their meager possessions—amber beads, jewelry, the metal clasps of belts, the remains of a fur hat, a child's wooden bank with two small coins in it, an iron house key in the hand of a 10-year-old, and the oil lamps with which the families had lit their way through the black night to their rendezvous with death.

Sealed in the volcanic rock and kept wet by groundwater percolating through the soil, the ancient bones were marvellously preserved, some still retaining bits of tissue and patches of hair. They comprise the first complete skeletons of the era ever recovered from Italy, for until Christian times, the Romans cremated their dead, and only plaster casts had been made of the bodies entombed in the ash at Pompeii. But once exposed to air the Herculaneum skeletons would quickly decay and crumble. To preserve and study them was the responsibility of physical anthropologist Sarah Bisel of the Smithsonian Institution. As each of the selected 39 skeletons was removed, she cleaned the bones, dipped them in an acrylic resin solution that hardens and seals them from the air, and stored them in open plastic boxes lining the walls of her laboratory from floor to ceiling.

Dr. Bisel's studies of the skeletons tells us more about the habits and physical characteristics of the Romans than we have ever known before. The men averaged 5 feet, 7 inches in height, the women 5 feet, 2 inches. They were generally well nourished, muscular and healthy, although a few showed evidence of arthritis, anemia and lead deposits which were probably derived from the lead vessels in which their wine was prepared. Their teeth were in exceptionally good shape, and they kept most of them into old age, which may be attributable to the absence of sugar from the diet and the hard food they ate. Because Roman children were nursed up to the age of three or four and did not suck their thumbs, there was good dental occlusion.

But Bisel's analyses go far beyond surface characteristics. "The bones like attention," she says. "They talk to me, and tell me the story of their lives." She gave the Pretty Lady her name because the contours of her skull show she had a lovely face, perfect teeth and a dainty nose, and her torso and slender leg bones are graceful. She was about 35 years old, and from the well developed muscles indicated by the arm bones and the way she used them, Bisel suspects she may have worked as a weaver.

The Patrician Lady was a relatively tall, well-nourished matron of about 45, who had led a comfortable life. She was not only rich, but had excellent taste as the quality and design of her jewelry prove. The woman called Portia had not enjoyed a comfortable life, or death. Her shattered skeleton was found on the beach onto which she had been blown by the surge, or had jumped to avoid it, landing on her face. Although in her late 40s, with extreme buck teeth and anything but good looking, Bisel believes she might have been a prostitute because the outgrowths on the bones of her pelvis are much like those of modern prostitutes she had examined.

The Soldier on the beach revealed a great deal about himself. "He was a well built, big-nosed, macho type of about 37, well above average height," Bisel recalls. The muscle attachments of his arm bones were enlarged, probably from holding a heavy shield and wielding a sword. A bony crest had developed on his right shoulder from hurling javelins much of his life. Bisel concludes that he was a cavalryman due to the distinctive musculature and en-larged ends of his thigh bones, derived from riding a horse bare-back (the Romans did not use saddles). The man had also seen a lot of action either in battles or brawls. Three of his front teeth had been knocked out and he had received a deep javelin wound on his left thigh which left an abnormal lump on the femur. As was expected of all Roman legionnaires, this one had a trade in addition to soldiering. The adz and chisels found on his back, which had probably been slung in a now disintegrated bag over his shoulder, show he was a carpenter.

Practically the only people Bisel has found who did not enjoy good health, enough nourishment or good treatment, were the slaves. "They were dreadfully overworked," she said. The leg bones of the stocky, 46-year-old male, mistakenly called the Helmsman, were flattened from incessant labor and poor nutrition. Heavy lifting had raised large crests on the muscle attachments of his armbones, and the constant strain on his back had twisted his spine. "He probably never had enough to eat, and his rotting teeth kept him in continual pain," Bisel observed. She was certain he was a slave because "a free man would have stopped when his body hurt as much as this man's must have."

Bisel was equally sure that the 14-year-old Nursemaid found holding the infant with the jewelry must have been a slave. The grooves in her teeth prove that she hadn't gotten enough to eat as a child. In fact, she had almost died of starvation or illness. The scars on the upper shafts of her humeri, where the pectoral muscles attach to the bone, were caused by doing heavier work than she should have. "Its sad to think of little kids having to work that hard," Bisel commented.

These are only a few of the many personalities Bisel had come to know from their bones. "They are all my friends," she said, "and they are very much like us." She saw their faces and figures on the streets of Ercolano, modern Herculaneum, every day.

The discoveries at Herculaneum may continue to make headlines for decades to come. With three-quarters of the ancient city still encased in rock beneath the modern city, it has been called "archeology's most flagrant unfinished business." Waiting to be exhumed are lavish temples, the theater, the magnificent Villa of the Papyri, a large covered market, acres of villas, dwellings and shops, and perhaps the stadium in which the gladiatorial helmets and weapons that have been found were put to bloody use. Out of the depths of Herculaneum may come unknown masterpieces of art and craftsmanship, and possibly manuscripts of the lost literature of antiquity.

And, archeologist Giuseppe Maggi predicts: "Somewhere in the ruins, or on the sections of beach and in the archways still to be excavated, will be found most of the missing population of the elegant city."

CHAPTER 14

The Fabulous Empires of the Andes

(800 B.C. to 1532 A.D.)

The Inca City of Machu Picchu, perched like an eagle's nest on a lofty peak high above the Urubamba River in the Peruvian Andes, is one of the most breathtaking archeological sites on earth. It is also one of the most baffling. Until its discovery by American explorer Hiram Bingham, in 1911, it lay empty for nearly five centuries. The Spanish never entered it because by the time they arrived in 1532, even the Incas had forgotten its existence. Not a single reference to it appears in any of the many chronicles written by the Spaniards, or by the Incas themselves after the conquest.

There were no smashed altars, demolished buildings or the ashes of conflagration to indicate that the city had succumbed to earthquake, invasion or revolution. The thatched roofs of the buildings and a few stones had fallen in, and water no longer coursed through the carved fountains and drainage canals. Otherwise the splendid city of over 200 palaces, shrine, dwellings, workshops and farming terraces stood intact. Yet sometime during the 14th century, the radiocarbon dates tell us, the people walked out, never to return, leaving a temple and other works still unfinished.

No one knows why the city was built so far from other population centers. Its impregnable location, and the stone-paved road connecting it with the great Inca capital of Cuzco, 70 miles to the south, would appear to make it a military outpost, intended to protect the rich valley. But if so, where was the garrison? Of the 141 identifiable skeletons found in its cemetery, 102 were those of women, five of children, and the remaining 34 were men over 60 years of age. There was not one male of military age among them. This has led some archeologists to theorize that Machu Picchu was a cloister, a city sheltering the famous "Chosen Women" or "Virgins of the Sun," who played so large a role in Inca religious life, and that the aged men in the cemetery may have been the eunuches who served them. But why they abandoned Machu Picchu, and what sin they could have committed to cause its very existence to be erased so quickly from Inca memory, is beyond imagining.

Still another wonder is how the Incas managed to construct the massive, superbly engineered, stone buildings at Machu Picchu and elsewhere without the aid of draft animals, wheeled vehicles, pulleys or iron tools. All they had were stone hammers, wooden crowbars, bronze chisels, fiber ropes and human muscles. With these primitive tools they split the granite blocks from the living rock in quarries, carved them to shape, dragged them with the aid of tree trunks and stone rollers up and down the sides of deep gorges and across rivers to building sites miles away, and lifted them into position. Then, using no mortar, they fitted them together so tightly that it is usually impossible to insert a pin into the cracks between them.

Sacsahuaman, the 370-feet-long, 28-feet-high fortress the Incas built to guard Cuzco, has been called "the greatest engineering feat ever attempted by primitive man." It is constructed of cyclopean, many-sided curved boulders, some of them the size of small houses, weighing up to 360 tons, the largest ever used in military architecture. Each of the monstrous stones would have to be moved, lifted and lowered, and its edges ground down with chisels, sand and water, dozens of times until it achieved a perfect fit with its neighbors on all sides. "We would have trouble building walls like that today even with power equipment and computers," an American civil engineer told me. "Stonehenge and the Egyptian pyramids are crude by comparison."

Equally awesome are the nearby bathing pools and long flights of steps carved out of single stones. The Spanish believed the feats were performed by wizards who knew how to melt rocks. Modern believers in the occult speculate they were accomplished with the aid of antigravity machines by visitors from other planets.

Actually the Incas, who arrived around 1300 A.D., very late in the history of pre-conquest Peru, did not originate the engineering and skills with which they are credited. They inherited them from earlier, far different cultures, each centered around a city that flourished for a few centuries, only to disappear as mysteriously as it had arisen.

The first city to reach prominence, between 800 and 300 B.C., was Chavin de Huantar, deep in the central Andes of Peru. Its three-story stone "castle," actually a temple, is an eerie place. Its walls are decorated with jutting stone heads with bulging eyes and jaguar teeth, and nightmare friezes of ferocious condors and jaguar-demons with writhing snakes in place of hair, long tongues where their legs and tails should be, and their backbones depicted as human mouths. We have no idea what the weird figures symbolized. The interior of the temple is honeycombed with rooms, passages and functioning ventilations shafts, only partially explored. In the center of the temple, kilted priests performed rituals around an intricately carved underground obelisk, 30 feet high, which seems to hang from the ceiling like a boa constrictor. Chavin appears to have been a religious center that attracted pilgrims from far and wide.

Gentler and more human was the culture that evolved in the Moche valley on the northwestern coast of Peru around 300 A.D. It was ruled by warrior priests from a city surrounding one of the most massive structures ever raised by man. It is a pyramid called the Shrine of the Sun (we don't know its real name) that measures 740 feet long and 450 feet wide, built of an estimated 130 million clay bricks, many indented with the trademarks of their makers.

In its glory, the pyramid must have been a dazzling sight, 120 feet high and covered with brilliant murals. But over the centuries the structure was attacked by the elements, pillaged by thieves who stole its bricks to build the modern city of Trujillo, and by treasure hunters who used gunpowder to blast their way into its inner recesses. Today it is a ruin. The few murals that survive have been covered over by archeologists to preserve them. Between the great pyramid and a smaller one, known as the Shrine of the Moon, lies a sand waste that was once a busy plaza where visitors can pick up shards of thousand-year-old pottery and figurines, and beads made of stone, copper, seashell, coral and llama teeth, with holes bored through them.

The legendary stone city of Tiahuanaco, almost a thousand miles to the southwest, is in better condition because it has been partially reconstructed. It stands on the desolate wind-swept altiplano near the Bolivian shore of Lake Titicaca, two miles above sea level. Its principal buildings, constructed of stone slabs held together by copper clamps in their corners, were completed around 600 A.D., and abandoned five centuries later. This cold and forbidding capital of a one-time empire is one of the most impressive archeological sights in the Andes.

Most dramatic feature of Tiahuanaco is the reconstructed Temple of Kalasasaya, a vast platform with a sunken courtyard whose walls are studded with stone faces. A massive staircase leads to the Gateway of the Sun, hewn from a single block of granite 30 feet long and 10 feet high. Carved on its surface is an enigmatic portrayal of the sun god, with rays emanating from its head. The god holds a quiver of spears in one hand and a spear thrower in the other. It is flanked on either side by creatures wearing condor and puma masks. The figure is called the Weeping God because tears, in the shape of tiny pumas, descend from its eyes. Elsewhere on the great square stand monoliths carved in the likeness of grim-faced men, clad in kilts. This is only a fraction of the original city, however. So many more ruins lie beneath the surrounding plains that archeologists estimate that it would take two centuries to uncover and restore them all.

As Tiahuanaco declined around 1000 A.D., the new kingdom of Chimor arose on the north coast of Peru. Legend says it was founded by seafarers who sailed in from the north on balsa rafts. Its capital, Chan-Chan, eight square miles in area, protected by adobe walls up to 50 feet high, may have been one of the largest cities in the world at the times, and perhaps the wealthiest. Within the outer walls lay ten separate walled labyrinths, each a city in itself. They contain elaborate temples, palaces, citadels, offices, council chambers, storehouses, burial vaults, huge walk-in water wells, sunken gardens, and workshops where textiles, pottery and metal objects were produced.

Chan-Chan is one of the few pre-Columbian Peruvian cities whose end we know. It was burned around 1467 by the conquering Incas, who transported most of its wealth and many of its skilled craftsmen to their own capital, Cuzco. Yet so much gold remained in the city's tombs that when Pizzaro and his conquistadors arrived 65 years later, they formed companies to "mine" the city, recovering an estimated $200 million in bullion, at today's prices.

Because of the lack of rain, many of the adobe buildings of Chan-Chan might still be standing today. It was largely torn down by vandals to recover its high quality bricks, which bring ten times the price of modern bricks on the black market. Only vestiges remain of the brilliant murals that once covered the plastered walls. But sculptured deep into the clay are intricate friezes of fish, monkeys, pelicans with anchovies in their pouches, and scenes depicting musicians and dancers, fishermen in reed canoes, and sequences of pictures that, like modern comic strips, tell a connected story.

It is astonishing that ancient Peru could have supported cities so large and cultures so rich because environmentally it is a hostile land. The area is divided into three vastly different regions. The coastal plain on the west is a desert, cooled by the frigid Humboldt current, but so dry that a resident may never have seen rain in his lifetime. The narrow valleys of the Andes in the center are well watered and fertile, but lie at altitudes of between 12,000 and 17,000 feet above sea level, where oxygen is scarce and breathing becomes painful. The eastern slopes of the Andes are hot, unbearably humid and covered with dense jungle. Only two percent of the land in Peru is arable. As in Egypt and Mesopotamia, civilization may have developed early there not because the living was easy, but because it was so tough, forcing the people to improvise.

Faced with a near total lack of rainfall, the inhabitants of the coastal plain were heavily dependent on food grown in fields irrigated with water from rivers that flow from the mountains only intermittently. As a consequence, they became immensely skilled hydraulic engineers, constructing colossal irrigation systems, with underground conduits and stone-lined canals extending for up to 100 miles. Many are still in use. In the mountains, the steep slopes were terraced and cultivated almost to a height of three miles above sea level, the upper limit of the tree line. The pre-Columbian Peruvians cultivated more land than is farmed there today and supported a much larger rural population. Because construction and maintenance of irrigation works and terraces requires a high degree of organization and leadership, a stratified class system, dominated by king-gods, priests and soldiers, had developed in Peru by 800 B.C.

From plants that grew wild in desert, sierra and jungle, the Peruvians managed to domesticate an amazing variety of crops, not one of which was known in the Old World at the time. They grew 200 varieties of potatoes, 300 types of corn and other cereals, many kinds of beans, sweet potatoes, yams, peanuts, along with manioc, guavas, avacados, melons, pumpkins and squash. Also grown were cotton in three colors, white, green and brown, chilis and plants for seasoning, along with quinine and herbs for medicine. On the coast, the diet was supplemented with meat from domesticated guinea pigs and ducks, shellfish, sea lions, and fish caught from balsa rafts and canoes made of tortora reeds. In the highlands, herds of llamas and alpacas provided meat, wool and leather, and their droppings were used for fuel in the treeless altiplano (high prairie). Unlike the Indians of North America, however, the Peruvians did not eat dogs.

To sustain themselves during the bitter winters, the Andeans developed comestibles that we think of as modern. They freeze-dried potatoes, grinding them into flour that could be reconstituted by adding water, and they smoked strips of llama meat into *charqui,* from which comes the North American "jerky" or "jerked" beef. By trading these products with each other, the ancient Peruvians enjoyed a richer and more varied menu than their unknown neighbors on other continents. In fact, 60 percent of all the food crops raised on earth today originated in America, most of them in Peru.

As important as food to the Peruvians, both then and now, were coca leaves from which modern cocaine is extracted. Mixed with lime from ground bones, limestone or seashells, the leaves were chewed by men, women and children, alike, in all classes of society. By inducing a state of passive euphoria, coca enabled its users to work, fight or march, for grueling hours in searingly hot or frigid temperatures, or at high altitudes, without feeling hunger, fatigue or pain. Human figures on pottery and bas relief are often portrayed with walnut-sized quids of coca bulging in their cheeks and are rarely shown without woven coca bags slung from their shoulders or belts.

The other Peruvian addiction was *chicha,* a milky, alcoholic beer brewed of ground corn. It was served in enormous quantities on ritual occasions both solemn and joyous, when the participants were expected to drink until they passed out. Intoxication was considered a religious act, rather than a vice.

As with agriculture, the cultural arts also appeared earlier in the Andean region than elsewhere in America. By 3000 B.C., the people had learned to manufacture ceramics and pottery and to weave cloth from cotton and alpaca wool. Gold and silver began to be worked around 2000 B.C., copper a millennium or so later, and by the time of Christ, they were alloying copper with tin and other metals to manufacture hard bronze weapons and tools.

Although these technologies had appeared earlier in the Old World, most archeologists believe the Americans developed them independently. However, there are some objects found in Peru, particularly, that raise questions. These include the 5,000-year-old Ecuadorian vases almost identical in shape to the Jomon pottery of Japan; the appearance around 200 B.C. of headrests like those of China; sitting Buddha-style figurines with one leg folded over the other; pendants in the shape of elephant tusks which were unknown in America at the time; and models of houses with saddle roofs common in the Orient. Equally mystifying is why Peruvian Indians who were beardless should have made effigy vessels in the sixth century A.D. portraying the faces of slant-eyed Orientals with culti-vated beards and others bearing the features of Africans and Arabs.

That there may have been contact between the Indians of Peru and Mexico, 3,000 miles away, seems possible, since the history and cultures of the two regions show some interesting parallels, and early European navigators encountered balsa rafts off the Peruvian coast carrying trade goods to and from Central America. Both people cultivated maize and cotton, although of different varieties; both built flat-topped pyramids; both used a decimal system of numeration, employing the concept of zero centuries before it was employed in Europe; and both areas told legends of bearded white gods who arrived from the sea, taught the people the arts of civili-zation, then sailed off promising to return some day. However, skeptics argue, if there had been close relations between the two regions, the Peruvians would surely have acquired the idea of a written language from the Mayas, the Mexicans would have grown potatoes, and if either region had contact with Europe or Asia, it would have learned the advantages of the wheel.

Much of what we know about the pre-Inca peoples of Peru has been learned from the objects found in their graves, some of which are magnificent. Visitors to the museums of Lima are unlikely to forget the 1,500-year-old startlingly realistic Mochica vases which portray, warts and all, the faces of snobbish nobles, smiling chil-dren, scowling soldiers, smirking beggars, pleading blind men, paralytics, humpbacks, and others whose cheeks and noses had been cut off, possibly as punishment for crime. Artists also depicted in ceramic vivid genre scenes from everyday life: weavers, farmers and fishermen at work; dancers, and singers with their mouths wide open; musicians playing flutes, trumpets, ocarinas and drums; and a busy textile factory in operation. Some of the ceramics re-enact scenes of the utmost intimacy, such as a woman washing lice from her hair, with the insects clearly shown, a baby being born with its head protruding between its mother's thighs, and graphic demonstrations of every variety of sexual activity known to man.

The textiles produced by the Peruvians are spectacular. From cotton, alpaca and vicuna wool, spun on crude stone or clay spindles, they wove filmy gauzes, rich brocades, tapestries, braided work, and lace finer than can be made today. There were also mummy shrouds and garments intricately embroidered, brilliantly colored, and sometimes ornamented with feathers, gold and turquoise. Preserved by the desert atmosphere, some of the textiles show as many as 190 different hues in a single fabric. Considering that it took up to 18 miles of thread to weave some of the garments, the output was prodigious. Regarded as more valuable than gold, many of the exquisite fabrics were created to be burned as sacrifices to the gods.

The Peruvians had no currency or other medium of exchange. All trade was done by barter. Precious metals were sacred, with gold viewed as "the sweat of the sun," silver as "the tears of the moon," to be used only for religious purposes and by the nobility. Common people were forbidden to own them. But they were produced in enormous quantities. The great walls of the Temple of the Sun in the Inca capital, Cuzco, were sheathed with sheets of gold from top to bottom throughout. In a courtyard inside, as reported by the three Spanish soldiers who had been sent to pillage the temple in 1532, lay a garden filled with flowers, cornstalks, trees and shrubs, hovering birds and insects, life-sized llamas and other animals, all meticulously fashioned of pure gold.

The dazzling Gold Museum in Lima offers glimpses of what the vanished treasures looked like. The objects on display range from delicately fashioned gold tiaras, jewelry, hair pins, musical instruments and toys, to heavy carved gold drinking cups, kettles, weapons, paddles, and statuettes of people and animals. Most of these exhibits were bought from grave robbers or recovered from the few tombs that had somehow been overlooked by looters through the centuries. Although there are hundreds of objects, they represent only a minuscule fraction of the gold that existed at the time of the Spanish conquest. With little appreciation of the exquisite work, the conquistadors threw most of the priceless ornaments into crucibles to be melted into bricks, sending back enough gold to make Spain the wealthiest country in Europe for two centuries.

As with all people, the calendar, based on the movements of the sun, moon and stars, was of the utmost importance to the ancient Peruvians. Their survival depended on knowing when to sow and to harvest, which meant knowing when the annual droughts and frosts were due, and when the snow would begin to melt in the Andes to fill the dry river beds with water. The Incas recorded the solstices by means of tall stone shafts, which cast shadows on sun dials beneath them, called *intihuatanas,* meaning "the places to which the sun is tied down" in the Quechua language. Cuzco relied on four towers for the purpose, and in Tiahuanaco in Bolivia, the people knew the spring equinox had arrived when the sun rose through the center of the Sun Gate at dawn. It is not known whether the Peruvians could foretell eclipses of the sun and moon, as the Mayas could, since they left no written records and the Spanish priests destroyed the solar observatories as pagan relics wherever they were found.

One of the most baffling of all archeological finds in Peru, indeed, in the world, are the long lines, geometric designs, and gigantic figures of birds, animals and insects, inscribed on the plains of Nazca, near the southern coast. They were "drawn" between 2,200 and 1,400 years ago by removing some of the dark brown stones that pave the desert in a prearranged pattern, to expose the lightcolored sand beneath. Far too large to be recognized from ground level, the figures were not discovered until 1940 when an archeologist flew over them in a plane. They have survived to the present day because the Spanish missionaries could not detect and destroy them, and because there have been few, if any, heavy rains in the area for the past 2,000 years.

What purpose the figures served, and how they could have been laid out so perfectly in such huge dimension, has been the subject of unending argument. Flying saucer enthusiasts claim the lines and geometric figures are navigational aids and landing strips for space ships from other planets, and that only their occupants would have possessed the technical skills needed to lay out the huge animal representations. But this seems unlikely, for the criss-crossing lines are far too many and overlapping to be useful for navigation, and the so-called "runways" cross ravines and obstructions that would wreck craft trying to land on them. Moreover, it is impossible to imagine why visitors from space would go to such enormous trouble to leave behind pictures of birds, a monkey, lizard, spider, whale and the like.

A more plausible explanation was offered by the late German-born mathematician Maria Reiche, who studied the Nazca figures for over 30 years. The criss-crossing lines, she believed, may be markers pointing to the positions of sun, moon and stars, at significant times of the year. The animal, insect and bird figures probably represent constellations of stars as the local Indians saw them. Just as the ancient Egyptians knew the life-giving Nile would flood when the Dog Star first appeared on the dawn horizon, the Nazcans may have known the river on which they depended for irrigation would fill up when particular constellations appeared. They replicated them on the ground large enough to be seen from the heavens to assure the constellations' return. Since some of the figures are exactly like those on Nazca textiles, they could have been copied from woven patterns, with each stitch enlarged to one yard. Whatever the reason for them, the figures were obviously important to the Nazcans since it required the labor of thousands of lifetimes to complete them all.

The ancient Peruvians' concern for survival extended beyond astronomy, however. Despite the great size and population of the city of Chan-Chan, the entrance to its compounds were so narrow that only one man at a time could get through, and they often led into dead-end passages in which invaders could be trapped and slaughtered. The precautions were necessary because wars among the local Indian peoples appear to have been fought in Peru, continuously and ferociously, from its very earliest days. Fortifications ringed the irrigated valleys of the coast. In the mountains, the villages were guarded by walled strongholds on nearby peaks to which the people could flee when attacked. The battles were brutal, fought with spears, sharp wooden swords, clubs topped with heavy metal, and slings that hurled egg-sized stones with deadly accuracy.

Prisoners captured in battle could expect no mercy. Vases and friezes show them stripped naked and bleeding, being led away with ropes tied around their necks or strung through holes bored through their shoulders, to be tortured and killed. Carvings dating to 1500 B.C. at Cerro de Sechin, in the Moche valley near the coast, portray the arrogant conquerors standing beside the severed heads of their enemies, who are shown as headless torsos with bellies slit and their entrails hanging out. Equally gruesome are the stelae at the museum in Huaras, in the Andes, which depict soldiers wearing severed arms and legs around their necks, holding trophy heads in their hands. The Incas added further refinements, making flutes of the shinbones of enemy leaders, drinking cups of their skulls, and drums of the dried, hollowed-out bodies, using the corpses' arms as drumsticks.

The religions practiced by the Peruvians varied widely and are only partially understood, but ancestor worship played a large role in all of them. The bodies of chieftains, priests and nobles were mummified in a sitting position, swathed in dozens of yards of richly woven textiles and ornamented with feathered headdresses, golden masks and jewelry, before being interred. Venerated as they were in life, they were not really considered dead. Each deceased emperor continued to live in his own palace where he was served by a retinue of servants who offered him daily meals, chicha and coca, exactly as if he were alive. During religious festivals, the mummy bundles were paraded through the streets of Cuzco on litters, and when the Incas fled the Spanish they took their mummies with them.

Human sacrifice in Peru never reached the extent it did in Mexico, but it was practiced nonetheless on important ceremonial occasions or in times of crisis. Children were the favored victims because of their innocence. Found in one kingly tomb were the headless skeletons of 600 young girls "stacked like cordwood," who were slaughtered to serve the ruler in the afterlife. At the coronation of the Inca Huascar, 200 young children, selected for their health and beauty, sumptuously dressed and jangling with gold ornaments, were made drunk on chicha, and strangled.

Displayed in a refrigerated glass case in a museum in Santiago, Chile, is the remarkably preserved body of a handsome boy, about nine years old, richly clad in Inca garments. Climbers found him surrounded by his toys and little bags holding his coca leaves, hair combings, nail parings and baby teeth. He was sitting in the eternal snow atop a mountain, where he had been left to freeze to death five centuries ago, for some unknown reason. Huddled against the cold, with his head resting on his knees, he looks as though he had just fallen asleep.

The origin of the Incas* is shrouded in myth. They claimed to be descendants of the sun god. The histories pieced together shortly after the Spanish conquest reveal that they were an Andean people who arrived in Cuzco around 1300 A.D. where for decades they struggled for survival with the warring tribes around them. But in 1438, they burst out of the city and in the next 50 years, under their warrior kings Pachacuti and Topa Yupanqui, they conquered all that was known to them of the civilized world. Cuzco was considered "the navel of the universe." By the time the Spanish arrived in 1532, the Incas ruled what was then the largest empire on earth, stretching 3,000 miles from the borders of modern Colombia in the north to halfway down the coast of Chile in the south, and eastward deep into Bolivia and northern Argentina. It had a population esti-

---

*Actually there was only one Inca, the king. But since we have no other name for them, historians apply the term to the entire people.

mated at 10 million, one-third more people than lived in Spain at the time and three times as many as in England.

The Incas resembled the Romans in a great many ways. They were unbeatable military strategists and superb organizers, but not cultural innovators. They acquired their knowledge of ceramics, textiles, metallurgy, farming, even their legends and religion, from the peoples they conquered. Like the Romans, they believed they had a civilizing mission, to bring the benefits of their superior culture to other peoples. Wherever possible they won their conquests through diplomacy, persuasion or the threat of force. If any enemy resisted, only the leaders were executed, the rest of the troops were sent home. Inca soldiers were under strictest orders not kill, loot, rape or offend the vanquished population in any way.

Their king Pachacuti warned: "It is not well to kill and destroy, for in the end the (conquered people) are all ours, and we should not destroy our own." To make sure the captured provinces remained loyal, the natives were allowed to worship their own gods and be ruled by their own leaders, under control of an Inca governor, bureaucracy and garrison. The sons of the local nobility were sent to Cuzco to learn Inca ways: the use of any language but Quechua was forbidden; and if the conquered territory still remained restive, up to half the population might be moved elsewhere and replaced by people from other parts of the empire.

What evolved was probably the most regimented, workaholic, welfare state the world has ever known, providing cradle-to-grave security for every inhabitant. But the price was high. The population, both men and women, was divided into age groups, each assigned specific duties, ranging from small children who gathered plants and berries in the woods, to oldsters who taught the young. In addition, every able-bodied male owed a labor tax which he paid by serving in the army, cultivating the fields of soldiers while they were away, working on roads and construction projects, or other chores.

All land and workshops belonged to the Inca, meaning the king, who allocated them to families on the basis of need. One-third of the crops and manufactures was set aside for the community. One-third went to the emperor, the bureaucracy and priests. The remaining third, stored in bulging granaries and warehouses, was used to supply the army, to support orphans, invalids, the aged and others incapable of working, and to meet emergencies. If earthquakes, flood, drought or other calamity occurred, couriers brought the news. The authorities immediately dispatched food, clothing, household necessities and repair crews to the afflicted area from other provinces.

Nobody lacked food, clothing or shelter in the empire, but nobody enjoyed a vestige of freedom, either. Rigidly ruled by the ubiquitous Inca bureaucracy, the people were told not only where to live, but when to sow their fields, what crops to plant, which designs they were permitted to weave, how to dress, how long to wear their hair, whom to marry, and how to conduct themselves. To enforce the rules, surprise inspections were made by officials called "see alls." Lying, laziness and adultery were punishable by death. Orderliness and cleanliness were also demanded. If an inspector found a home unswept, he could order the slovenly housewife to eat the dirt in public. Every person's life belonged to the Inca. At the age of ten, the most attractive girls, the Chosen Women, were taken from their parents and sent to school to be trained, some to spend their lives in religious duties as Virgins of the Sun, others to be awarded as concubines to men the king chose to honor.

The incredible network of highways built by the Incas held the far-flung empire together and made the benevolent despotism possible. Almost 10,000 miles in total length, the highways averaged 15 feet wide in the mountains and 24 feet on the coast. They were graded, paved, equipped with stone culverts, and lined with walls, where necessary, to keep out the drifting sand. One Spanish chronicler marveled, "there is not a stone out of place, or a single weed to be seen," along the carefully tended road.

Since the roads were designed only for people on foot, the litters of nobility, marching troops and llama trains—there were no wheeled vehicles or horses to worry about—the engineers took the shortest distances feasible. The roads zig-zagged over mountains up to 17,000 feet high on thousands of stone steps. They skirted precipices on wooden beams inserted in holes in the walls, and passed through obstructing rock in tunnels, some of which spiral upwards. They crossed swamps on causeways, low-lying rivers on stone bridges, and continued across 1,000-foot-deep gorges on suspension bridges woven of ropes and vines hung from masonry pillars on the banks.

Stone *tambos*, or inns, some of them palatial, were built at distances of a day's journey, averaging 24 miles on the flat lands and 16 miles in the mountains. There travelers could dine and spend the night. Between them were frequent rest stops fitted with stone benches, walk-in bathing pools, and shrines. At intervals of approximately three-quarters of a mile, considered the maximum distance a man could run at top speed, stood small post houses from which relays of barrel-chested couriers, called *chasquis,* carried messages, and occasionally precious goods, throughout the empire. The service was so swift that the royal Inca in Cuzco could dine on fish caught 48 hours earlier in the Pacific, 300 miles away. The Inca roads remained the principal means of travel in Peru until well into the 19th century, and many are still used by Indians and hiking tourists today.

Impossible as it may seem to us, the vast Inca empire with its intricate system of government, highways, and social welfare, was managed without the use of a written language or numerals. All news, messages and reports, were sent to the capital by word of mouth, to be committed to memory by professional *camayocs* (re-memberers),. and all accounts were kept on *quipus,* collections of long, knotted strings of various lengths and colors, which worked like abacuses, each string and series of knots representing a different set of statistics.

With the aid of the *quipus,* the *camayocs* could tell down to the last pot, length of cloth or bushel of corn, how much goods was stored in each of the thousands of warehouses throughout the empire. They also kept an accurate census of farmland, domestic animals and population. A Spanish official reported to his king in Madrid that "the emperor in Cuzco has a complete record of every pair of alpaca sandals beside every bed or hammock in the realm."

It is no longer clearly understood how the records were kept, because the Spanish destroyed all *quipus* they could find without bothering to learn how to read them. Very few can be decoded today. Yet the system worked to perfection. With information provided by *quipus* and *camayocs,* relayed by fleet-footed *chasquis,* the Incas could muster armies of up to 200,000 men from various parts of the empire in a matter of days, set them marching toward an objective, and supply them with weapons, food and other necessities for months at a time—logistic feats difficult to perform even today.

That this rich, powerful and superbly organized empire could be overthrown in the year 1532 by a mere 168 Spanish adventurers was due largely to coincidence. Francisco Pizarro and his men arrived exactly at the end of a disastrous five-year civil war over succession to the throne which had decimated the armies and left the government in shambles. Split into dissident factions, some of the subject peoples and Inca nobility joined the invaders.

Remembering the ancient legend of the benevolent white men who had brought civilization to Peru, then sailed away promising to return, the Inca Atahuallpa entered the Spaniards' camp at Cajamarca at the head of unarmed troops in the belief they had come to help him. Pizarro and his men promptly slaughtered the troops and seized the Inca. Atahuallpa finally realized that, for some incomprehensible reason, the barbarians were after precious metals. He promised to fill the large hall in which he stood—it can still be visited—once with gold, and twice again with silver, if they would release him. Although he fulfilled his promise, the Spanish strangled him anyway.

With its god-king gone, the paralyzed empire disintegrated. The Spaniards enslaved the people to work the gold and silver mines. Succumbing to overwork and European diseases against which they had no immunity, the native population dropped from an estimated 10 million to one-half million in the next two centuries.

It was a tragedy from which Peru has not yet recovered.

CHAPTER 15

The Underground Cities of Turkey

(100 to 700 A.D.)

In 1963, a farmer in the village of Derinkuyu in the Cappadocian region of central Turkey discovered that a section of his cellar had fallen in, leaving a gaping hole in the earth. Descending into the cavity, he found himself in a broad underground passage that led to one of the most phenomenal archeological discoveries of recent times—a huge underground city whose existence had been forgotten for nearly a thousand years. Once home to 20,000 people, it had been dug into the bowels of the earth and inhabited by Christians during various periods between the second and tenth centuries A.D. Two years later, under the nearby village of Kaymakli, a second subterranean city of equal size was uncovered.

The reason for the cities is not hard to find. Situated at the crossroad between Europe, Asia and Africa, Cappadocia had been a battleground from time immemorial. It is also a high plateau

devoid of building stone and timber, making above-ground fortifications unfeasible. There was no place for the people to go but
underground, if they were to save themselves from slaughter, en-
slavement or forced conversion to other religions.

To explore the strange cities—at least, the sections of them that
have been lighted and opened to visitors—is to experience a fantasy. Imagine if you can a community nearly two square miles in
area, without a single window in it, extending 240 feet deep into
volcanic rock on eight levels, with 10 miles of tunnel streets
branching off in all directions. Lining the passageways are hundreds of room comprising living quarters, storerooms, wine cel-
lars, workshops, and large chambers which served as chapels,
meeting places and schoolrooms. Here and there, where several
streets come together, the passages widen into broad underground
public squares. The layouts are so labyrinthine that, were it not for
the guides and helpful arrows placed on the wall, it would be
difficult to find your way out. Visitors who enter without guides
sometimes have to be rescued.

In physical terms, the subterranean cities rank with the greatest
engineering achievements of antiquity. The volcanic rock is fairly
soft, hardening only when exposed to air. Nevertheless, it took
centuries of patient labor to chisel and scrape out the miles of
passages, rooms and air ducts, with nothing more than hand tools.
No one actually knows how long men, women and children could
have endured to live in the eternal darkness, without ever seeing the
sun or daylight. Archeologists doubt that the cities were intended as
permanent residences. They believe they were places of refuge in
which the villagers slept at night when danger threatened, moving
into them as the enemy approached. They probably stayed for only
as long as it took the invaders to plunder their homes, ravage their
fields, and depart, which would have taken a few days or weeks at
the most.

Nevertheless, the cities were occupied on and off for eight centuries, and life in them was reasonably comfortable. The passages
and rooms were lit by oil lamps and torches placed in niches in the
walls. Fresh air was provided, as it still is, by ventilation shafts

nine feet in diameter that rise 240 feet (24 stories) to the surface, with openings at each level. In fact, you nearly always feel a slight breeze in your face in Derinkuyu, coming from 52 main airshafts and hundreds of smaller one, and the temperature remains at an air-conditioned 55 degrees Farenheit (12 Celsius) both summer and winter. Fresh water was also plentiful, drawn up from wells sunk deep in the earth. Visible on the sides are the notches that held the rods from which the buckets were suspended, and the deep grooves made by the ropes over the centuries.

Each city is divided into self-contained residential sections, six in Derinkuyu and 11 in Kaymakli, which may have been added on at different times as population expanded. Families lived in suites of rooms, some of them spacious, with box beds and shelves hewn in the walls, alcoves to serve as closets and cupboards, and cavities in the floor in which jars were set to receive human wastes. Babies slept in cradles tied to loops in the rock. Each residential section was served by one or more communal kitchens, built around fire-pits in the center, or stove-like fireplaces in the wall, with chimneys to carry off the smoke. Here women gathered at mealtimes to carry hot food to their families and perhaps take turns doing the cooking. Lining the walls of the kitchens are glazed, jar-shaped niches to store wine, oil and food, some of which held thousand-year-old kernels of wheat when found. Nearby are smaller rooms housing the millstones on which the grain was ground. In the corner of one kitchen stands a large, round stone with egg-shaped indentations on its surface in which spices were pounded with pestles.

Although green vegetables were probably scarce, the people enjoyed a varied diet. Apples, pears, onions, oranges and melons, can be stored in the cool vaults for months without spoiling. They supplied the vitamins needed for the long spells underground. Meat, milk, and perhaps eggs, were also available. Large byres occupied the topmost levels of the cities. Hollowed in the walls were feed bins for cattle, sheep, goats and chickens.

One curious feature of the cities is that they had facilities for producing far more wine than the inhabitants could possibly have consumed. Cappadocian wine was famous in antiquity, the prov-

ince's major export, and the underground dwellers are believed to
have made and stored it for sale, when conditions permitted. The
grapes, harvested on the surface, were dropped through a chute to
the topmost level, then carried in baskets to shallow stone basins on
other levels where they were treaded out by human feet. The juice
flowed from the troughs through gutters and pipes carved through
the walls into huge storage vats in the rock where it aged and
fermented.

Despite the amenities, the cities were not built for comfort, but
for defense. To get from one level to another, one must climb in a
doubled-over position, through low corridors or staircases too narrow to use weapons, or admit more than one person at a time. It is
no place for claustrophobes. Situated at the end of each corridor are
guard posts fitted with peepholes through which an intruder could
be seen coming. Alongside each guard post is a niche holding a
huge stone wheel, up to seven feet wide and two feet thick. In case
of danger, the wheel, which weighs two or three tons, could be
rolled across the passageway into an indentation in the opposite
wall, completely sealing the interior.

Although the wheels were installed over 1,000 years ago, they
are so well rounded and balanced that I could roll many of them
back and forth without aid. Even if an enemy managed to dig his
way around the first wheel—and there is evidence that invaders
tried to do so—it would do little good, since a few feet farther on
was another wheel, then another, and another. There are reputed to
be 800 in Derinkuyu alone.

With fresh air and water assured, and the storerooms on the
lower levels stocked with sufficient food to withstand sieges of a
year or more, the cities were virtually impregnable. The occupants
could not be smoked out, for the air was drawn in from below
through hundreds of hidden ducts. The shafts where the air exited
branched out at the surface in dozens of apertures disguised to look
like animal burrows, not all of which can be located, much less
plugged up. There were underground hospitals for the sick. The
dead, too, were provided for, with crypts scattered throughout the

communities in which bodies could be piled up until they could be taken to the surface for burial.

But the occupants of the shelters took no chances. If an enemy did manage to penetrate all the defenses into the heart of the city, which never appears to have happened, there were numerous secret tunnels leading to hidden ravines through which the inhabitants could flee. One escape passage in Derinkuyu consists of a staircase that spirals 240 feet up through the rock. Another is a tunnel six miles long that connects Derinkuyu with the neighboring subterranean city of Kaymakli. Not yet open to visitors, the passage is reported to be wide enough for three people to walk abreast.

Even finding the cities would have been difficult for an invader. In place of the broad portals through which visitors enter today, their original entrances were small, unobtrusive holes, similar to dozens of others in the rock, and unlikely to be found unless one knew exactly where and what they were. Like the air ducts, the outlets to the chimneys from the kitchens were dispersed so that little smoke would be seen. The original excavators took still another precaution. They avoided creating vast piles of the rubble dug out of the rock, which would have betrayed the existence of the subterranean dwellings. Instead, they transported the debris for long distances, scattering it over the terrain or dumping it into rivers where it would be unnoticed. The safeguards worked so well that the cities remained undiscovered for nearly a thousand years.

The people, safe in their underground refuges, led a well-organized existence. Women took care of their families, the cooking and household chores, and perhaps helped with the wine-making and the livestock. Children went to school and doubtless played in the dimly-lit passageways. Men tended to their weapons, fashioned new ones in charcoal forges that have been found in the workrooms, and took turns standing guard at the entrances to the connecting tunnels. Some doubtless might venture to the surface at night to spy on the enemy. And everyone prayed six times a day, as their sainted bishop, Basil the Great, had ordered them to do. The Cappadocians were famed for their Christian fervor. A large room with benches carved in the rock which lies just beyond the entrance in Derinkuyu, is believed to have been a training school for missionaries. There are religious chapels to be found on every level of the cities, with altars and baptismal fonts still in place, and here and there, crude crosses have been scratched into the walls of corridors.

The largest, most elaborate rooms in the cities are the churches, which may have also served as administrative and military headquarters, since the communities are believed to have been governed by priests. Kaymakli's main church, located on the fourth level down, 60 feet below the surface, is an unusual structure, adorned with twin apses and Maltese crosses carved in the walls. The principal church at Derinkuyu, lying seven levels beneath the surface, 200 feet down, is a splendid chamber. Excavated in the form of a cross, it is 80 feet long, 32 feet wide and 11 feet high. Opposite the church lies another impressive hall adorned with stone columns which is believed to have served as a council chamber, court room, and perhaps a prison. Holes bearing the marks of chains can be found bored in two of the columns. They are called the "pillars of punishment" because malefactors are believed to have been shackled to them for their misdeeds.

The Cappadocians had turned to Christianity very early. The borders of their province were only 150 miles north of Tarsus, the birthplace of St. Paul. The Roman writer Libanius described them as an uncouth, but gentle, people who "smell of fried fish and stew, and say to everyone they meet, 'I love you,'" which was a common Christian greeting at the time. But as followers of Christ, they had aroused the hostility of the normally tolerant Roman emperors who could not abide a faith that refused to recognize their divinity. Many Cappadocians were martyred. To strengthen their resolve, St. Peter addressed a letter to them and other threatened Christian communities—it is now part of the New Testament— in which he advised: "Forasmuch as Christ had suffered for us in the flesh, arm yourself likewise with the same mind; for he that suffered in the flesh has ceased from sin." (I Peter, 4,1)

As the persecutions mounted and Persian armies invaded Cappadocia during the second century A.D., the Christians began to go underground. They were not the first to do so. From the archeological evidence, the topmost level at Derinkuyu had been occupied by Hittites 2,000 years earlier, and subsequently by other peoples. The military commander Xenephon, who led his mercenary band of Greek soldiers through the region in their flight back to their homeland in 401 B.C., wrote in his celebrated account of the retreat, the *Anabasis:* "The dwellings in these villages are underground; they have entrances like the mouth of a well, but the rooms are spacious. They keep stores of corn, rice, vegetables and barley wine, in large jars. The livestock live in separate caves; the men descend by ladders."

The early Christians expanded the caves into small subterranean towns, abandoning them when Christianity won official recognition, then reoccupying them again during the frequent wars that followed. The worst onslaughts the Cappadocians had to endure occurred between the years 650 to 1050 A.D., when the marauding Moslem Arabs repeatedly raided the province. Not strong enough to retain what they captured, the Arabs' strategy was to strike, plunder, slaughter the inhabitants, and ride away before the Roman legions arrived. It was during these troubled centuries, with their populations at a peak, that the refuges expanded into the subterranean metropolises we see today.

Since the discovery of Derinkuyu and Kaymakli a quarter-century ago, 36 additional subterranean cities have been located, including one near the village of Ozkonok that is estimated to have accommodations for 60,000 people. Adding their capacities together, archeologists calculate that as many as a half-million people lived underground at one time or another in Cappadocia. A more striking testimony to the indomitability of the human spirit would be difficult to find.

However, these were not the only strange communities to appear during that era, for Cappadocia had turned to monasticism on a scale never known before. Tens of thousands of men and women flocked to the religious orders, along with many lay families who chose to live and work with them. True to local tradition, they put their buildings below ground. For protection, they chose some of the most bizarre settings to be found on earth, inaccessible valleys weirder than moonscapes, where eons of wind, rain and vanished rivers had sculpted the volcanic rock into gorges, pyramids, castles, obelisks and conical needles up to 100 feet high, called "fairy chimneys," some with rocks perched on their pinnacles. These monastic villages are smaller than the underground cities. They were dug into the earth above ground level, rather than below it, and the rooms have windows.

The most famous community is at Gorême, a few miles north of Kaymakli and 200 miles southeast of Ankara, the Turkish capital. Gorême lies in a large rocky amphitheater protected by narrow passes. The peaks, crags and fairy chimneys that make up the community are little more than stone shells. Their interiors had been hollowed out from top to bottom over the centuries into hundreds of rooms, chapels, passages and staircases. Secreted in the cliffs are monasteries, convents for women, and apartment houses for lay families. The rooms are furnished with tables, seats, beds, shelves and closets, all carved in the rock, as well as lavatories supplied with running water. There are communal kitchens and large refectories with individual rock benches for diners. They sat at stone tables indented with recesses for platters, hot pots, runnels for gravy, and bowls in which the diners crushed grapes for their juice. The outer walls of the habitations are honeycombed with thousands of cotes for pigeons, whose droppings were used to fertilize the fields and vineyards below.

But the glory of Gorême lies in its churches. Hidden in practically every cone and pinnacle, they crowd the valley, often lying side by side, in clusters, or on top of each other. No two of the churches are alike. Some are entered through crude holes in the rock, others through beautifully carved doorways, or by perilous climbs up stone staircases worn smooth by centuries of use. The impressive interiors of the churches are carved in the shape of crosses or basilicas, with vaulted ceilings, domes, cupolas, columns and arches, and often galleries two stories high.

Multicolored frescoes cover practically every inch of the church walls. Some have faded or have been defaced, but many glow with vivid and imaginative pictures of saints, patriarchs, and biblical scenes designed to raise the spirits and reinforce the faith of the worshippers. Odd folk myths are also portrayed on the walls. The Devil is seen attending the Last Supper; the newborn Christ is shown emerging from an egg; the Jesus the Magi meet in Bethlehem is sometimes portrayed as a youth or grown man instead of an infant.

Painted over a period of five centuries, the scenes range in style from archaic depictions that pay little attention to anatomy, proportion or perspective, to the most sophisticated achievements of Byzantine art. There are also impressionist renditions that look modern enough to have been done by Picasso or Chagall. The most memorable Gorême murals include the earliest known Last Supper in the so-called Dark Church, which is as inspiring in its way as the one painted several centuries later by Leonardo da Vinci; the scene in the Church of the Snake showing the Cappadocian-born St. George spearing a dragon that looks very much like a boa constrictor; and, in the Church of the Apple, the figure of St. Christopher holding in his palm a world that is as round as an apple, indicating that these early Christians did not believe the earth was flat.

Despite the haven they offered to harried Christians, and the good works performed, the religious communities did not enjoy a quiet existence. Their problems came not from foreign invaders, but from fellow Christians, the Iconoclasts (image smashers), who held that the Bible forbade the portrayal of the human form and regarded the worship of saints and relics as idolatry. They also opposed the growing wealth and influence of the monasteries. In 730 A.D., the Byzantine emperor in Constantinople, Leo the Iconoclast, ordered the removal of all images and murals depicting people from all the churches of his realm and condemned the veneration of saints. The struggle rocked the empire for more than a century. Monasteries were closed, secularized or converted to barracks. Monks and other supporters of icons who refused to obey the edicts were excommunicated, imprisoned, flogged or condemned to death. Nuns were given the choice of marriage or torture.

Cappadocia escaped the worst of the oppression because of its frontier location, far removed from Constantinople, the capital of the Eastern Roman Empire. A few churches removed their statues and overpainted their murals with crosses, foliage, landscapes or geometrical designs, but most did not. Before the persecution finally ended in the year 843, over 50,0000 anti-iconoclasts had fled to Cappadocia, taking shelter in the grotto communities and underground cities. Among them were hundreds of religious painters who resumed their work to make the province the world's leading repository of Byzantine art.

In 1071 A.D., the Turks finally captured Cappadocia, which they have retained ever since. They tolerated Christians so long as they paid their taxes. With the centuries of warfare ended, the underground cities fell into disuse, eventually to be forgotten completely. The grotto communities, however, continued to flourish. Many of the churches remained in use until 1924, when the Christians, practically all Greek, were exchanged for the Turks living in Greece. Since the 1950s, the Turkish authorities have done what they can to preserve the ancient sites. When French priest Guillaume de Jerphanion visited Goreme in 1920, the churches were so filled with debris that only the ceilings and upper walls were visible. Today, they have nearly all been cleared.

But it has been impossible to protect all of the nearly 1,000 ancient churches in Cappadocia. Many of the honeycombed cliffs have eroded and collapsed leaving the interiors of the churches exposed to the elements. Thousand-year-old frescoes have been disfigured by graffiti, obliterated by fire, or gouged out in the search for hidden treasure. Other churches are used today as stables, dovecotes, granaries and workshops. The rooms in the Gibralter-like volcanic rock at Uchisar have been wired for electricity, fitted with glass windows, and converted into apartments. Turkish families live in many of the ancient fairy chimney dwellings. Others have been turned into restaurants and hotels.

The subterranean cities, too, have returned to partial life. Forty thousand tourists visit them annually. Villagers have dug private corridors to the rooms beneath their houses, which they use for fruit storage and animal shelters, as their ancestors did in Xenephon's time. One of the large rooms under Kaymakli has been converted into a discotheque adorned with peasant rugs and colored lights, where visitors sip drinks and listen to the music, unaware that the cubicles in which they sit are ancient burial vaults.

CHAPTER 16

The Dazzling Treasure Caves of China

(366 to 700 A.D.)

Of all of China's myriad archeological treasures, few are more magnificent, and none more fascinating, than those hidden in the ancient man-made caves of Dunhuang, Yunkang and Longmen. It is not surprising that the caves are less well known than the Great Wall, the Imperial Tombs, and the other marvels of the country. They were remote, inaccessible until recently, and had been neglected for so many centuries that the Chinese themselves had almost forgotten their existence. Not until the government opened the caves to visitors in the late 1970s have they been recognized as among the richest repositories of ancient art on earth.

Dunhuang, an arid, windswept, and sparsely inhabited oasis on the edge of the Gobi Desert, 1,200 air miles from Beijing, is not a place you would choose for its charm. But during the 1,500 years of its glory, between the first and 16th centuries A.D., it was one of the busiest and most famous trading centers in Asia, a lush green island in the desert, surrounded by irrigated fields and orchards. The city teemed with travelers, hostelries and merchants speaking 17 languages. For this was the eastern terminus of the famous Silk Road that led across the Roof of the World to the Mediterranean.

From here camel caravans began their long journeys westward laden with the Chinese silk so coveted in Europe, as well as furs, cinnamon, exquisite ceramics and lacquer work. They brought back with them woolens, linens, ivory, coral, amber and, far more important, new ideas and religions. Manichean and Nestorian Christian missionaries arrived in the seventh century, Moslems in the eighth, and in the ninth century came an influx of Jews who flourished in the eastern city of Kaifeng for centuries, and still retain their identity although they have lost nearly all memory of their religion.

In the first century A.D., missionaries from India brought in Buddhism. Promising hope, remission of sins and an afterlife, Buddhism replaced fatalistic Confucianism and Taoism as the most popular religion in China. It transformed Chinese art, morals and everyday life, as profoundly as Christianity changed Europe.

The Buddhist faith was ancient by the time it reached China. It was founded in northern India six centuries before Christ by a prince named Siddartha, also known as Sakyamuni, Gautama and other names, who gave up his position, family and worldly possessions in the search for enlightenment. The Master taught that to escape from the eternal cycle of reincarnation, suffering and death, and attain immortality in Nirvana, blessed oblivion, the people must surrender all worldly desires, including the desire for life itself, and spend their lives in comtemplation of the Divine.

As originally propounded, Buddhism required a spirituality and self-discipline that few can attain. But it soon broke up into a variety of sects that people could more easily assimilate. The Mahayana Buddhist (Greater Vehicle) doctrine which reached China was a religion vastly different than the Master had envisioned, requiring little sacrifice or self-denial. The doctrine held that during eons of time countless worlds had come into existence and were destroyed, and that the historic Buddha of the past, Sakyamuni, had been preceded by other earthly Buddhas, and would be followed by Maitreya, the Buddha of the Future, a messiah who would someday come to the aid of suffering mankind.

The Mahayana heavens were filled with disciples, angels, gods, demons and *bodhisattvas*, or saints, who deferred their entrance into Nirvana in order to help humanity. Two of these saints were particularly important: Amitabha, ruler of the blissful Pure Land of the West into which devout Buddhists could be reborn simply by appealing to him from the depths of their hearts; and Avaloki-teshvara—Kuan-yin to the Chinese—who was originally a male, but was gradually transformed into a compassionate female ma-donna who answered people's prayers in this life.

In the year 366 A.D., the pious monks of Dunhuang began dig-ging caves into the hard clay of a nearby 140-foot-high river bank to serve as shrines for pilgrims and for merchants starting out on the perilous Silk Road. The work continued for the next nine centuries. Financed by kings, nobles and rich merchants, seeking to earn merit in heaven, the grottos ranged in size from cubicles holding a single image to great caverns, three stories high and 60 feet wide, that could accommodate scores of worshipers at a time.

No one knows how many caves existed, since many have col-lapsed or were destroyed by people who lived in them during the centuries after the abandonment of the Silk Road. When British archeologist Aurel Stein visited the site in 1907, it was guarded by a single illiterate monk who allowed him to cart off to the British Museum eight wagonloads of priceless ancient manuscripts and paintings. Similar hauls were made by French, Russian and Ameri-can art dealers, who also took with them a large quantity of other treasures. Many of the marvelous statues, paintings, friezes and murals you see in American, European and Japanese museums and private collections were looted from the caves of Dunhuang.

In 1962, finally realizing that the grottoes are among the richest art treasures on earth, the Chinese government placed them under state protection and later launched a program to restore them. Of the 492 caves that survive in Dunhuang, 53 are open to the public, connected by a five-tiered walkway clinging to the face of the cliff.

A visit to the caves is an esthetic experience unlike any you have ever known. The guidebooks suggest that you devote three days to it. But actually three weeks would not suffice, for each cave is a miniature Sistine Chapel, with every inch of its walls and ceiling blazing with frescoes, murals and colored clay statuary. The sculptures, molded of clay and then painted, tend to be garish. But the paintings are superb. Protected from the elements and preserved by the dry desert air, some look almost as fresh as the day they were finished, others are faded with the patina of centuries. Sweeping across the walls and ceilings of the caverns in a kaleidoscope of fantasy and realism that holds the viewer spellbound are the lively figures of flying angels and bejeweled saints, of arrogant kings and snarling warriors with their feet planted on squirming demons, of disciples riding miraculously through the sky in chariots drawn by lions, dragons and elephants. Interspersed among them are life-sized portraits of donors, both male and female, with their names and titles carefully inscribed beside them.

Representing the changing art styles of a millennium, no two caves are alike. The earliest figures are recognizably copies of Greek, Roman, Persian and Indian prototypes, gradually becoming Oriental as native artists replaced their foreign tutors. At first the Chinese figures are ascetic and emaciated, as profoundly religious in feeling as the pictures of saints in early Christian basilicas. Later they become robust and muscular, full of the joy of life, painted with a knowledge of perspective which western artists would not discover for another thousand years. Toward the end, the figures are almost impressionist in appearance, delineated with the vigorous, eloquent brushstrokes of a Cezanne.

There are literally countless figures of Buddha—a reputed 10,000 in one cave alone. He is shown standing, praying, seated cross-legged in meditation, preaching to the enraptured multitudes, and reclining on his left side, as the Buddhist scriptures relate, "on the night he turned in his sleep and quietly passed into the great silence." Varying from 50 feet to less than an inch in size, each

Buddha is framed in an aureole representing the sacred flame and bears the characteristic signs of divinity—the head surrounded by a halo, surmounted by a topknot or protruberance indicating super-human wisdom, large ears and the circle on the forehead, denoting a third eye, which enable him to hear and see all that goes on in the world, and on his face, always, the seraphic, almost Mona Lisa smile of serenity.

Like the wall paintings in the tombs of the pharaohs, the Dunhuang murals also depict in vivid detail how the ancient Chinese lived, worked and amused themselves; the pagodas, palaces and houses they built; how they coiffured their hair; and the clothes they wore, down to the slit skirts of the women. There are colorful scenes of weddings, funerals, banquets, and children at play, of fishing, farming, livestock breeding and pottery making, of criminals in the stocks, nuns being tonsured, and physicians healing the sick. There are fascinating glimpses of a man and woman in the act of love, of scantily dressed dancers, of acrobats performing their feats, and of orchestras absorbed in the music they are playing, including one in which the flutist keeps time with his big toe.

There are also marvelous portrayals of merchants returning from a journey, of a caravan being robbed by bandits, of troops marching with drums beating and banners flying, and of a violent battle with soldiers charging and arrows flying, amid fallen horses and slain men. Among the ancient paintings are some that would be considered masterpieces in any culture. They include scenes of a groom struggling to hold a rearing horse; a frightened deer fleeing from a mounted hunter; a sumptuously dressed donor attended by servants bearing swords, feather fans, and an umbrella to shield him from the sun; and a genre scene in a butcher shop showing a bound sheep awaiting slaughter, meat hanging from hooks, and a butcher carving a carcass while his dog waits open-mouthed for scraps to be thrown him.

Perhaps the most interesting paintings at Dunhuang are the many Jataka murals, illustrated parables describing the good deeds performed by the Buddha during his incarnated lives before he was reborn a prince. They are arranged like modern comic strips to present a connected story. One tells of a prince who threw himself from a cliff so that a starving lioness and her cubs could feed on his body; another, of a king who fed hungry doves with slices of his own flesh; a third relates the famous tale of the 500 robbers whose eyes were gouged out for their crimes. But as the pictures show, the stories all have happy endings. The self-sacrificing prince and king earn Buddhahood for their sacrifices, and the 500 robbers have their eyesight restored when they appeal to heaven and become monks.

The paintings on which the Dunhuang artists lavished their most exuberant efforts, and were undoubtedly the most popular with worshipers, were the 125 large murals depicting the Pure Land of the West, which Mahayana Buddhists hoped to enter when they died. The Pure Land was far different from the Nirvana envisioned by Buddha, where the soul itself is annihilated. It was a place of ineffable beauty, happiness and delight, enlivened by festivals, banquets, music and dancing, where the blessed inhabitants clad in heavenly raiment wandered through jeweled forests to the most sumptuous dwelling places the imagination of the artists could conceive.

Although Dunhuang remained popular until the closing of the Silk Road, it was a long way from the rest of China, and as Buddhism spread eastward, more accessible places of meditation and pilgrimage were needed. In 460 A.D., the Wei rulers of northern China ordered a new set of caves to be dug into a sandstone cliff at Yunkang, 10 miles from their capital at Datong, near the center of China. Working under fearfully hard conditions, thousands of sculptors and stone masons, many of them war prisoners, labored for 35 years to chisel out of the rock cliff 53 enormous and numerous smaller cave temples.

Before restoration began in the 1970s, the caverns were in deplorable condition. Local peasants stabled their mules, and stored their farm implements and coffins amid the 1,500-year-old statues. During the Cultural Revolution, the local militia had to stand guard to prevent them from being destroyed by the rampaging Red Guards. Because most of the wooden temples that originally protected the porticos had long since burned down, the sculpture in some of the grottos were badly weatherworn, and others had collapsed. But thanks largely to the debris and weeds that blocked their entrances, the rest were all preserved, although 1,400 of the images were damaged or missing. Foreigners who managed to reach the caves before 1949 had paid the natives to chop out the friezes, statues or heads they wanted, often with the connivance of the authorities. But with 51,000 sculptures remaining, the damage is hardly noticeable.

The caves at Yunkang were built largely as a state enterprise, rather than by the efforts of individuals. Consequently, they are far larger and grander than those at Dunhuang—cathedrals, as compared to chapels. And though their interiors do not glow with the same exuberant warmth as the painted clay walls of Dunhuang, the splendor of the sculptured ornamentation that covers their stone surfaces is overwhelming. The colossal figures of Buddha that fill the first five caves constructed are actually portraits of Wei emperors. It is a thrill to stand in semi-darkness at the foot of one of these immense figures, your eyes traveling upwards until, with your head almost bent over backwards, you see the face of the Buddha, illuminated by a window, smiling down at you from a height of 50 feet. One can imagine the emotions the sight must have aroused a thousand years ago in the hearts of worshipers, to whom the figure was sacred.

More appealing esthetically, however, are the caves supported by square, multi-tiered stupas, or columns, in their centers, around which worshipers walked in ritual circumambulation. Carved in relief on each of the four sides of the columns are deep niches holding statues of Buddhas of the Past, Present and Future. The figures are endowed with an indescribable air of introspection and detachment that seems to fill the cave with timeless tranquility. An amalgam of Greco-Roman, Indian and native styles, the statues are among the most inspired and abstractly beautiful religious sculptures ever created.

Among the more intriguing depictions molded in stone are those of performing acrobats; of musicians playing panpipes, guitars, flutes and drums; of a Buddha who wears a stone cape with a thousand tiny Buddhas woven into the design; and exquisite friezes of water weeds, fish and birds, three of which were carried off to New York's Metropolitan Museum. But the best known sculpture at Yunkang—in all of China, in fact—rests in a cave whose outer walls collapsed seven centuries ago, leaving the 55-foot-high Buddha staring out across the countryside. Its enigmatic smile has been described as expressing "secret irony, full of indulgence toward the spectacle of universal folly and vanity." You may see the figure and the smile in practically any Chinese travel folder.

In the year 494 A.D., the Northern Wei dynasts moved their capital from Datong to the more centrally located city of Loyang, and began digging a new set of shrines into a rock cliff at nearby Longmen (Dragon Gate). It was excruciatingly difficult work to carve the huge grottos into the dense gray limestone, which is harder than the sandstone of Yunkang, with nothing more than hammers and chisels. According to the records, it took 25 years and 800,000 working days to hollow out and decorate the most ornate cave. Yet, by the time the digging ended four centuries and seven dynasties later, the nearby hills were honeycombed with over 1,300 caves, containing an estimated 100,000 statues, both free standing and in relief, and 3,600 stone tablets whose inscriptions provide a detailed history of the period and some of the finest examples of ancient Chinese calligraphy in existence.

The statuary and friezes of Longmen represent the supreme achievement of Chinese sculpture. Apparently using living models for inspiration, the unknown artists attained a sensuous refinement and grace in the molding of the figures and the drapery of their garments equal to the finest work of classical Greece. Never again were Chinese sculptors to produce such masterpieces. But few sites in China were more viciously despoiled by art thieves. A thousand heads of images which pious worshipers had dedicated to the divinities are missing from one cave alone. To see what are probably the two finest friezes created at Longmen, you must visit museums in New York and Kansas City.

But what remains is still magnificent. The Buddhas and saints at Longmen attain a spirituality unknown elsewhere. The feet of some of them have been polished smooth by the hands of the generations of students, who came to pray for help in passing their exams. The walls of the oldest cave, 36 feet high, are lined from top to bottom with the full-length figures of political administrators and generals. Their faces, full of character, strength and wrinkles, are almost certainly portraits of real people. The Medical Cave has become the most popular grotto. Its walls are inscribed with over a hundred prescriptions for ailments ranging from stomach ache and piles to madness. Chinese visitors often jot down the prescriptions apparently for use, although pharmacologists warn that many are poisonous.

By far the most dramatic sight at Longmen is the huge recess open to the sky in the center of the cliff, in which sits a colossal image of the Buddha Vairocana, the supreme cosmic Buddha, flanked by monks, saints and gods. Half-naked, bulging-muscled guardian kings protect the deity on either side. Their ferocious expressions and contorted poses were designed to frighten away evil spirits. The startling violence of the figures are a fitting tribute to the cruel and lecherous dowager empress Wu Tse-tien, who ordered the tableau constructed after slaughtering her way to power in the eighth century A.D.

With the completion of the Longmen complex, the practice of building underground shrines declined. But they left a rich legacy. Many of the sculptural, decorative and painting styles that were later adopted by Japan and other Oriental countries, and which influence western art today, were born by flickering lamplight in the darkness of these ancient Chinese caves.

CHAPTER 17

The Strange Disappearance of America's "Ancient Ones"

(700 to 1300 A.D.)

In the winter of 1888, cowboys Richard Wetherill and Charlie Mason set out to search for cattle in the desolate Mesa Verde of southern Colorado. They stopped to peer into a canyon during a snowstorm and blinked in disbelief. They thought they saw, shimmering through the falling snow, the outlines of large buildings where no buildings ought to have been.

Tethering their horses, the men climbed down into the canyon on tree trunks. In a large recess halfway to the bottom of the cliff, they entered a splendid little city of multistoried stone dwellings, tall towers, small plazas, and circular kivas used for worship. Inside the structures they found pottery, stone tools and metates used to grind corn, and the ashes of cooking fires that had lain untouched for 600 years. The site, now famed as Cliff Palace, was one of the habitations of the most remarkable, and mysterious, prehistoric Indians of what is now the United States.

We do not know what the people called themselves, since they disappeared abruptly in the 13th century A.D. The later-arriving Navajos referred to them as Anasazi, the Ancient Ones. They occupied a domain larger than California spread across the Four Corners area of the southwest, where the borders of Colorado, Utah, New Mexico and Arizona, meet. It was, and still is, a bleak desert region, an unlikely place for primitive farmers to hope to do more than scratch out a subsistence. Yet the culture the Anasazi developed was brilliant. The engineering and architecture of the stone cities they left behind are so impressive that early archeologists could not believe they had been built by local Indians, and attributed them to Egyptians, Phoenicians, or to the Toltecs of Mexico 1,500 miles to the south.

There is no longer any question that the Anasazi were native to the region since their cultural evolution can be traced back for millennia. Over 60,000 of their sites have been mapped so far, and a great many more may still lie undiscovered. The reason so many of the buildings are so well preserved after centuries of blast furnace summer heat and buckling winter cold is partly due to their sturdy construction, but principally to the superstitions of the later Indian tribes who shunned them for fear of angering the spirits of the Ancient Ones.

Many might still be intact were it not for the avarice of white residents who ripped them apart, as they still do, to recover the valuable artifacts they held. Also to blame was the ignorance of early archeologists who excavated with dynamite, fueled their campfires with ancient roof logs whose rings are now used to establish the dates of the buildings, and did other incalculable damage. But even in their ruined state, the monuments speak to us with an eloquence that no words can express. The largest Anasazi concentrations, and some of the most notable ruins, lie in the Mesa Verde and Hovenweep regions of southwestern Colorado and adjoining Utah. Others are in the Kayenta territory straddling the

Arizona-Utah border, with a smaller but marvelous group of sites in picturesque Canyon de Chelly in eastern Arizona.

By far the most important Anasazi center, however, is in Chaco, a canyon 15 miles long and a mile wide in northwestern New Mexico, where around the year 1050 A.D., the people experienced a burst of creative energy so unprecedented, and sudden, that archeologist refer to it as the "Chaco phenomenon." In the space of a few decades, they constructed a complex of 12 elaborate towns lying within a few bowshots of each other, which blossomed into the religious, political and commercial capital of the Anasazi world. Together with its suburbs, the canyon held an estimated population of 6,000, extraordinarily large for a stone age desert society.

The first city dwellers north of Mexico, the people lived in multistoried apartment houses containing hundreds of rooms, which were not equaled in size in the United States until larger ones were erected in New York eight centuries later. Why such concentrated living quarters were necessary with so much empty land available is a mystery. Each of the Great Houses, as they are called, was constructed of as many as 30 million blocks of sandstone, and up to 30,000 pine, fir and spruce roof beams, which had to be hauled for distances of 35 miles or more without the aid of draft animals or wheeled vehicles. The masonry is splendid. The stone blocks were meticulously chiseled to shape with crude stone tools, cemented together with a thin layer of mud to form an attractively patterned wall, then lovingly veneered with smaller stones. Esthetically pleasing, the buildings harmonize so well with their surroundings that they look like part of the natural scenery. But the Anasazi were never satisfied with their accomplishments. Compulsive builders, they were forever adding to and remodeling their pueblos. Beneath the floor of some of the structures often lie the remains of several older ones.

Grandest of the Great Houses was Pueblo Bonito (the names are all of Spanish or later Indian origin). A D-shaped structure covering three acres, its five terraced stories held some 800 rooms. Although the building took 50 years to complete, according to the tree ring dates of its roof timbers, it was pre-planned from the beginning, architects point out. The foundation walls were built massively to bear the weight of the multiple stories above them; the walls of the succeeding stories were made progressively thinner and lighter. As in a modern steel-reinforced concrete skyscraper, each floor became a working platform on which the next one was built. The upper apartments were reached by means of wooden ladders stretching from the roof of one story to the terrace of the next.

Kivas, of which there are 37 in Pueblo Bonito alone, were among the most important features of Anasazi life. In addition to their religious functions, they are believed to have served as club-houses for the men. (Since Anasazi society is thought to have been matriarchal, men may have been mere boarders and providers in their wives' homes.) Constructed in imitation of the underground dwellings of the earlier Anasazi, the kivas are usually circular in shape, covered with a beehive roof of timbers on top of which earth and rubble was packed to form a public patio. Each kiva had a fire pit for warmth and a sacred hole in the ground, called a *sipapu* by modern Hopi Indians, through which spirits passed from the under-world. There was also a foot drum, a low-walled rectangular pit covered with boards on which men danced.

Spectators sat on a circular stone bench built into the wall to watch the ceremonies. Ventilation was provided by underground stone ducts through which fresh air flowed from the outside. The only entrance was a ladder through a hole in the roof. Niches in the kiva walls served as repositories for religious objects and valu-ables. Most of them have long since been looted, but one over-looked sealed vault in Chaco yielded a wealth of jewelry, including 17,000 beads of turquoise and shell in strands up to 17 feet long.

Near Pueblo Bonito stands another remarkable village, Chetro Ketl, whose three-story-high wall, still intact after 900 years, is almost as long as a football field. Its most intriguing feature is a cloister-like porch supported by columns, whose spaces were later blocked up, which is reminiscent architecturally of the far distant Toltec and Mayan porches of Mesoamerica.

A third structure, Casa Rinconada, is the largest kiva in Chaco, over 63 feet in diameter and 15 feet deep. Its acoustics are so good that a whisper can be heard form one end to the other and a sneeze is amplified to a roar. Since the Great Kiva can hold hundreds of people, archeologists believe it may have been a communal temple, or theater, for the whole of Chaco. And like a modern theater with trapdoors under the stage, Casa Rinconada had a secret underground passage through which masked and feathered priests could crawl to spring from the smoke before the spectators like emanations from another world.

Curiously, in no two of the Chaco villages are the architecture, masonry and layouts exactly alike. This leads to the speculation that rather than being a single people speaking a common language, the Anasazi may have been a confederation of tribes, sharing a common culture but speaking as many different dialects as do the present day Pueblo Indians, who are their descendants. Thus, the villages, constructed over the span of 150 years, may have been built by different groups of people who followed their own architectural traditions. The masonry of the Kin Kletso, the last Chaco pueblo erected, is in the distinctive style of the Mesa Verde Anasazi who lived 200 miles to the north.

The Great Houses were probably built by their residents. The Chacoans also constructed and maintained irrigation systems, roads and other communal undertakings. Political organization of a high order would be needed to supervise such public works and to adjudicate the disputes of the many communities squeezed into so small an area. Anthropologists believe that a hierarchal social structure existed, in which priests, elders and skilled engineers, directed the work of the common people. The buildings of the villages surrounding Chaco were much cruder and their rooms smaller than those of the Great Houses, indicating that the capital itself may have been home principally to officials and the privileged.

Each Chaco family occupied a suite or rooms, some of which were used for storage, turkey pens, trash disposal or, occasionally, burial chambers. The walls of the living rooms which were of larger proportions, up to 12 feet long and eight feet high, were finished with white plaster and often decorated with frescoes, whose traces can still be seen in places. Windows and doors, some built in a T-shape, were kept small to reduce heat loss in winter. Warmth was provided by open fires in the rooms which left the ceilings black with soot. As there are no chimneys, the fires must have filled the interior with smoke.

Their burial remains reveal that the Anasazi were stocky people, the men averaging 5 feet, 4 inches in height, the women two inches shorter, about the same size as Europeans of that era. Men wore their hair shorter, in long braids, women cropped theirs short, using the rest to make string. As with most primitive people, they suffered numerous ailments. Grit from the stone metates on which their cornmeal was ground wore their teeth to the gums, causing horrendous dental abscesses. They also suffered from arthritis and other bone diseases, forcing them to use wooden crutches that have been found. Fractures, probably caused by falls from canyon walls or the upper stories of the pueblos, were also common. Fire was an even greater peril, since the wooden ceilings of the dwellings were readily flammable. The remains of almost 50 children were found in the charred debris of a kiva at Salmon, a Chaco colony 50 miles to the north. They had probably been playing in the courtyard above the roof of the kiva when it collapsed.

The Anasazi apparently took care of the aged and crippled members of the family who could no longer work. They treated their dead with reverence, binding the bodies in fetal positions, surrounded by the adornments, tools, pottery, sandals and other goods they would need in the afterlife. The dead were interred in caves, cracks in the cliffs, in sealed rooms in pueblos, or in trash heaps where the digging was easy. But these account for only five percent of the many thousands of bodies that should have been found in Chaco, and what happened to the rest is still another mystery.

A greater puzzle is why, with so many more favorable sites available, the Chacoans should have chosen to settle in a desolate, thin-soiled and arid canyon, lacking a running river, springs, forests, or even much vegetation. One theory was that the climate and resources must have been better in the southwest 1,000 years ago. But modern research shows that environment was as harsh then as it is now.

Investigators now believe that it was the Anasazis' mastery of irrigation that made their florescence possible, enabling them to support a considerably larger population than occupies the area today. They evolved a system of dams and cisterns to collect and hoard the precious rainwater that flowed down the canyon walls, funneling it through sluices, ditches and watergates, to the terraced plots where they raised corn, beans and squash. They also gathered wild berries, seeds, plants and pinon nuts, bred turkeys and dogs, hunted deer, antelope and small game. The greatest fear was drought, which is frequent in the southwest. To survive, the Anasazi had to set aside enough food during bumper years to see them through the lean years, which may account for the inordinate number of storerooms found in their pueblos.

Despite the hardships, the Anasazi lived a rich life. They dined on stews of meat, corn mush, squash and wild vegetables, together with cornmeal tortillas baked on stone griddles. They wore sandals made of fiber or rabbit fur, and robes of hides, fur, feathers and woven cotton, sewn with needles and fibers of the yucca plant, which they tied with colorful sashes made of finely spun cotton. They created marvelous pottery, some in the shape of birds and animals, painted with striking geometric black and white designs. They fashioned exquisite jewelry of turquoise and shell, and finely woven pitch-coated baskets in which to store water. For amusement, or in religious rites, they played music on drums, rattles, wooden pipes, and flutes made of bird bones.

Enthusiastic, if not always talented artists, the Anasazi covered the interiors of their homes with frescoes and painted or pecked pictures on cliff faces. The illustrations range from abstract designs whose significance can only be guessed, to whimsical depictions of birds and animals. There are also elongated caricatures of people, and of mythical beings such as Kokopelli, a humpbacked flute player with gargantuan phallus, who was probably a fertility god. To achieve special effects, the Anasazi used some surprisingly modern techniques, such as spattering the paint, applying it with fingers, blowing it on through tubes, sometimes incising the painted surface with sharp tools to give it texture. Although they had no writing or known system of numeration, the Anasazi were skilled surveyors and astronomers. The great Kiva of Casa Rinconada is so perfectly aligned with true north that the Pole Star hangs directly over the entrance. To keep track of the seasons on which their agriculture and religious rites depended, they installed diagonal doorways and put windows at strange angles in their pueblos, which catch the rays of the sun or light from particular stars only on key dates in the calendar. They also built celestial observatories on cliff tops. The best known is located on Fajada Butte in Chaco Canyon, where thin shafts of sunlight— archeologists call them "sun daggers"—fall on spiral disks to register the advent of the solstices, equinoxes, and the eight periods of the year between. The 800-year-old devices are held to be as accurate as those used today.

Since the Anasazi were active traders, they may have acquired their astronomical skills second- or third-hand from the distant Mayas. In fact, Chaco appears to have been a busy commercial center whose prosperity and eminence largely depended on trade. The Chacoans are believed to have bought corn and raw cotton, which they could not raise, from more climatically favored Anasazi communities elsewhere, and perhaps dried buffalo meat from the plains Indians farther east. Beyond the Anasazi world, they imported copper bells, and macaws prized for their plumes from Mexico, seashells from the Pacific coast, and fine flint for implements from Wyoming. Because the Chacoans lacked sufficient wood to fire their kilns, 80 percent of their pottery was also imported, as can be told by the varied styles and materials of which they are made.

What the Chacoans had to offer in exchange was turquoise, which they obtained from a mine 150 miles away. Vast quantities of the blue-green gemstones, in both raw and finished form, have been found in the ruins, a half-million pieces in Pueblo Bonito alone. Archeologists believe that the city became a turquoise manufacturing center, which exported its delicately crafted necklaces, bracelets, inlaid pendants and other ornaments, as far as Central Mexico.

Helping to maintain Chaco's commercial dominance was the network of roads that radiated from the canyon in all directions. The surprise is that, instead of the trails one might expect to find in a land where all travel was on foot and goods were carried on men's backs, these roads were surfaced and carefully engineered. They are a consistent 30 feet in width (broad enough for automobiles), expanding in one place to a four-lane highway. There are almost no curves in the 300 miles of roads that have been traced through the sand and sagebrush so far, which may be a mere fraction of their total extent. The highways run arrow-straight through the rough terrain. They cross gullies on causeways, are supported by stone curbs and retaining walls on hillsides, and climb cliffs on broad stairways carved into the rock. Every eight to ten miles lie the ruins of small pueblos which are believed to have been rest stops for travelers and porters. Also sited on mesa tops near the roads are the remains of isolated stone towers, once assumed to be shrines. They now appear to be signal stations from which messages were relayed by means of fire, smoke, or possibly mirrors made of mica or obsidian.

The need for a communications system is apparent, but why the Chacoans should have invested the prodigious labor and expense to build the amazing highways is more difficult to understand. The most plausible explanation is that the roads were needed to accommodate the large throngs of traders and pilgrims who flocked to Chaco for the trade fairs and religious festivals held there. One possible proof lies in the inordinately deep layers of refuse deposited intermittently in the trash mounds, which are believed to have been created by seasonal gatherings of large numbers of people.

Significantly, many of the roads converge on Pueblo Alto, a Great House whose extensive storerooms, accessible only from the outside, were capable of holding several times the quantity of food and goods that could have been produced in Chaco in a year. The site was apparently used as a distribution center where corn and other necessities were collected and stored, to be sent out where needed in a drought or other emergency. It would have been a means of managing and stabilizing the region's limited resources.

Around 1150 A.D., seemingly at the height of its power and prosperity, the Chaco culture suddenly collapsed. The inhabitants of the canyon and its satellite communities abandoned the splendid cities in which they had resided for almost two centuries, and left the area. Their departure poses the most baffling of all the mysteries surrounding the Anasazi. Various authorities attribute the city's collapse to overpopulation, leading to political stresses or social trauma, to a severe and prolonged drought, to the advent of colder weather and earlier winters which shortened the growing season, or to the cutting down of the forests for miles around, depriving the people of the wood needed to cook their food. Others speculate that centuries of overcultivation, and flash floods which washed away the thin topsoil, had eroded the basin into a dustbowl in which little would grow. Archeologist Julio Betancourt of the University of Arizona contends: "The people beat the hell out of the environment and had to move."

There may be a graver reason, as well. During the centuries of their existence, the Anasazi appeared to have lived at peace with each other and with neighboring tribes. Of the hundreds of human bones unearthed, only one—the skull of a woman with an arrow protruding from it—shows any sign of violence. But in the mid-12th century, a curious thing happened in Chaco. The people of Pueblo Bonito and the other habitations walled up the doors and windows of rooms facing to the outside of the Great Houses as if to protect themselves from intruders. They also blocked up the main entrances of the pueblos with stone, allowing access only by ladder which could be drawn up in case of attack. Still, nowhere in the ruins have any mutilated bodies, charred rooms, or other signs of war or revolution been found. Who the hostiles may have been is not known, since the marauding Comanche, Apache and Navajos did not enter the region until three centuries later. Whatever the reason, the Chacoans left the basin they had occupied for centuries never to return.

At the same time that the Chacoans were departing, and perhaps for the same reason, the Anasazi of Mesa Verde and elsewhere left their exposed villages on the mesas and built new pueblos in the canyons below. The crudity of the earliest construction indicates that they moved in haste. The building of the later stone towers, kivas and multistoried dwellings, on the sloping floors of the caves required skillful engineering, and the hauling up of great quantities of stone and timber. The walls were composed of rectangular sandstone blocks shaped to give them a dimpled surface. They are less sophisticated and pleasing to the eye than those of Chaco. But to compensate, they were plastered over with white pottery clay, then polished to give them a smooth, lustrous surface that is attractive indeed.

Nestled in the caves and overhangs of the cliff walls, the toylike "cities" of Mesa Verde and Canyon de Chelly, and of Betatakin and Keet Seel in Kayenta, are among the most delightful prehistoric sites to be found on earth. To modern visitors who reach them on steel-and-concrete staircases, they are miniature Disneylands, where you climb up and down ladders, squeeze through crevices in the rock, crawl on hands and knees through narrow tunnels, clamber in and out of tiny doorways, and lie on your back to see the murals.

To their inhabitants, however, the cliff dwellings must have been difficult places to live and raise children. Although sheltered from rain, snow and storms, they are in shadow most of the day, rendering them dank in summer and deathly cold in winter. And they were exceedingly difficult to get to. The only way many of them could be reached was by hand and footholds carved into the cliff faces, a hard climb for a vigorous adult, an impossible one for small children or old people, and positively dangerous when carrying food, firewood, or babies on one's back.

The one thing the cliff dwellings did offer was protection from enemies. They are set too far into the walls to be bombarded by rocks dropped from above. Their entrances, just wide enough for one person to pass at a time, could be protected by a single man or woman with a club. Intruders climbing from above or below could

be picked off by bow and arrow. To withstand sieges, the inhabitants stocked food in rooms wedged into cracks in the cliff above the
dwellings. Water was stored in jars, or was available in pools in the
backs of the caves which were replenished by moisture seeping
down through the limestone. But we have not a clue as to who the
attackers could be—or whether there actually were any. Some archeologists suspect the communities may have been feuding among
themselves over water rights or scarce arable land. Yet, as in
Chaco, no signs of pitched battles, sieges or assaults on the cliff
pueblos have ever been found.

A further aid to defense may have been the stone towers up to
four stories high—early explorers mistook them for castles— that
guard the approaches to pueblos in Mesa Verde and Hovenweep.
Some of them are connected with nearby kivas by tunnels through
which the defenders could crawl without exposing themselves to
enemy arrows. Yet they, too, pose a puzzle, since some of the
towers stand inside caves or in places where they could not be used
for defense or even lookouts, and other lack windows or doors. The
guesses are that they were built as signal stations, celestial observatories, granaries, ceremonial innovations, or for just plain show.

For a time, the Mesa Verdeans prospered. They even sent colonists to occupy the abandoned Chaco cities at Aztec and Salmon in
New Mexico, where they remodeled the kivas to their own taste,
and divided the big Chaco rooms into the smaller ones they were
used to, with partitions of their own distinctive masonry. But the
winds of disaster that had driven the Chacoans from their homes a
century earlier, pursued the other Anasazi as well. In 1276 A.D., the
tree ring dates reveal, a savage drought struck the southwest that
lasted for 23 years. As the crisis deepened, the Mesa Verdeans
appear to have turned to prayer, converting many of their rooms to
kivas. As though in a last desperate effort to appease the rain gods
and avert starvation, they began building a magnificent temple on
the rim of Chapin Mesa at Sun Point.

The temple was never completed, for shortly afterward the Anasazi of Mesa Verde and the rest of the Anasazi world began leaving.
From the evidence, it was not a mass exodus. As in Chaco, they

departed gradually by groups, families or villages, leaving their cliff dwellings intact, filled with pottery, grinding stones and other household goods they could not carry, as though going on a trip from which they expected to return. But they never came back. By 1300 A.D., archeologists believe, few, if any, Anasazi were left in their once wide domain.

Although the Anasazi lost their identity as a people, they did not vanish. They moved to more favorable locations where they built new stone pueblos, which they occupied for a few decades or generations before leaving again. Fanning southward into Arizona, and eastward into New Mexico and the upper Rio Grande valley, they became the forebears of, or merged with, the Hopi, Zuni, and other tribes which carry on some of their religious and social traditions, and live in adobe pueblos that are reminiscent of the fine stone dwellings of their ancestors.

But the fame of the Ancient Ones persisted, spreading as far as Mexico City, where the legend arose that they lived in seven cities of gold. In 1540, acting on the report of a Spanish friar who said he had seen the cities from afar and that they were, indeed, made of gold, Francisco de Coronado led an expedition north to find and loot the fabulous habitations. He spent two years searching the territory, opening it to Spanish colonization. But he found no treasure.

The friar's mistake is understandable, however. For when viewed from a distance, with the rays of the afternoon sun reflected from their lustrous surfaces, the ancient ruins do look as though they are fashioned of gold.

CHAPTER 18

The Bloodthirsty Children of Coyolxauhqui

(1250 to 1500 A.D.)

On a night in February, 1978, workmen were digging a conduit for telephone cables in the heart of Mexico City. Fifteen feet below street level, they came across a red stone with carving on it. Work immediately stopped—it's the law in Mexico—and archeologists were called in. Working with brushes and spoons over the next two days, they unearthed the most sensational Aztec relic ever found, a huge stone disk, 11 feet in diameter and a foot thick, weighing eight tons. Carved on its surface in high relief lay the dismembered body of the Aztec moon goddess Coyolxauhqui (pronounced Coyol-*shau*-kwee). Except for a crack across its face, caused by the vibrations of trolley cars that had rumbled over it for decades, the disk was in perfect condition. Realizing that this was part of the *Templo Mayor* (Great Temple) of the Aztecs, whose location had been forgotten for almost four centuries, the government razed the buildings, parking lot and street that covered the area and began an intensive excavation.

What the diggers uncovered was phenomenal, "infinitely more than we ever expected," said chief archeologist Eduardo Matos Moctezuma. They found not one structure, but the remains of six more pyramids nested one on top of the other underneath it. Twin shrines were erected on their flat tops, one dedicated to the patron deity of the Aztecs, Huitzilopochtli (Weets-ilo-*posht*-lee), the god of the sun and war, the other shrine devoted to Tlaloc, the rain-fertility god.

The hieroglyphic inscriptions indicate that the earliest pyramid was built in 1325 A.D.; the last one, covering an area the size of four football fields, was completed in 1498. Some were built to honor the accession of new kings to the throne, others to thank the gods for survival at the end of each 52-year-long century, a dread occasion when the world might come to an end—as it had four times in the past, according to Aztec cosmology. There were also 28 partial reconstructions made necessary by the sinking of the land.

Perhaps to avoid arousing the wrath of the gods to whom it was dedicated, a pyramid-temple was not destroyed when it was replaced, and no attempt was made to salvage anything from it. It was simply covered over with earth and buried, statuary and all, and a new, larger pyramid was built over it. The last temple, reached by 114 steps flanked by serpent's heads, all brilliantly painted and covered with murals, according to the Spanish conquistadors who saw it, is estimated to have towered 180 feet (18 stories) high, taller than most European cathedrals. Representing the culmination of 5,000 years of Mexican artistry, the temple was "of a size and magnificence that no human tongue can describe," wrote Spanish leader Hernan Cortés to his king in Madrid.

Only the foundations and lower steps of the later pyramids remain, because the Spanish invaders razed them in 1521, using the stones to build their churches and homes. However, the earlier pyramids had sunk so deeply into the marshy ground on which they stood that the Spanish were unaware of their existence. Digging upward through the earth by floodlight beneath the structure that covered it, the archeologists discovered the second temple, built in 1390, to be almost completely intact.

Two colossal feathered serpents, emblems of the god Quetzal-coatl, project from the bases of the balustrades of the wide stair-ways. The front of the platform is decorated with coiled snakes and large stone frogs, with holes in their backs for insertion of poles topped with banners. Protruding like gargoyles from the side walls are the stone heads of eagles and carvings of marching warriors.

On the flat top of the pyramid, the searchers found parts of the painted walls of the two sanctuaries in which religious rites were conducted. Still standing in place in front of the shrines were an ominous, rough-hewn black stone of volcanic rock, 20 inches square, and a remarkable reclining polychrome figure called a *chacmool*, with an urn on its chest, whose functions will be explained.

Digging outward from the main temple, the excavators un-earthed smaller temples to lesser gods; the foundation of the pavil-ions of the priests and the Eagle Knights who guarded the temple; a carved dais on which gladiatorial combats were fought; the remains of a ball court; pediments whose sides were carved with 240 massed stone skulls, and much else. A great deal more could be discovered, for the sacred enclosure is reported to have contained 78 separate buildings. But to uncover all of the vast temple complex would require the demolition of almost the entire center of old Mexico City, including the National Cathedral, the National Pal-ace, and other historic buildings which are themselves centuries old. So the excavations have ended.

But more treasures awaited the archeologists inside and around the multi-layered pyramids, including burial crypts and over one hundred caches of offerings never before found in Aztec sanctuaries. Piled up like toys in an attic lay some of the finest pieces of early Mexican art ever unearthed. There were golden bells, precious stones, jewelry fashioned of gold, and of mother-of-pearl, turquoise, jade and greenstone, which symbolized water and fertility. There were stone masks whose purpose is unknown, bearing the insignia of

50 tributary cities, and another from the ancient Olmec culture that must have been 2,000 years old when it was buried. There were figurines of smiling horned gods, previously unknown, magnificent painted vessels of stone and ceramic bearing the effigies of numerous other deities, including the bulbous-nosed god of pulque (Aztec beer). Two ornately incised ceramic urns were found which may contain the cremated ashes of the emperor Moctezuma I.

There were humbler objects as well, including seashells, corncobs, fish and animal remains, household utensils, flutes and rattles, and numerous obsidian knives, some decorated like faces with eyes and teeth. The excavators also encountered grimmer relics: the torsos of men without arms or legs, the headless skeletons of women and children, and elaborately decorated human skulls, some with stone knives protruding from their eye and nose sockets. "These objects have given us insights into Aztec civilization we never had before," noted Matos Moctezuma.

Most fascinating, and puzzling, of all are the sculptures found in the temple. Some of them, such as the statues of eight standard bearers laid horizontally on the steps of the forth temple to protect them before it was covered over, are as primitive and grotesque as if carved by children. But when they wished to, Aztec craftsmen were capable of creating art equal to any on earth. The stone carving of a giant spiral conch shell is a masterpiece of design, as are the elegant little alabaster deerheads, and the sophisticated sculptures of fishes, turtles, frogs, eagles, jaguars and other animals. After viewing the gold ornaments Cortés had sent back to the Spanish monarch in 1520, before they were melted down, the great German artist Albrecht Dürer noted in his diary: "All the days of my life I have seen nothing that rejoiced my heart so much as these things."

But for reasons that can only be guessed, the principal gods were invariably portrayed as monsters. The Spanish who saw the idol of Huitzilopochtli that stood in the Great Temple described it as "a devil from hell," half man and half lizard. The rain god Tlaloc is invariably depicted wearing heavy goggles around his eyes, with fangs protruding from his lips. The statue of the earth goddess

Coatlicue, in Mexico's National Anthropological Museum, is one of the most hideous ever conceived. Her face is formed of the heads of two serpents, her toes are ferocious claws, she wears a skirt of writhing rattlesnakes, and a necklace of human hearts, chopped off hands and a skull. The figure looks as though carved under the influence of narcotics—as it may well have been. For to bring themselves closer to the gods, the Aztec priests are known to have smoked marijuana and to have taken peyotl, a drug distilled from mushrooms that produces violent hallucination.

The Aztecs were comparative latecomers on the Mesoamerican scene. They are related linguistically to the Utes and other peoples of the western United States. They arrived in the Valley of Mexico late in the 13th century A.D. from a mythical mountain called Aztlan somewhere in the north, carrying a wooden image of their tribal god Huitzilopochtli with them. Their savagery was legendary. Seeking to establish his people, the Aztec leader arranged a marriage between his son and a daughter of the lord of the rich city of Colhuacan. But when the Colhuacanos arrived for the ceremony, they were greeted by a dancing Aztec priest clad in the skin of the girl, who had been flayed alive. Driven from the mainland by their outraged neighbors, the Aztecs settled on a swampy island in Lake Texcoco (since drained) where, as a tribal prophecy had foretold, they found an eagle perched on a cactus devouring a snake. This has since become the Mexican national symbol, appearing on the country's flag.

But the Aztecs were not to be denied. Considering themselves a chosen people destined to rule the world, their armies soon dominated the Valley and eventually conquered an empire extending across the breadth of Mexico, from Guatemala in the south, to the deserts in the north. Although still living in the Stone Age, lacking metal tools, wheeled vehicles or draft animals of any description, they built their island city, known as Tenochtitlan ("the place of the cactus"), into the largest, most magnificent metropolis on earth. With a population estimated at over 200,000, it was six times the size of contemporary London. With its ornate palaces, vast market-place, lofty temples, teeming canals and broad causeways and viaducts connecting it with suburbs and neighboring cities on the shore, "it is the finest city ever seen," Hernan Cortés reported. To conquistador Bernal Diaz it seemed "an enchanted vision, a first glimpse of things never heard of, seen or dreamed before."

Borrowing from the Mesoamerican civilizations that preceded them, the Aztecs also developed a brilliant culture. Their libraries were filled with hundreds of illustrated books written in hieroglyphs on a form of paper, every one of which was burned by the Spanish priests, although a few were later reconstructed from memory. They were accomplished astronomers, capable of predicting eclipses and the transit of the planets. Their complicated calendar was considerably more accurate than that of their conquerors, and they employed the concept of zero in arithmetic centuries before it was used in Europe. Particularly marvelous to the Spanish were the botanic gardens, animal zoos and bird aviaries of the city, which did not exist in Europe at the time.

Although abstemious in their personal habits—adultery and drunkenness were punishable by death—the people lived and dressed extremely well, largely on the tribute exacted from the empire. They dined on a wide variety of foods totally unknown in the Old World at the time, including maize, beans, peanuts, squash, tomatos, avocados, chiles and other exotic fruits, and a drink called *chocolatl* brewed of cacao beans. They also ate the meat of turkeys, iguanas, a species of duck, and fat, hairless dogs, bred for the table (game was scarce, and cattle, horses, sheep and goats were unknown to them). They celebrated 200 religious festivals a year, some of them joyous. They played a variety of games, including a board game called "patolli" which, unaccountably, was identical to the game of parchesi developed in India, and a sacred game resembling basketball, in which rival teams, using only their padded thighs, arms, bodies and buttocks, attempted to drive a heavy rubber ball through a hoop set vertically in the wall.

The Aztecs also wrote sensitive lyric poetry and songs, loved music, and danced to the accompaniment of flutes, bells, drums and percussion instruments (they had no stringed instruments). They possessed a passion for butterflies, bright feathers, and particularly flowers, which trailed from roofs and window boxes all over the city. Men wore them in their hair and carried them in their hands. Upper class children were sent to schools where, along with reading, writing and religion, they were taught singing, dancing and fastidious rules of etiquette, including the proper way to smoke tobacco and to hold and smell flowers.

But the Mexican civilization also presents an enigma that historians have not been able to explain. In violent contrast to the refinement of the rest of their culture, their religious rites were phenomenally brutal—"maniacal" is the word one anthropologist uses. The principal function of their temples was to sacrifice humans. Admittedly, many other primitive religions in the world indulged in human sacrifice at one time, until the ameliorating effects of civilization, or popular resistance, led to the substitution of animal sacrifice and the offering of fruits and plants.

But the practice of human sacrifice continued to flourish in previous Mesoamerican cultures, and it reached a crescendo among the Aztecs. Spanish chroniclers reported that to celebrate the last reconstruction of the Great Temple, 30 years earlier, 20,000 men (some said 80,000) had been sacrificed in four days, with the priests replacing each other at the altars in relays as their arms tired of the killing. Hernan Cortés' men counted 136,000 heads in the skull racks when they captured the city. All told, historians estimate, 250,000 people were sacrificed in Central Mexico every year. The reason: the gods lived on an exclusive diet of human blood and hearts, the Mesoamericans believed, and unless they were fed daily, the sun would not rise, the rains would not fall, crops would cease to grow, and life on earth would end.

To understand the Aztecs' particular ferocity brings us back to the dismembered figure of the malevolent moon goddess Coyolxauhqui. According to Aztec legend, she and her 400 brothers, the stars, were all children of the widowed earth goddess Coatlicue (she of the serpent skirt), who lived on a mountain. One day, a feather from heaven fell on Coatlicue's breast rendering her pregnant. Furious at being dishonored by their mother, the moon goddess and her brothers plotted to kill her. But as they approached to carry out their intention, the unborn sun god, Huitzilopochtli, sprang from his mother's womb fully grown and girded for battle, his face arrayed in war paint. Wielding a serpent of fire (the sun's rays), he drove off his brothers and killed Coyolxauhqui, cutting up her body and hurling the pieces down the mountainside.

The cosmic drama was reenacted every day from then on. In his war to save his mother, the earth, and dispel the darkness, the sun must fight his way into the sky each morning, slay the moon and drive away the stars before making his journey across the heavens. The eternal battle exhausted him, threatening his life. As People of the Sun, who had promised them mastery of the earth in exchange, the Aztecs had made a covenant with the god to provide him with the human blood needed to rejuvenate him. When the Spaniards urged Moctezuma to end the practice, the emperor warned them that if the sacrifices were discontinued for even a single day, the sun would not have the strength to arise next morning, the world would be plunged into eternal darkness, and they along with the rest of mankind would assuredly perish.

The Aztecs obtained their victims partly from slave dealers and as tribute from conquered territories; one subject tribe, the Totonacs, was required to supply 30 young men and women every 80 days. But the majority of the men sacrificed were prisoners captured in the incessant wars the Aztecs fought as a sacred duty. Historians point out that the reason Cortés and a handful of Spaniards managed to escape from Tenochtitlan on the *Noche Triste,* the night of sorrow, when surrounded by enemies who outnumbered them by thousands to one, was that the Aztecs did not seek to kill them, but to take them alive to be sacrificed, as a great many were.

In one skirmish, Cortés himself was pulled from his horse by enemy warriors, any one of whom could have slain him with a spear thrust. But none of them struck the fatal blow. In times of peace, when the holding pens of victims were depleted, the Aztecs fought mock battles, called "flower wars," with neighboring cities in which the contenders sought not to kill but to capture each other for their respective altars.

To the Spanish who witnessed the spectacle enacted daily in the Great Temple, it was "a scene from hell." To the accompaniment of a terrifying dirge of pounding drums and blasts from conch shell trumpets, the prisoners shuffled in a long line up the steps of the pyramid, which was a replica of the mountain on which Huitzilo-pochtli had performed his deeds. As each man reached the platform on top, he was expected, or forced, to dance in honor of the god. Then, he was thrown on his back across the sacrificial stone, with his head, arms and legs, held down. A priest sliced open the victim's chest below the ribs with a razor-sharp flint knife and tore out the beating heart, holding it up to the sun for a moment before throwing it into the urn implanted on the chest of the recumbent *chacmool.*

After sacrifice, the lifeless bodies were tossed or kicked down the stairs of the pyramid, which were steeply built so they could roll unimpeded to the bottom. They landed, symbolically, on the disk bearing the dismembered body of Coyolxauhqui. The heads were cut off to be skewered through the temples and hung on skull racks. The arms and legs were severed to be "cooked in a sauce of peppers and tomatos," and eaten by the nobles, priests and war-riors. The torsos were thrown to the animals in the zoo.

Blood was everywhere, the Spanish noted. The magnificent shrines on top of the temple were smeared and spattered with gore. It cascaded in torrents down the staircase. Although a great deal of sweet-smelling incense was burned, it could not disguise the stench of the decomposing heads in the skull racks. Particularly disgusting to the Spanish was the sight of the black-garbed priests of the temple. As Bernal Diaz describes them, their faces were streaked with pitch, their bodies and clothing stained with gore, their long hair, which they were forbidden to cut or wash, infested with insects, and so black with clotted blood that no comb could pass through it.

Only men were offered to the sun god. The rain god in the adjoining temple was propitiated with women and children, who were sacrificed by drowning, strangulation or decapitation. The children were beaten before being put to death, since their tears were harbingers of copious rain. Xipe Totec, the god of gentle spring, was welcomed annually by intoxicating the victims with pulque, breaking their necks, then flaying them. Their dripping skins were draped over the bodies and faces of soldiers or priests, who are depicted wearing them like shirts and masks, dancing in them, shaking rattles, and imploring the god to permit the crops to grow. The grisly garments were worn until they dried and cracked off, symbolizing the bursting of the skins of planted corn kernels from which new life emerged.

Despite the documentary and pictorial evidence, some historians are suspicious of the Spanish accounts of the slaughter. Since they were all written after the conquest, they hold them to be inventions or, at least, exaggerations intended to justify the Spaniards' own savage treatment of the Aztecs. The eating of the flesh of the victims is an even more controversial and sensitive issue. A few authorities doubt that it happened. The majority view it as a symbolic ritual. It has been practiced by a great many primitive cultures around the world in the belief that ingesting a slain warrior's flesh enables the conquerors to absorb his strength and courage.

But anthropologist Michael Harner of the State University of New York attributes the cannibalism in ancient Mexico to a shortage of animal protein. Human flesh constituted an important complement to the diet because deer and other game had been almost exterminated and no large domesticated food animals existed, he says. The number of male skeletons lacking arms and legs found in the Great Temple seems to confirm Harner's claim. The Spaniards saw their own Indian allies feasting on the limbs of their captives, and in the cities they entered, they found wooden cages in which men, women and children were being fattened for sacrifice and food. Although few historians agree with Harner, a mural by famed painter Diego Rivera in the National Palace of Mexico shows human arms and legs hanging from hooks in the meat markets of ancient Tenochtitlan. The meat may have been cut up in a stew called *tlacotolli*, which is said to mean "dried maize with human flesh"in the Aztec language.

Human sacrifice did not seem as gruesome or unjustified to the Aztecs as it does to us. The Spanish missionaries who deplored it "repeatedly stress that there was no intent of cruelty, punishment or blood lust, connected with the offering of human life," notes historian Patricia Anawalt. "It always took place in the most reverential circumstances, the supreme religious act of a deeply devout people." As the chosen people of Huitzilopochtli, the sun god, the Aztecs felt they had a sacred duty to nourish him and the other gods, thereby preserving humanity and the world.

In compensation, the victims were assured a glorious afterlife. The souls of the sacrificed men were immediately wafted to heaven where they were accorded the divine honor of accompanying the sun god on his daily rounds. (Women who died in childbirth were similarly honored, since they too were considered as having sacrificed themselves to preserve mankind.) Women and children sacrificed to Tlaloc, along with the souls of people who were accidently drowned or killed by lightning, went to a paradise called Tlalocan, where they spent their days playing, dancing and chasing butterflies. The rewards for dying for the gods were so great, in fact, that captives who were offered their lives sometimes chose death instead, and on critical occasions, even nobles offered themselves or their wives and children to the knife.

These barbarities should not be allowed to obscure the glories of Aztec civilization, however. They were scarcely worse then the burnings at the stake and other excesses committed in Europe a little later in the name of a gentler god, or the horrors perpetrated by the Nazis. Nevertheless, their barbarism helped to destroy the Aztecs. Seething with hatred because of the continual slaughter of their people and the never-ending tribute exacted from them, the neighboring tribes needed little persuasion to join the Spanish in exterminating their brutal overlords.

With the capture of Tenochtitlan, after a 90-day siege, the brilliant civilization was snuffed out. The Spanish priests burned the sacred books, together with every other pagan vestige on which they could get their hands. The shrines atop the Great Temple were blown up with gunpowder. The pyramid itself, along with all the other great buildings, were leveled in order to fill the canals that once ribboned the metropolis, and a new European city arose on their ashes.

But the Aztecs obtained partial revenge when they were employed to build churches for their conquerors. Embedded under altars and inside stone crosses before which generations of Christian Mexicans have worshipped are the sacrificial stones and other relics of the ancient religion. And still buried somewhere beneath Mexico City, awaiting some future ditchdigger's shovel, lie the idols of Huitzilopochtli, Tlaloc and other gods and treasures, which the Aztec priests smuggled from the Great Temple and hid, before it was destroyed.

CHAPTER 19

How Amateurs Help to Unearth the Secrets Buried in a Cornfield

(7500 B.C. to 900 A.D.)

Until recently, archeological excavations and research were carried out almost exclusively by professionals, aided by their students or paid workers. Amateurs wealthy enough to finance their activities were welcome, or at least tolerated, so long as they did not interfere. Others were likely to be regarded as nuisances.

However, the surging public interest in archeology, plus the increased costs of excavation, have changed professional attitudes. The enterprise described in this chapter represents the new approach. It was one of the first instances of an important project that was instigated by amateurs, and carried to a successful conclusion through the hard work of volunteers, directed by professionals. Such cooperative archeological ventures have since become the rule in Western countries, rather than the exception.

241

Archeology professor Stuart Struever of Northwestern University suspected a hoax when he first examined the collection of Indian spear points and pottery shards brought to him by Illinois farmer Harlin "Alec" Helton in 1966.

"You couldn't have picked them all up on the surface in the same place," he explained patiently, "because some of them were made thousands of years apart. It's like finding automobile hubcaps and Roman chariot wheels in the same trash heap."

But Helton was a stubborn man. He insisted the artifacts had all come from the cornfield of his neighbor, Theodore Koster, on the lower Illinois River in the southwestern part of the state. Moreover, he badgered the archeologist so relentlessly that Struever finally went out to look at the place two years later, "largely to get him off my neck," he later admitted. What his trained eye detected in the little valley were the outlines of one of the largest prehistoric villages he had ever seen, 25 acres literally strewn with pottery fragments from the 1,000-year-old Jersey Bluff Culture. But mixed in them were stone artifacts of much earlier eras. How could they have gotten there?

As Struever pondered the mystery, it began to rain, and the water pelting down the denuded hillside gave him a clue. Could it be that the rain cutting through the layers of earth on the steep slope had washed the artifacts of earlier millenia down to the valley floor? And if so, did these same ancient strata extend below the present surface?

To find out, Struever returned to the cornfield with a small crew in the summer of 1969 to dig a few test holes—thereby making archeological history and winning permanent fame for farmer Koster. For the site proved to be one of the richest ever discovered in the United States. It contained no less than 13 separate "horizons," or layers of black organic material stacked one on top of the other, which indicate that human beings had lived in the cornfield on and off for nearly 10,000 years.

Radiocarbon dating of the debris from the stratum in Horizon 4, four feet below the surface, showed that it had been occupied 2,000 years before the birth of Christ. In Horizon 8, named the "Helton

Culture" in honor of the persistent Alec, the diggers unearthed the post holes, foundations and bits of burned plaster of houses built prior to 5000 B.C., the oldest permanent structures yet discovered on the continent north of Mexico. In Horizon 11, they came across the skeletons of a ceremonially buried dog and an 18-month-old infant, covered with powdered red ocher, who had died 8,400 years ago. The settlement in which they were found, 34 feet below the surface, was contemporaneous with some of the early villages of Asia Minor and more than five millenia older than the Egyptian pyramids. Below Horizon 13, a thousand years older, the diggers could not go because they had reached the water table.

Although not the earliest repository of human artifacts in North America—evidence of human occupation found in the Meadowcroft rockshelter in Pennsylvania dates back 19,600 years—Koster was the kind of site archeologists spend their lives trying to find. For unlike caves and overhangs, where the relics of different periods are often jumbled together, ruined by dripping water or falling rock, the ancient remains at Koster were not only abundant and undisturbed, but extraordinarily well preserved. "It was a fossilized layer cake, with each period of occupancy neatly packaged in its own impermeable blanket," said Struever. "We could not only tell exactly how old they were, but by comparing them we could trace cultural evolution through 9,000 years."

From the artifacts and thickness of the organic material in the horizons, it was evident that some of the villages or camps had been lived in for only a few decades, others for over 500 years. As each group of people abandoned the site, for whatever reason, dust blown in by the winds or washed down from the hills covered their habitations under several feet of sterile soil. "It is unlikely," Struever believes, "that a new group of migrants, arriving at the site centuries later, would have any idea that the place had previously been occupied by other people."

With the climate turning warmer and drier as the great glaciers receded, life in ancient America had changed dramatically some 10,000 years ago, when the history of Koster began. Men were still primarily hunters, but with the giant mammoths, mastodons, sloths and other huge animals having disappeared, they did not wander as far. Their flint projectile points shrank in size and their other tools and weapons became more refined as they had to rely on smaller animals, birds and fish, for sustenance. Baskets and kitchen utensils had begun to appear as seeds, plants, nuts and berries became more important in their diet.

Struever is certain that the site's superb location is what attracted archaic man to Koster. The 100-foot-high bluffs to the north and west protect the little valley from winter winds and snow, and a gushing spring, in which pigs now wallow, has provided it with fresh water from time immemorial. It was near the Illinois River, which served as an important highway, yet high enough to be safe from its floods. "Ecologically, the place was a Biblical land of milk and honey," said Struever. "Its food resources were tremendous and the taking was easy."

The people lived on roasted white-tailed deer, wild turkeys and smaller game caught in the woods, on turtles from the creeks and mussels which they steamed or cracked open, with an occasional fat puppy served up on special occasions. After the spring floods, they scooped up vast quantities of fish from the ponds and lakes, left behind by the receding waters, which they dried or smoked on special racks. In the fall, they dined on migrating ducks, geese and trumpeter swans, which they trapped in the reeds by flinging nets weighted with smooth stone plummets.

Other charred remains found in the roasting pits indicate that the Kosterites also ate wild grapes and berries of several kinds, hickory nuts, hazelnuts and wild pecans, which they boiled or ground to flour in heavy metates, or grinding stones. They also consumed the seeds of wild sunflowers and other plants now considered weeds, such as marsh elder, lamb's-quarters and pigweed. They stored their food in baskets woven of roots and twigs, and made nets, fishing lines and rope from the fibers of milkweed and similar plants. In fact, their dependence on plants was so great that by the time European explorers reached the area, they found their descendants using 275 species for medicine, 130 for food, 31 as magical charms, 27 for smoking, 18 in beverages or for flavoring and 54 for manufacturing purposes.

The richness of the evidence gleaned from farmer Koster's cornfield made it, for a time, the busiest archeological site in North America. Headquarters for the expedition, which numbered over 120 in the summer, were located in the hamlet of Kampsville (population 400), nine miles away across the Illinois River. The university professors on the staff, headed by the dynamic 41-year-old Struever, lived in boarding houses, the crews in sagging frame dwellings which had been empty for years. Ten laboratories, a library and computer center, were located in abandoned stores, the museum in a former meat market, and the zoology lab in what was once a church. Struever's own office was in an ancient hotel that had served the river boats a century earlier.

As a largely self-financed operation, the Koster excavation set a pattern that has since been copied elsewhere in the United States and the world. Directed by a small professional staff, some of the diggers were archeology buffs—middle-aged business executives, housewives, teachers and high school kids—who volunteered their labor for a week or two in the summer. But the majority were college students of both sexes from universities throughout the United States and Canada.

The labor they performed proved more grueling than most of them had ever believed possible. Awakening at dawn, they downed a quick breakfast in the public school cafeteria before boarding buses to the dig. At 6:00 A.M., armed with picks, shovels, trowels and notebooks, they climbed down the ladders into the excavation, 34 feet deep in places, to begin their 11-hour day. Working on hands and knees, they carefully scraped the six-foot-square columns of earth with trowels and slivers of bamboo, recording the exact location, depth, and probable meaning of every scrap of charcoal, bone and stone they came across. Later they ground the remaining dirt, sifting it through half-inch wire meshes to make certain that nothing of interest escaped, then shoveled the debris over their heads to ledges where other youngsters hauled it away. Under the blazing sun, the temperature in the pit often exceeded

100 degrees. When it rained, the mud was so thick that the diggers were sometimes hauled up by ropes and hosed off before they are allowed back into the buses to Kampsville at 5:00 P.M.

"If convicts were forced to work that hard under those conditions there would be a national uproar about cruel and inhuman punishment," observed the local sheriff. Yet the students not only enjoyed the work, but actually paid for the privilege of doing it—$750 for two weeks, plus $100 for room, board and Band-Aids. What did they get out of it? "Well, you earn three credits toward your college diploma, and you lose a lot of weight," explained a dirt-smeared co-ed, who was flown to Kampsville in her father's private jet, "but it's the excitement that keeps you coming back. We've discovered things that have never been known before."

Indeed they did. The thousands of bits of evidence they unearthed each day, all carefully tagged and bagged, were cleaned, classified, counted and weighed, then sent to the laboratories for analysis. Zoologists studied the animal remains to determine how they were killed, and by counting the rings in ancient fish scales through microscopes, ichthyologists could tell the season of the year they were caught. Examination of the pollen and snail shells in the strata enabled other specialists to reconstruct the climate in each period. And to find out how edible were the pigweed and other strange plants found in the cooking pits, young botanist Nancy Asch actually lived on them for a time. "Digestible," was her verdict, "but not appetizing."

Particulary significant were studies of human skeletal remains made in the osteology laboratory. Infant mortality appeared to have been appallingly high, around 50 percent, and even adolescence was a dangerous age. Of the nine burials discovered between Horizons 11 and 6, nearly all were of teenagers. People suffered from bad teeth and a variety of diseases, including syphilis—the New World's gift to the Old. A number of women were found with arthritic growths in their necks, believed to have resulted from carrying heavy loads in tumplines suspended from their foreheads.

Finally all of the bits of data from the laboratories were fed into a computer which, in a matter of days, was able to reach conclusions that formerly could not be arrived at for years, if ever. A computer-produced isometric model of one of the ancient horizons, for example, showed that benches or shelves had been built into the walls of the houses, the uneven ground was terraced, and that there may have been division of labor in the village, since the distribution of bones and artifacts indicate that special areas had been set aside for butchering animals, cracking mussels, making tools and depositing garbage.

Unlike other archeological digs which were surrounded by "Keep Out" signs, the public was welcomed to Koster because Stu Struever believes archeology is, or should be, everybody's business. Thirty thousand visitors a year came to the excavation and museum, where trained guides explained what was going on. There was no admission charge, but the postcards and brochures they bought, and the memberships to which many subscribed, ranging in price from $5 to $5,000, helped finance the expedition. The local people helped out too. Farmer Koster charged no rent for the cornfield taken out of production. Alec Helton installed conveyor belts at his own expense. Equipment manufacturers contributed tractors and earth movers, which local mechanics repaired at no charge. Farmers donated corn, vegetables and fresh meat to provide a welcome change in the expedition's standard luncheon menu of bologna and peanut butter-and-jelly sandwiches. And the citizens of Kampsville held fish fries which netted around $700 apiece for the dig.

The findings at Koster not only filled great gaps in our knowledge of life in ancient America, but changed ideas that have been held for generations. The existence of permanent houses and well-kept cemeteries indicated that these early hunter-gatherers were not as nomadic as had been believed, but were actually a sedentary folk living in the valley the year round, or returning to it regularly during certain seasons of the year.

"Life in the Stone Age was not as nasty, brutish and short, as had been pictured," says Struever. "In fact, people enjoyed security and a good deal of leisure." They had time to breed and train dogs, carve stone pipes into fanciful animal shapes, make flutes and

whistles of bird bones, manufacture beads, jewelry and bone hairpins, tattoo their bodies with colored pigments and stone needles,
and play a game something like lacrosse and another that involved
spears and round, flat stones about the size of hockey pucks.

They also carried on an astonishingly extensive trade, importing
obsidian from Yellowstone Park, red pipestone from Ohio, alligator
teeth and conch shells from Florida, and mica from the Carolinas,
which they cut into silhouettes of animals and people. From the
shores of Lake Superior they obtained copper which they shaped
into exquisite little snake charms and heavy ear spools. Judging
from the pigments and few stone carvings that have survived, these
ancient Indians must have been superb wood carvers and colorists.
In later centuries, they may also have had contact with Mexico, for
among the artifacts unearthed in Horizon 1 were colored clay
figurines similar to those found at Teotihuacan (see Chapter 12),
and heads carved of turtle shell all bearing the long, pointed nose of
the patron god of Aztec traders.

But Koster also poses some mysteries. As long as 5,000 years
ago, in Horizon 6, the inhabitants were lining the bottoms of fire
pits with beautifully formed, baked clay pans in which they probably boiled fish. But not until 3,000 years later, around 500 A.D., did
pottery appear in the area. "Why the incredible delay?" Struever
asks. "Was it because people were resistant to innovation, or did it
take that long for the human mind to make the connection between
a clay receptacle in the ground and one that could be carried
around?"

The discovery of seeds of wild cereal-like plants in Horizon 6
signifies that the Kosterites may have known how to cultivate them
5,000 years ago. Yet it was not until the time of Christ that people
in the lower Illinois Valley started raising crops in any quantity, and
not until 800 A.D. could they actually be called farmers. Again
why? The only answer that can be adduced is that population began
to exceed the natural food resources.

But this poses another question. If the area around Koster provided such an abundant larder prior to that time, why did the
inhabitants repeatedly abandon their snug valley over the millenia?

It could have been disease epidemics, sudden drought or other natural disasters, Struever concedes, although there is no evidence of them, but he believes the more likely cause may have been lack of firewood. "When they had cut down all the trees for miles around with their 20-pound stone axes," he speculates, "they may have reached the point where it became easier to move the village than to drag logs to it. When the area reforested itself, after a few generations, new people would return to repeat the cycle all over again.

But the reason people abandoned the last village at Horizon 1 a thousand years ago, never to return, appears to have a grimmer explanation. For the first 10,000 years of human existence north of Mexico, there is no evidence of war or murder. Of the 500 bodies found in a burial mound dated around the year 1 A.D., only one shows signs of having met a violent death. Warfare did not begin until the advent of the Mississippian Culture around 900 A.D., and Horizon 1 was a Mississippian village. Many of the skeletons in the graveyards of the period were found with crushed skulls or arrows stuck in the bones. Once war became a way of life, Koster had to be abandoned, because the little valley was indefensible.

When the last possible artifact had been recovered in 1978, the Koster excavation was filled in and the site abandoned. However, the village of Kampsville still serves as a field training center and administrative headquarters for other nearby excavations, under the aegis of the University of Chicago's Center for American Archeology. But Stu Struever has gone on to other digs in the hope of finding traces of even earlier Americans, perhaps those of migrants who actually took the long walk across the land bridge from Asia in the days of the mastodons.

A Parting Word

In this book we have relived various episodes in the human adventure ranging in time from the appearance of man four million years ago to the disappearance of the Aztec civilization less than 500 years ago. The accounts are based on the latest information available. Yet, sooner or later many of the facts, opinions and theories offered here are certain to be revised in the light of new findings, and some may be rejected altogether.

For archeology today is in a ferment of activity. There is scarcely a university worthy of the name that does not boast a department of archeology or anthropology, staffed by professionals. Students in unprecedented numbers are graduating with degrees in these disciplines. More new discoveries, and reassessments of old discoveries, are being made than ever before, and the pace is accelerating. The new findings will inevitably render obsolete some of the ideas that are accepted as scientific fact today, just as modern researchers reject the one-time certainties that human beings evolved in eastern Asia and that the major arts of civilization all originated in the Middle East.

251

This is an exhilarating prospect. The new findings may answer questions and solve some of the mysteries that have baffled us for centuries. They may unlock the dark closets of prehistory to give new insights into how we became what we are today, and enrich our lives by opening unsuspected vistas into the past. The discoveries may be difficult to keep up with, but they are something to look forward to.

Appendix

If you would like to participate in archeological explorations—
More opportunities are available to amateur and student volunteers in archeology than ever before.
For information about openings at projects in the United States and abroad, *which charge fees:*

- Look for the ads in science magazines such as *Archeology, Smithsonian* and *Natural History,* copies of which are available in public libraries;

- Write to Earthwatch, 680 Mt. Auburn Street (or P. O. Box 43), Watertown, MA 02272, an environmental organization which sponsors ecological and archeological projects in 22 U.S. states and 46 countries;

- Send a check for $8 to Archaeological Institute of America, 675 Commonwealth Ave., Boston, MA 02215, asking for its annual *Archaeological Field Work Bulletin,* which provides names, dates, addresses and telephone numbers of each project, plus the hardships likely to be encountered;

- Send a check for $6 to American Anthropological Association, 1703 New Hampshire Ave. N.W., Washington, DC 20009, requesting its annual *Anthropological Field Schools* guide, which provides much the same data.

For information about government archeology projects in the United States only, *which do not charge fees* (and may pay expenses):

- Write to National Park Service, Interpretive Division, 2101 L Street, Washington DC 20013, requesting a *VIP (Volunteers in Parks)* brochure and application;
- Write to USDA Forest Service, Cultural Resources Management, P.O. Box 06090, Washington, DC 20090, asking for the Service's *Opportunities for Volunteer Archeologists.*

For information about unlisted projects in your own part of the country consult the archeology or anthropology department at a nearby university.

Happy digging!

Index

255